NOT A ONE-WAY STREET

There is, to my mind, no element in
business more essential than loyalty.
Loyalty—to the organization, to its
management and to other workers—is
the cement which binds an organization
together. It is necessary to the success
of any undertaking. . . .

Loyalty is not a one-way street.
No organization is loyal to a leader
unless he, in turn, is loyal to those who
are working for him. The example
must always come from the top. No
leader should ever ask his staff to do
more than he is prepared to do himself.

From Chapter 28,
The Harvest of the Years

NOT
A ONE-WAY
STREET

the autobiography of
JAMES S. DUNCAN

CLARKE, IRWIN & COMPANY LIMITED
TORONTO/VANCOUVER/1971

PRINTED IN CANADA

Thanks are due to:

Massey-Ferguson Limited for supplying photographs.

The Toronto *Globe and Mail* for permission to quote an article
that appeared in the July 5, 1938 issue.

The Macmillan Company of Canada Limited for permission
to quote from *What's Past is Prologue* by Vincent Massey.

Preface

My HISTORIAN FRIENDS HAVE, over the years, spoken with distress of the limited number of biographies of the industrial, financial and commercial leaders of Canada. The few that have been written—some as autobiographies—are treasured. They are as rare as diamonds.

In this volume, a much respected and honoured Canadian industrialist and community leader has unfolded the record of a life as notable for its liveliness as for its personal achievement. He has written with candour and balanced judgement about war, mergers, industry, expansion, politicians and businessmen.

James S. Duncan spent forty-six years with the globally expansive Massey-Harris Company and its successor, Massey-Ferguson.

During those years, he worked on the factory floor; demonstrated farm machinery to people of far-flung lands; built factories; created merchandising organizations; put together mergers; converted a succession of annual losses to a long era of profitable prosperity; fought stockholders' battles, including at least one mighty struggle involving control. In all these ways he helped to build one of the world's great "multi-national" corporations.

But Jim Duncan's association with Massey-Harris is only part of his story. The satellite responsibilities of a business leader—to his country, to his community, to the challenge of human welfare, national security, education and culture—were always willingly accepted by this remarkably busy executive. The diversity of his public work is a measure of the man. He fought with British troops in World War I. He was Deputy Minister for Air in World War II, with special responsibility for the magnificently successful British Commonwealth Air Training Plan. His links with France (where he was born) led to his heading up the Free French in Ontario during World War II. His links with Britain (land of his ancestors) led him to take on dedicated work as the organizer and chairman of the Dollar-Sterling Trade Board, which helped the U.K. to emerge from its post-war world trade problems. It led him also to take on the chairmanship (and fund-raising job) of London House, a home for Canadian scholars in Britain. His links with Australia led him to become the head of the Australian-Canadian Committee. In Canada, he was president of the Board of Trade of Toronto; chairman of the Canadian Committee of the International Chamber of Commerce; chairman of the United Appeal of Toronto; a governor of the University of Toronto, and chairman of its committee for the Royal Conservatory of Music.

He has served also on the boards of other prestigious companies: Canadian Imperial Bank of Commerce, Canada Cement, International Nickel, etc.

After his retirement from the chairmanship of Massey-Ferguson, Jim Duncan responded to the appeal of the Prime Minister of Ontario to take on the multi-billion dollar Hydro Electric Power Commission of the Province. There he saw through the vast power developments associated with Canada's share of the St. Lawrence Seaway.

Honours have been showered on Duncan: the C.M.G.; LL.D. from Dartmouth College; Chevalier of the Legion of Honor; King Haakon VII Cross; Croix de Lorraine. He has been "Canadian Business-man of the Year" and was once described by Dartmouth College as conducting an "unremitting private ambassadorship to a score of nations."

Now he lives with his lovely Spanish-born wife, Trini, in an historic old home in Bermuda. He busies himself with writing. This volume of autobiography deals chiefly with his career as a businessman. But the full story of this never dull life calls for yet another volume, in which, it is hoped, we will meet a few more of Mr. Duncan's friends in many countries and get a fuller account of his travels, particularly of his two trips to post-war China and three trips to the U.S.S.R.

FLOYD S. CHALMERS

Office of the Chancellor
York University, Toronto

Foreword

THIS BOOK has been written in response to a wish expressed by my wife, who, affectionately prejudiced no doubt, believed that she saw in my personal experiences throughout a long and varied life an interest which should be shared with others.

Later, as they grew older, my children, who have always been very close to us, joined their mother in urging me to place on record some of my reminiscences.

My family's suggestion fell on fertile ground. I have always deplored that some of my older friends, alas no longer with us, whose lives had been intimately connected with many of the great events of their time, should have left no record of their useful and colourful lives. Had they done so, many of our young people might have read with profit and enjoyment some of the experiences of these eminent men, and having thereby acquired a better understanding of the recent past, with its problems, its difficulties, its struggles, its disappointments, and its solid achievements, might have been better able to bring into clearer focus the perplexing problems of their own generation.

For these and other reasons, I decided about two years ago to write the simple story of my life, with its ups and downs, the stirring events I have lived through and at times been associated with, and the great leaders whose friendship I have enjoyed.

There are readers who might feel that I have dealt in too much detail with the fascinating story of the growth of the world-wide organization I was privileged to serve. To them, I say that I could not write the story of my life and deal only summarily with the history of the organization in which I spent forty-six years.

Much that was dynamic, constructive, and colourful in my experience was connected with the growth and development of this great organization, in which I rose from office boy in Berlin, Germany, to become its chief officer for twenty-one years.

In writing these memoirs I have been greatly handicapped by the fact that I never kept a diary. I have had, therefore, to rely on my memory, the one or two records dictated at the time, covering some important development, and the notation of my various daily appointments kept by my efficient secretaries.

As is the case with many who attempt to write their biography, a fair sprinkling of mistakes may have crept into mine, some through fault of memory, others through incorrect assessment of passing events. I cannot, therefore, vouch for the complete accuracy of all the statements made, nor the figures quoted. I do believe, however, that I have set forth a valid summary of past events.

When I look back over the years, I realize that I have been greatly privileged and rewarded, probably beyond my deserts. Like all who have lived an active and meaningful life, I have experienced disappointments, but they have been so overwhelmed by satisfactions that if I had the chance to live my life all over again, I would not wish it to be very different.

The ups have far outnumbered the downs, and I am content.

JAMES S. DUNCAN

Somerset House
Paget, Bermuda
January, 1971

Contents

To Trini, Rosa Maria, Maruja and Jimmie

NOT A ONE-WAY STREET

I

My First Job in Canada

IT WAS ON A FEBRUARY DAY IN 1910 that I first set foot in Toronto. Three days later I started to work on a full-time job. I was not yet eighteen.

Canada was teeming with new immigrants from Britain and Europe. Jobs were not hard to find. But adaptation to the New World was more difficult for most of them than it was for me. I had been sent to learn the farm implement business from the factory floor up and a job was assured.

I already knew a great deal about ploughs, harrows, rakes and threshing machines. My Scottish-born father, James Stuart Duncan, was manager for France, Belgium and North Africa of Canada's famous Massey-Harris Company. I had divided my boyhood between schooling and working with Massey-Harris salesmen and engineers in the harvest fields of France and Germany. It had long been planned in our family that I should go to Canada when I was old enough to start in earnest my career with the Massey-Harris Company.

The president of the Company, Senator Lyman Melvin-Jones, and other senior officials used to make frequent visits to France. Mother and Father, who were most hospitable people, always asked them to lunch or dinner in our home. When the

3

meal was drawing to a close, and coffee was being served, I was allowed to come into the dining-room, where I used to sit, wide-eyed with breathless interest, listening to the stories of our guests about life in Canada.

On one unforgettable occasion, in the summer of 1907 when I was nearing the age of fourteen, the Senator turned to my father when dinner was over and the cigars and cigarettes were being passed around, and said, "Duncan, that young son of yours has all the earmarks of becoming a real implement man. Send him out to Canada when he is a little older and we will put him to work in our factory and teach him the business." Then and there my father accepted the offer. My heart was beating so hard and so fast from the excitement of this proposal that I thought all of those sitting around the table must have heard it.

I had lived with the thought of going to Canada ever since that memorable day, and when my father announced my early departure for Toronto, I hailed the news with joy and enthusiasm.

No boy of seventeen ever set out from the shores of Europe on his way to the New World with higher hopes or greater anticipation. I have travelled widely throughout the world ever since, but I have never recaptured the thrill, the elation, the wonderment even, of my first contact with North America.

Everything was different, new and exciting. Everything seemed to be of outsized dimensions: the Statue of Liberty with its vast proportions which, to the trusting eyes of the Italian immigrants clustered on the deck of our trans-Atlantic liner, represented the freedom they had come to seek in the New World; the tall buildings of New York which I gazed at in fascination as I passed them on my way to the railroad station; the large number of cars and trucks, the size of which contrasted so strangely with the smaller and less numerous motorized vehicles to which I was accustomed in the streets of Paris.

Perhaps what struck me most was the unbelievable dimensions of the train in which I travelled to Canada: the massive and imposing locomotive with its clanging bell, the commodious freight and passenger coaches, three times the size of any I had ever seen before.

The unusual arrangement of the sleeping cars was another source of interest; the friendly coloured attendant, the inconvenient upper and lower berths where one had to struggle to undress behind a curtain, the wash-room-cum-smoker at either end of the coach equipped with washbasins, huge brass spittoons, and a comfortable couch where male passengers sat and smoked while others shaved, brushed their teeth, washed their faces, and carried out their morning or evening ablutions which, in France or in England, were undertaken only in the privacy of individual compartments.

That first night, too excited to sleep, I lay in my lower berth and looked out of the window as we sped through the sparsely populated, wintry country, past the clapboard farmhouses and barns with their blankets of heavy snow as they stood out under a full moon. I watched the sleighs on the wide country roads, their drivers wrapped in buffalo robes, and the pine forests, heavy with snow, the frozen lakes and the small towns, so different from those of the Old World. All along the way, the bell on the locomotive clanged its note of warning.

Toronto was a relatively small city in 1910. On my arrival, I was shown the way to the Walker House Hotel, close to the station, where my father had reserved a room for me which, with all meals included, cost $2.50 a day. I stayed there two nights. Such high living was well beyond my budget.

The arrangements my father had made for my journey were simple. I left home with a trunk full of clothes, my fare was paid to my destination, and I was given sufficient money for incidental expenses and two days in the hotel. After that I was on my own.

These arrangements suited me very well. I did not have to look for work because our president had arranged with my father that on my arrival I should be employed by the Toronto works of the Massey-Harris Company at a salary of $9.00 a week.

While enjoying the Walker House's generous breakfast the morning after my arrival, a breakfast very different from the more modest *café au lait et croissant* I was accustomed to in France, I reflected with eager anticipation on the new life opening up before me. I was warmed by a feeling of independence which sprang from the satisfaction I was to experience of earning my own living.

When I arrived I found that Senator Melvin-Jones, the only person I knew in Toronto, was away in western Canada. This was a disappointment, but I was taken to see the general manager, Thomas Findley, a great man in his own right, who gave me a hearty welcome and, in his kindly and fatherly way, tried to make me feel at home in my new surroundings.

Thomas Findley was a very religious man who neither smoked nor drank. He was a leader in his church, a teacher in a highly successful Bible class to which he devoted much of his time, and a tower of strength in the Toronto West End Y.M.C.A. over whose destinies he presided.

I took an immediate liking to him, but I am afraid I made a very poor start on that first morning. Shortly after I sat down in his office, he asked me what church I belonged to. In true French fashion, I did not belong to any. He was greatly shocked, and I was correspondingly embarrassed.

He asked me, however, to come to his home for lunch the following Sunday. But he suggested that before doing so we should foregather at the door of the Bloor Street Presbyterian Church, so that I could share his family pew for the morning service. After the service, I was introduced to Dr. Wallace, the minister, who befriended me throughout my stay in Canada. Then I walked home with the Findley family, all of whose members became life-long friends.

On Monday morning, two days after I had arrived in Canada, I commenced work in the King Street plant at 7:00 a.m.

I was given the job of helper to a couple of men who were working at a bench setting up seeding machinery. They were inclined to take rather a dim view of my English accent and my Continental manners. In the intervals between chewing tobacco and expectorating on the floor, they exchanged rude jokes with their fellow workers about the new addition to the factory's work force. It took me a few weeks to adjust myself but in time I became accustomed to their rough ways, and after a few weeks we got along splendidly together.

Working conditions before World War I were very different and a great deal harder than they are today. We worked fifty-nine hours a week from seven in the morning to twelve, and from one o'clock to six, excepting Saturday when the works closed at 5:00 p.m. In those rugged days, no organization existed in our plants to look after the interests of the workers. Labour unions were still many years away.

In 1910 each worker, myself included, carried a little brass check with his number on it which he dropped into a box as he entered the factory in the morning and when returning to work after lunch. If by any chance a worker was delayed, and dropped his brass check into the slot even one second after the factory whistle had stopped blowing, one hour was deducted from his already painfully small earnings.

Summer holidays were still unknown to factory workers. Their days of rest were limited to such statutory holidays as Christmas Day, New Year's Day, Easter, and Dominion Day.

After I had become accustomed to the hard manual labour and the fifty-nine hour week, I began to thrive on it.

My requirements were modest. I was too tired after the long days in the factory to do anything else in the evenings but go to bed. I found that I could live satisfactorily on my weekly pay of $9.00, and even, by careful budgeting, save between fifty and seventy-five cents a week. Paris had not obliterated my Scottish background.

Having had a good deal of experience in field work at home, I was singled out at the end of the first year to undertake occasionally, mostly in the summer time, the much more interesting work of setting up and demonstrating machinery to the farmers throughout Ontario. This was a rough but most enjoyable experience. My pay was not increased, but I received $1.50 a day to defray all my expenses excepting rail travel.

When the ripe wheat had been harvested, it was the turn of the itinerant threshing crews to move in. Their threshing machine was installed in the barn. They stayed three or four days or more, depending on the size of the crop. The crews consisted of half a dozen men, and at mealtimes all of us would sit around the kitchen table while the farmer's wife, aided usually by a neighbour, cooked and served the meals.

I shall never forget the heat in those kitchens during the height of summer, aggravated as it was by the wood- or coal-fired stoves, nor the swarms of flies which, notwithstanding the various and ingenious models of fly-catchers hung from the ceiling or placed on the table or sideboard, invaded the kitchen during meal hours.

After I had spent a little over two years as a manual worker, and had become well acquainted with conditions in the Province of Ontario, it was suggested that I should try my hand at selling. I did so eagerly, but with only modest success.

On many occasions throughout my life I have had to handle difficult situations which required a certain amount of intestinal fortitude. I cannot recall, however, any which drew more deeply on the reservoirs of my stamina than the experience of travelling several miles in a sleigh during a bitter winter day, and, on arrival at a farm, stepping out from the cutter into the deep snow, with cold reaching down to the very marrow, and setting out to sell a farmer a plough, a drill, or a binder which he had no intention of buying until the following spring—or perhaps not at all.

To my great relief, a few months later I was appointed to an office job. My salary was increased to $14 a week, I no longer had to carry a time check, and the work day started at 8:30 instead of 7:00. I had joined the ranks of the white-collared workers.

Shortly afterwards I was given my first responsible job. I was put in charge of a group of some twenty men who travelled as I had done throughout Ontario setting up and repairing machinery.

During the settlement season in the fall of the year, the Company's books were closed. A number of us were called on to work several extra hours in the evening over a period of two months, for which overtime was always paid. I threw a monkey wrench into the procedure by refusing to accept overtime. I needed the money badly enough, and I didn't want to get in wrong with my fellow workers, but I couldn't bring myself to accept payment for overtime.

I had the rather unsophisticated view that the Company's interests were always paramount. If management felt that overtime was required I was happy to accept their decision—but not for extra remuneration. My attitude in this respect did not endear me to my fellow workers who accused me of trying to curry favour with the bosses. It took time to live this down.

Throughout my early years in Canada I lived a Jekyll and Hyde life.

During the week I was a working man, sharing an inexpensive boarding house near the factory with other workers, lunching and dining in cheap restaurants, wearing overalls and rough clothing.

But on Sundays life was different. Due to the kindness and hospitality of many of our directors, I lunched or dined in their homes, went to church with them, and dressed as they did in a morning coat and top hat which was customary in those days.

Every Sunday, after attending the Bloor Street Presbyterian Church, I lunched in the friendly atmosphere of Thomas Findley's home. He and his charming wife always made me feel as if I were a member of the family.

In the afternoon, I usually attended my host's Bible class, and dined or rather had high tea in the hospitable home of J. N. Shenstone or other directors who invariably took me with them to the evening church services.

My family in Paris were not church-going people, but by the time I had spent three years in Canada, I felt with some justification that my long-term average of church attendance left nothing to be desired.

Once or twice a month, on Sunday evenings, Sir Lyman Melvin-Jones (he was knighted in 1910) used to invite me to dine with him in his home at 145 St. George Street. In size and construction it resembled the home of his next door neighbour, George Gooderham, which has long since been taken over by the York Club.

For some reason which I never understood, this great industrial leader, this unchallenged chieftain who ruled the affairs of our Company with an iron hand, whose judgement was never questioned by the directors or the members of his staff, whose point-of-view was never opposed, took a liking to me.

He had only one daughter in his family, who by that time was married to the Rev. Crawford Brown, the minister of St.

Andrews Presbyterian church. He lived, therefore, alone with his wife, who was frequently away from home, or chose not to come down for dinner on Sunday evenings.

Sir Lyman and I would dine alone, on cold partridges or prairie chickens which he had shot himself, and a bottle of French wine from his excellently stocked cellar. To me, as a young man still in my very early twenties, these were most enjoyable occasions.

Sir Lyman did nearly all the talking; I was an avid listener. He recounted stories of his early youth on the barren and ill-conditioned farm, where life was hard and unproductive; of his early experience in the local town in which he worked for a few months; of an illness which proved to be the turning point of his career, because the local doctor told him that he should find a job in which he could work out in the open air.

This led him to apply for a position with the Harris Manufacturing Company in Brantford to set up, repair, and sell agricultural machinery. Young Lyman was able and ambitious. He showed early signs of a highly developed mechanical sense and was soon recognized by Alanson Harris and his partners as a coming man.

In 1879, the Harris Company decided to open a branch office in Winnipeg to introduce the Harris line to the sparsely populated prairie provinces. Lyman-Jones was chosen for the job and proceeded to Winnipeg through St. Paul, Minnesota, and the Red River Valley which was the usual access to Winnipeg from Ontario at that time.

He soon became a person of importance in the booming little town of Winnipeg. Only a few years after he had landed there, he was elected mayor.

He was so outstandingly successful in the development of the Company's business in western Canada, and made so many valuable suggestions concerning the improvement in the Company's line of machinery, that in 1888 he was recalled to Brantford and made general manager of the Company.

His contribution to the development of the Harris line could not well be overestimated. The open-end binder he designed, and for which he took out many patents, was a major success in Canada and in Europe. It was copied by manufacturers in England, the United States, and Canada.

Three years after Lyman Jones had risen to be the senior executive officer of the Harris Company, he became one of the architects of the amalgamation between the Massey and the Harris groups under the leadership of Hart A. Massey. When the amalgamation was completed in 1891, he became general manager of the newly formed Massey-Harris Company.

Thus was founded, two and a half years before I was born, the Canadian company which carried the name of Massey-Harris to every country where wheat was grown, and which in later years became second in importance among all the farm-implement organizations in the world.

My four years in Canada were soon to be interrupted by the outbreak of World War I.

According to French law, having been born in France, I was considered a French citizen until I reached the age of twenty-one, at which time I had the right to exercise my option either to remain French or to adopt the nationality of my parents. I chose the latter. I was seriously considering remaining in Canada where I thoroughly enjoyed my work and where I was sustained and exhilarated by the buoyant atmosphere of this young and dynamic country.

I was firmly convinced that Canada would be called on to play a great role in world affairs, and I wanted to become a Canadian and to be associated with the expansion which I felt was about to take place.

Fate decreed otherwise.

On July 2nd, 1914, Sir Lyman called me into his office and showed me a telegram he had just received from my father. It contained the news that practically all his French staff had been mobilized, that a moratorium on all payments of debts had been declared, and that he was endeavouring almost single-handedly to carry on the business.

Sir Lyman was a man of action. Turning to me, after reading out the cable, he said, "Jimmie, you speak French and you have learned a good deal about this business. Get yourself on the first boat for France to see what you can do to help your father during these distressing times." He got up, shook me by the hand, and wished me good luck in my new endeavours.

It was the last time I was ever to see him. He died towards the end of the war from an infection following a serious operation from which he would have recovered in a few weeks had medical science been as developed as it is today.

2

Early Background

THE WAR WAS A CRUCIAL TURNING POINT in world history. It was also a crucial turning point in my own life and in that of my father. Before recounting the colourful and tragic events of those days, and the manner in which they influenced my life I feel I should go back a few years to my earlier background.

My sisters and I were born in Paris towards the end of the 19th century. My father and mother had been living there ever since their marriage in 1883.

Our summer vacations were frequently spent in the hospitable home of our grandparents in Banff, a little town north of Aberdeen on the rugged coast of Scotland.

It was from the stories our grandparents used to tell us, and the records written in their family Bible, that we learned all we know about our forefathers.

All of them came from the Highlands of Scotland. They were hardy, modest living, well educated, hard working and God-fearing people. Some were merchants, others farmers; others again sought their fortune in foreign lands as Scottish people are wont to do.

I have always been grateful that I come from a race of people whose physical and moral fibre were toughened by the harsh and forbidding conditions that existed in the Highlands of Scotland throughout the past centuries.

Some of my forebears were among the many who left the shores of Scotland either to serve their country in foreign wars, or to settle in North America, South Africa, Australia, and other distant lands where conditions were more rewarding.

There was Solomon Shearer, born in 1774 in the north of Scotland who enlisted as a youth, fought under Sir John Moore in Ireland and under Wellington in the Peninsula war, was shipwrecked in the Channel on the way home and settled down in Banff to live to the ripe old age of 87.

His only daughter, a handsome and charming young woman, married my grandfather, Alexander Milne, in 1836. I remember her kindly presence, her fine features, and dignified bearing when, as a very young boy, I spent summer vacations at St. Ann's Hill, my grandfather's home in Banff.

My grandfather's grandfather was Commander George Lyons, who skippered the two-masted, square-rigged brigantine, which was captured on May 30th, 1813, by the American brig, *Yankee*. This naval encounter is documented by a statement signed by the commander of the *Yankee* and his officers:

> Dated at sea on board the *Yankee*, 3rd June 1813. This certifies that George Lyons of the Brig *Thames* and crew were captured on the 30th of May, 1813, by the Brig *Yankee*, Elish Snow, Commander, belonging to the United States of America. This day have given their parole of honor not to take up arms against the United States of America during the continuance of this present war, unless regularly exchanged, under pains and penalties attached to a break of parole. The said George Lyons defended his vessel like a brave and intrepid Commander, to the last extremity, and in our opinion is worthy of the confidence of any gentleman.
>
> Signed: Elish Snow
Witnessed: Thomas James, 1st. Lieut.
Samuel Barton, 2nd Lieut.
George A. Bruce, 3rd Lieut.

The brig *Yankee* set sail for Jamaica where Commander George Lyons, who was allowed to keep his sword in recognition of his gallant conduct, was put ashore with all his crew.

Commander Lyons settled down in Jamaica to await the arrival of a British ship in which he and his crew were to be repatriated to Scotland. But this was not to be. Yellow fever, that scourge of the British West Indies in the 18th and 19th centuries, broke out in Jamaica. Commander Lyons, his son who had also served on the *Thames*, and nearly all the members of his crew died of the epidemic.

My Duncan grandfather was born in Buckie, Banffshire, in 1826 and emigrated to Australia as a young man, lured by the exciting news of a gold rush which was taking place in Ballarat, sixty-five miles northwest of Melbourne. He found no gold, other than one rather remarkable nugget which remained in my family's possession until it was stolen from my mother's home on the French Riviera, which was occupied by the military after the Italians entered the war against France in the early part of World War II.

Disappointed by his experience in the gold mines, my grand-father reverted to his old profession and established a contract-ing business close to Melbourne where he built roads, bridges, and highways. He would probably have remained in Australia all his life had he not been thrown from a runaway horse. He almost died of concussion, and was invalided home to Scotland as a result.

My father was born in Melbourne in 1856. He was eight years old at the time of his father's accident. Together with his parents and his two half-brothers, he embarked on a square-rigged ship which carried wool back to England.

The trip was a memorable one, for the ship was nearly lost in the treacherous and wind-swept mountainous seas while rounding Cape Horn. Later it was becalmed in the North At-lantic and ran short of water. The trip from Australia took four months and a week.

A few years after their return to Scotland, my grandfather, who had recently been appointed factor of the home farm of Lord Ashburnum at Battle Abbey, died of a gunshot wound while out hunting. My grandmother was left with her five children of which my father at the age of fourteen was the eldest. The youngest was three weeks old.

Two years later, the family moved back to Banff, where my father, then sixteen years old, entered his uncle's business as an apprentice. This was an important step in his career, because his uncle, J. W. Murray, was the owner of a foundry and a manufacturer of simple farm tools. There my father learned the rudiments of the farm-implement business which was to become his life's work.

After a few years in his uncle's firm, where he became cashier and accountant, my father decided to strike out on his own and travelled to London in 1877 in search of greater opportunities.

Here he went through a harrowing experience. He knew no one and had no capital other than a keen brain and an unusual capacity for hard work. Jobs were hard to find. Day after day he walked the streets of London looking for work. The small savings he had brought with him from Scotland were nearly exhausted when at last he found a job of minor importance in a firm of tea merchants.

Six weeks later, while walking to work one day, he met the senior partner of the firm of Ben Reid & Company, farm-implement manufacturers, with whom he had become acquainted while he worked for his uncle in Banff. Father was immediately offered a position as a salesman in Scotland and Ireland, which he readily accepted. He was back once again in the farm-implement business and remained in it for the rest of his life.

A year later, the company decided to open a branch in France. My father, who was then twenty-two years of age, was chosen as their representative in that country. Although without knowledge of the language or the customs of the country, he succeeded beyond expectations, and his qualities of salesmanship, his organizational ability, his enthusiasm, and his activity soon brought his firm and himself to the forefront.

The rapidity with which my father acquired a knowledge of French and of the farm-implement industry attracted the attention of one of the European representatives of the D. M. Osborne Company, an important farm-machinery manufacturer of Auburn, New York, which was then making strenuous efforts to enter the European market. In 1881, when my father was twenty-five, he was appointed European General Manager of the D. M. Osborne Company and set out to establish agencies in nearly every country in Europe, including Russia, and in Algeria and Tunisia on the North African continent.

Father was now well established, and earning a substantial income. His thoughts turned to the charming Scottish lassie he had met in the days when he was working with his uncle in Banff, and with whom he had kept in touch by frequent exchange of letters. Late in 1883 he returned to Scotland, married my mother, and the young couple travelled to France for their honeymoon.

My mother had just entered her twenties when she became engaged to my father. From the early photographs I still have of her, she was a very beautiful young girl.

She spent most of her life in France, and I will always recall her as a warm-hearted, kindly, handsome and dignified woman. She remained that way until her death in Toronto at the age of ninety-two. She would undoubtedly have continued to live in France had she and my sister not been obliged to evacuate their home on the Riviera during the early stages of World War II.

Like my father, she had been quick to learn French and became completely bilingual, although, unlike him, she retained throughout her long life, when speaking French, overtones of the Scottish accent she had brought with her to France from the Highlands of her native land.

My mother invariably accompanied my father on his business trips all over continental Europe and North Africa. Few people knew Europe as thoroughly as he did in those days when travel was so much more burdensome and difficult than it is today. Unfortunately, the long train journeys, the discomforts of travel in Russia, the Balkans, and North Africa, began to tell on his health, which had always been somewhat precarious. In 1886, following the advice of his doctors, and my mother's urgings, he resigned from the D. M. Osborne Company and founded his own business in Paris as an importer and distributor of agricultural implements.

In those early days Britain was the largest exporter of farm machinery to the continent of Europe. My father represented two of the leading British manufacturers, but American and Canadian industrialists were beginning to take a greater interest in the European market.

Hart Massey, the owner of the Massey Manufacturing Company of Toronto, and the grandfather of the Rt. Hon.

Vincent Massey, was one of these. My father took over the exclusive representation of this Canadian firm for France, Belgium, and North Africa. Although I was not born at the time, this decision was to affect my entire business career.

Throughout the decade which followed, my father's business expanded rapidly and his firm became one of the three largest in the implement business in Europe.

In those days, and until his death in 1921, there was no more familiar or conspicuous figure in the French and Belgian agricultural implement trade than my father. His spirit of enterprise, his initiative combined with his outstanding personality, and his irrepressible sense of humour left an impression on the trade as a whole which is vividly remembered to this day.

His French was perfect and, enjoying, as many Scots do, an appreciation of the well turned phrase and the appropriate word, he spoke and wrote both languages with exceptional facility and brilliance.

His success was all the more remarkable since he was in delicate health throughout his life. My boyhood was coloured with the family's anxiety over his frequently recurring illnesses, and the predictions of his early passing which, fortunately, proved to be overly pessimistic.

3

A Paris Boyhood

WE LIVED in a section of Paris built in the 1880's which, although far removed from the more fashionable quarters,
boasted of its wide streets and its proximity to the Buttes Chau-
mont, a small but charming park with an artificial lake, to which
Mother took us every day to romp and play, and watch the ducks
disporting themselves in the water.

The broad avenues in our part of town, the wide streets, the
architecture of the apartment houses, had undoubtedly been
influenced by the famous town planner, the Baron Haussmann,
who, during the reign of Napoleon III, changed the face of
the capital city.

Our apartment, on the rue Meynadier, just a stone's throw
from the Park, had a bathroom, a somewhat rare occurrence in
our part of the town in the 1890's. Other less favoured tenants
of the neighbouring apartment houses hired the use of a tin
bath from a man who made his daily rounds from street to
street, leading a little pony cart specially constructed to accom-
modate the bath and two large metal water containers.

The streets of Paris during the last years of the 19th century
were the subject of constant interest to a little boy watching the
proceedings from his balcony. Street life was more leisurely

19

and more exciting and colourful than in our present age of mechanization and of greater abundance.

In those distant years, no taxicabs, trucks or motor-buses honked their urgent way through the ever-growing traffic, filling the air as they went by with polluting fumes.

The cabs, or *fiacres*, filled me with delight. They had four steel-rimmed wheels; the coachman sat up on the box clothed in a fawn-coloured three-tiered cape over a greatcoat with large round white buttons.

It was the rattling hand-carts, however, pulled or pushed by men, or more frequently by women, which elicited my greatest interest. These were the colourful street vendors who, hawking their wares from door to door with their familiar cries, would bring the housewives running into the street to purchase their supplies for the day. The hand-carts were full of fresh vegetables, meat or fish purchased from Les Halles, a central market, often before dawn, and then trundled and rattled across the city to their accustomed or allocated sales area.

Further up our street, an open-air market was installed each Sunday and Thursday morning. Awnings were placed over the hand-carts and stretched on poles across the pavement so as to shelter the purchasers from inclement weather.

Goods of all kinds were displayed and their merits loudly proclaimed, with more enthusiasm than veracity. On display were groceries, flowers, fresh fish, game, skinned rabbits, chickens—killed and dressed, or tied by their feet in their coops —eggs, and even inexpensive dress materials.

Trade was brisk in these open-air markets, and on a strictly cash-and-carry basis. Costs were low and well within the reach of the pocketbook of the average residents in our part of town. They were not inflated as they are today by expensive wrappings, attractive packaging, tin containers, nor by the high cost of delivery, of credit, of expensive rentals, of advertising, or of attractive display windows.

In those more modest days there were only two profits between the producer and the ultimate customer; those of the farmers, who carted their goods to Les Halles, and those of the vendor, who sold them to the ultimate purchaser.

Our streets was always full of intriguing sounds. In the morning and in the evening little boys with an arm full of newspapers would come running through the streets shouting out the exciting headlines. At other times itinerant and poorly dressed singers or violin players would take to the streets in the hopes of making enough to keep body and soul together through the generosity of those who would drop them a coin as they passed by. My mother, whose heart was always touched by the underprivileged, would give my sisters and me coins to toss down from our balcony.

With the regularity of migrating birds, as winter approached and the leaves began to fall, hundreds of *marchands de marron*, the toasted-chestnut sellers who hailed from their native villages in the mountainous center of France, descended on Paris to earn enough money during the winter months through the sale of their locally grown chestnuts, to see them through the rest of the year. They could be seen everywhere, pushing their little carts laden with chestnuts, and equipped with a charcoal grill on which these were roasted as the vendors went their rounds through the streets of Paris. They attracted the attention of their customers by the shrill sound of a whistle activated by the steam generated by the charcoal furnace. These Auvernois usually did a brisk business.

Printer's ink never seemed to harm anyone in the '90's for everything that was edible—fish, meats, fruits, vegetables—was wrapped up in newspapers. The only exception seemed to be those long loaves of delicious bread carried unwrapped under the arms of little ragged messenger boys who, ill-kempt and unwashed, delivered them from door to door.

These were the days when the great double-decked buses known as *impériales*, pulled by dapple-grey Percheron horses, ensured passenger service between the various parts of the city. About once a week, my mother would take me with her when shopping in the center of Paris. As we always left our home early in the morning, we were usually successful in obtaining two seats on the top of the bus, right beside the driver. Occasionally, if he was a friendly fellow, he would let me hold the ends of his reins, which made me feel very important, but never, unfortunately, his whip which I coveted greatly.

One day, as I was walking with my father to his office, he

pointed out an interesting innovation: a cab with hard rubber tires. It took its place proudly in the cab stands on the corner of our street, an aristocrat among the lesser steel-tired vehicles.

On a later occasion my father took me for an exciting drive in one of these modern conveyances, free from the rattle and the noise of the steel-tired wheels on the cobblestones of Paris, and people would stop and watch us as we silently drove by.

Sometimes of a Sunday afternoon, my father and mother would take my sisters and myself on a bus to the Grands Boulevards where, after a long walk and a lot of window shopping, we would be installed on the terrace of the Café de la Paix, at the corner of the Place de l'Opéra, or at some other pavement café, where white-aproned waiters bustling about with incredible activity would serve us hot chocolate and *croissants* on round white marble-topped tables, while my mother and father partook of more sophisticated beverages.

At other times our parents would take us to the open-air *guignol* shows, of which there were several in the Champs Elysées. There we sat on little wooden benches and gazed, wide-eyed with interest and emotion, at the intriguing and exciting convolutions of the puppets activated by unseen operators, hidden from the public eye by a wooden stage drop.

Those were the days when the city was exclusively lit by gas. In the evening, when it was becoming dusk, uniformed employees of the gas company would go from street to street with a long pole in their hands, ingeniously equipped so as to enable them to turn on the jet and light the gas at the same time. We used to watch their progress from our balcony as one lamp-post after another sprang into light.

Our apartment house was modest but well built. It had no elevator, but although we lived on the third floor this was never a problem, at least for us youngsters. The corridors and staircases were lit by gas jets. There was something very cozy about this form of lighting. In the evenings our sitting room was deep in shadows, but the large table in the center was brilliantly lit by a large petrol lamp, and the whole family gathered around it, the children to do lessons, my mother to sew or knit, and my father, from whom I later caught the habit, to work diligently on papers he had brought home from his office.

The ceilings in our apartment were high, the walls were ornamented with wood frame patterns as was customary in the better houses in those days. The ceiling of our drawing-room was embellished with paintings of soft white clouds against a blue sky.

In those days people worked a lot harder to earn their living than in our present age. The six-day week was a standard practice, and many worked also on Sunday morning until twelve o'clock. My father always did.

Frequently he would take me down to his office on a Sunday morning and entrust me with the opening of the mail. He warned me that no envelope should be thrown away, but carefully split open and speared on a nail ready to be used for scribbling pads.

Like the majority of educated men of his time, my father wrote in a fine, legible, flowing style, an achievement which all my past and present secretaries will attest was never emulated by his son.

All the letters in my father's office were written by hand with copying ink. Sometimes I was given the responsible task of making copies under a press set up in the corner of his office.

Although we had a gas jet in the hall which gave off a small flickering light and a rather unpleasant odour, we used lamps in the other parts of our home which mother, or our servants—we had two of them at the time—would carry from room to room, wherever the family was assembled.

In those days few people could afford to travel to the seaside or the mountains for their summer holidays. Certainly our family couldn't. Although occasionally we children were sent to Scotland to stay with our grandparents in Banff, we usually spent our holidays in a small villa which my father rented in a village called Olnay in the outskirts of Paris. We used to spend three months there, and my father commuted by train every day from Paris.

In 1898, my father and mother decided that we should

move permanently to the country. We rented a large house at a place called Gagny.

Father was a very enterprising man. He had already made two visits to the United States and he was one of the first importers to introduce American typewriters and bicycles to the French market, and the first in our whole neighbourhood to equip our new house with central heating.

When we rented our new home in Gagny, it had only one bathroom, which was installed in a room off the stables and carriage house. As the carriage house was at least a couple of minutes' walk from our house and had a strong odour of stables —which even in France was regarded as undesirable in a bathroom—my father decided that this impractical arrangement should be discarded and that two bathrooms should be installed in our house. This unprecedented action was widely commented on by all our neighbours. They took a dim view of these new-fangled American ideas, and felt that installing central heating and two bathrooms in the house, with all the dangers of leakage which such dispositions would probably entail, was a very unsound and hazardous procedure.

Our proprietor was so outraged when he heard about it that he threatened to sue my father for having made these unheard-of innovations without consulting him. He was only pacified when my father signed an agreement that he would compensate him for any damage that might occur to the house during our tenancy. He also agreed to remove the offending bathrooms and central heating when our lease expired.

Perhaps the most vivid recollection of my early childhood was when, on December 31st, 1899, my father and mother decided that my sisters and I should be allowed to stay up to see in the new century.

It was a great occasion. Father had invited a few friends from Paris to celebrate with us; champagne was brought up from the cellar, and as the old grandfather's clock, which my mother had brought with her from Scotland, struck twelve, all the assembled company raised glasses and drank to the new century.

Father had brought back, from a recent trip to the United States, an Edison phonograph, with a long brass horn supported on a tripod, over which we children had a habit of tripping with disastrous results, and in consequence of which the horn had a somewhat battered appearance. On this occasion, after we had toasted the new century, a wax record, which had already been put into the phonograph, played "God Save the Queen," during the rendition of which we all stood at attention. It was an exciting and emotional evening.

4

Formative Years

WITH THE NEW CENTURY, a crisis overtook my father's affairs. His business, as an importer of farm machinery from Canada and from Great Britain together with bicycles and hardware from the United States, had grown rapidly and prospered greatly. But France suffered in 1899, 1900, and 1901 from a serious agricultural depression which resulted in an abnormal accumulation of inventories—one of these periodic recessions which have always bedevilled the agricultural-implement industry.

This situation was aggravated by the very considerable expense incurred in connection with the 1900 world exhibition. My father had a very large stand exhibiting all kinds of farm equipment, and he participated in many competitive and costly field trials in the environs of Paris, and in many other large cities throughout France.

The upshot of it all was that my father's firm found itself short of working capital.

He was not alone in this. His two chief competitors, representing the McCormick and the Deering lines, both manufactured in the United States and long since absorbed by the International Harvester Company of Chicago, were in the same position. The financial standing of these three firms was good, but their liquidity was impaired through excessive inventories of unsold machinery.

Each of them appealed to their respective suppliers to grant them an extension of credit beyond their specified payment dates, so as to give them time to sell off their inventories and recover their liquidity. The American companies agreed to this arrangement, but the Massey-Harris Company, which was at that time my father's most important supplier, insisted on payment at due date, a condition which he could not meet.

The choice lay between bankruptcy and the somewhat invidious proposal that Massey-Harris should take over my father's business, move into his premises, and that he should henceforth continue to operate the organization as their manager, and gradually divest himself of his other lines of activity.

Business in those days was more ruthless by far than it is today. The Massey-Harris Company had father over a barrel, and for a man of his high moral standing there was no alternative but to accept their proposal.

Without compensation, therefore, the Canadian company took over the organization which father had founded, to which he had devoted many years of work, and which had grown so rapidly under his leadership. Thereafter, working for a salary only, he continued as head of the company which used to be his own.

I was too young at the time to know what was going on in my father's mind, but no doubt this change in his fortunes was a serious blow to him. At no time, however, did I ever hear him complain. On the contrary, he carried on the promotion of the Massey-Harris Company's business with the same dedication and success as if it were still his own.

During that period I had my first taste of the farm-machinery business. From what I saw of it, I liked it. I have ever since.

My father owned a carriage with a pair of Shetland ponies, which he frequently drove himself. Every Sunday during the summer months he would take me out with him to watch our farm machinery operating in farms situated in the vicinity of the small village in which we lived.

We left early in the morning and as we travelled along the country roads I could see the harvesters, men and women, carrying their scythes over their shoulders, two large round loaves of bread with a hole in the center slung over their left arm, and holding in the other a wicker basket containing their breakfast and luncheon of bread, a large hunk of cheese, and several bottles of red wine.

All day long in the broiling sun, the men would cut the golden wheat with the rhythmic swing of their scythes while the women followed behind, tying the fallen wheat into sheaves with a cord of straw which they fashioned as they went along. At ten in the morning, and again at noon and at four o'clock, they were allowed short periods of rest, during which, sitting under the shade of a tree, they would eat their bread and cheese, and drink generously of their wine. And so they worked throughout the long day until the sun had set, when they returned home in the gathering dusk.

Here and there the modern farmers, who were few and far between, would be operating one of our Canadian binders, much to the disapproval of the harvesters, who looked on the use of this new-fangled device as a threat to their continued employment.

It was still customary in the early days of the new century to hold country fairs throughout France where farm implements were exhibited and took part in competitive trials. These affairs were taken very seriously. Judges, well versed in farming operations, used to choose the winning machine and its runner-up, and at the close of the day present the winning firms with a handsome gold or bronze medal.

Sometimes, if one of these fairs was held not too far from Paris, my father would take me with him, in pursuance of his policy of training me in the various activities of the farm-implement business.

When we got to the fair grounds, father would introduce me to his agents, his travellers, and sometimes his competitors. Throughout the early part of the day, I would listen to men's talk about farm machinery. Later, I would thrill with pride when, as frequently happened, our Canadian machine carried off the *Grand Prix* from its American and British competitors. My father, looking very elegant and debonair in his grey topper, would step forward to receive the gold or bronze medal from the judges.

When I was about eleven years old, my father suffered from a serious attack of pneumonia, which almost cost him his life.

During the frequent bouts of lung congestion from which my father suffered, my mother, in her distress, used to tell me of her fears for the future, and how the time might come, sooner than I expected, when I would be the head of the family. She used to encourage me to work hard so that I could equip myself for this role. All this, I am sure, had a profound effect on the early moulding of my character.

My boyhood was happy in that I was living in a relatively modest but comfortable home surrounded by love and affection; but mine was also a serious boyhood in which work played a much more important part than recreation.

My education took place entirely in France. I have never attended an English school.

After kindergarten and primary schools, I spent two years at the Collège Rollin, an excellent but rather forbidding institution, where the hours of study were long and sports programs non-existent. A small gravel courtyard was our only recreation field.

According to my father's judgement, private tuition at home in the subjects which, in his opinion, would best equip me for a business career, plus a knowledge of foreign languages was the most desirable program. This was probably not a very good plan, and certainly it would be a very bad one in our present era but it never stopped me from earning my living!

My father was influenced in his choice of this somewhat unusual educational plan by the fact that there was never a time throughout my boyhood or as I began to grow up that I had ever entertained any doubt about what I was going to do with my life. It was always a foregone conclusion that I was going to follow in my father's footsteps in the farm-machinery business.

When I was still going to school, and later when I took private tuition at home, I used to spend Thursdays, which was the weekly school holiday, and Sunday mornings, erecting farm machinery in my father's warehouse. I was paid for it on a piece-work basis and usually earned one dollar for a ten-hour day.

The farm-implement business in France in those days was still in its infancy. Every time a new machine was designed and built, the head office in Toronto used to send mechanics over to France during the summer months, to introduce these machines to the dealers and the farmers. They travelled from place to place throughout France, attending pre-arranged trials to which hundreds of farmers and many dealers had been invited.

As none of these Canadian experts could speak French, my father hit on the plan of sending me to accompany them and to serve as interpreter during the summer holidays. This proved to be an invaluable experience. When I was still little more than a youngster, I became accustomed to talking to large groups of people. It gave me an insight, too, into the operations of the farm machinery in the field.

By the time I was fifteen, my father used to send me out occasionally alone to carry out demonstrations and book orders when dealers or farmers became sufficiently enthusiastic over the performance of the machinery to make a purchase.

Before I was sixteen, my father decided that it was time for me to improve my English, and I was sent to Banff, the home of my grandparents. Here I was given tuition by a retired professor of the Banff Academy, James Allan, to whose respect for a well turned phrase, a correct and precise choice of words, and the suppression of superfluous verbiage I will be eternally grateful.

When I returned from Scotland, my father sent me to Berlin, Germany to learn the language. I remained there just under one year.

The arrangements were that I should spend the mornings working in the Berlin office of the Massey-Harris Company, and my afternoons taking private tuition in German.

Because I lived in a German home and spoke either German or nothing at all, I became quite proficient in this language within seven or eight months. Then, following my experience in France, I was sent out with Canadian experts who came to demonstrate new designs of machinery, to interpret for them. We travelled together all over Germany. I thoroughly enjoyed my eleven and a half months in that country.

Two evenings a week I took night lessons in draftsmanship and mechanics at the Charlottenburger Hoch Schüle. On other evenings, with friends of my own age, I used to roller skate on the Charlottenburger Chaussee, where occasionally we were halted with all the rest of the traffic as Kaiser Wilhelm II drove at high speed from his Berlin residence to Potsdam, usually in a large open car, preceded and followed by others occupied by members of his family, his entourage, and an imposing contingent of military guards.

I would have stayed longer in Berlin had it not been that a friend introduced me to a young and, to my undiscriminating eyes, fascinating German vaudeville girl, of whom I became very fond. Max Stoevandt, the manager of our German business, who had served in his youth in the Prussian army and had never lost his military bearing or his rigidity of outlook, came to the conclusion, which was probably not erroneous, that if I stayed around Berlin much longer, my young German vaudeville friend would teach me more than the German language! He took it upon himself, therefore, to write to my father and, somewhat to my dismay, I was summoned home to Paris with what seemed to me quite unseemly haste.

My experience in Germany had been rewarding. I had learned another language and widened my experience in the affairs of our Company. I had enjoyed and come to understand the German people, and, generally speaking, my horizons had been broadened.

5

The Miracle of the Marne

IT WAS NOT LONG AFTER I returned to Paris from Germany that I was shipped off to Canada for four years, as I have recounted in the first chapter of this book.

When I left Germany, I had no premonitions of the military and political holocaust that was to follow just four years later.

But in August of 1914, when I returned to France from Canada, Armageddon had come. The events of that time are clearly etched in my mind.

On August 4th, the day after Germany had declared war, I sailed for France from New York. The trip was uneventful but the suspense and lack of news of the towering events which were taking place in Europe was a strain on the passengers.

On August 12th, our ship docked in Southampton, and when, after the gang-plank had been lowered, the news boys came on board with the daily papers, they were soon sold out.

We were stunned to read that neutral Belgium had been invaded the day after we had left New York. We read with optimism of General Joffre's offensive, of his triumphant crossing of the frontier into Alsace-Lorraine. Most of us came to the sadly erroneous conclusion that the war would be short and that Germany would soon be defeated.

From the deck of our ship we watched large groups of British soldiers, members of the expeditionary force, awaiting convoys to take them to the Continent.

Along the walls of the Customs House were men pasting up recruiting posters, illustrating the stern face and penetrating eyes of Lord Kitchener, his finger pointing straight at the reader over the legend, "Your King and Country Need You." We were soon to be told that the War Office had instructed that this compelling poster should be displayed on every hoarding in the land.

A military band was playing martial music as our boat left the dock for the French port of Le Havre, having taken on board a large contingent of troops and equipment. They parked themselves all over the decks. Good humour, enthusiasm, and boisterous spirits prevailed. The soldiers seemed to be keenly anticipating their arrival in France. Many expressed the hope that they would get to the front before the war was over.

The weather was sunny and the sea was calm as our ship headed out across the Channel, and the coast of England was clearly delineated on the horizon. Few among those gallant young men seemed to feel any foreboding that they might be looking at the cliffs of their native land for the last time.

We landed in France on August 13th. After a tedious journey of almost twenty-four hours, in a train crowded with French troops, which was switched to sidings at nearly every station to allow troop trains to pass us on their way to the front, we arrived in Paris on the morning of August 15th.

As I drove through the streets to my father's home, the city seemed deserted. Nearly every store was closed and signs were pasted on the steel shutters saying "Fermé pour cause de mobilisation." Civilian traffic was reduced to a trickle.

In all the squares and open places young recruits, still in civilian clothes, were being drilled, taught to march and to form fours.

As we turned into the rue Lafayette, traffic was halted as an infantry battalion, in red-and-blue uniforms and headed by a military band, was marched down the street, to entrain for the front at the Gare du Nord. The martial music and the beat of marching feet brought men, women, and their children to almost every balcony on both sides of the street. They cheered the soldiers as they marched by, some waving, others throwing flowers to them.

At the Place de la Concorde, my attention was immediately drawn to the statue of Alsace-Lorraine, which, ever since this province had been lost to France in 1871, had been covered with wreaths and flowers as a symbol of mourning. It was now standing out in all its majesty as if it had risen from the ashes of the past, symbolic of the faith of all Frenchmen that their lost province would be restored to them once again.

There had been no exaggeration in my father's cable to Sir Lyman Melvin-Jones. All our staff, excepting a few oldsters, had been called to the colours. Although July and August were normally the busiest months of the year, nearly all the rolltop desks were shut down. Our office reminded me of its appearance on a Sunday afternoon.

From my family and friends, I soon learned that the optimism which had prevailed in the early days of August was rapidly giving way to concern and apprehension. Little more was heard about France's triumphant offensive. Joffre's communiqués were noncommittal. The great forts of Liège had fallen on the day of my arrival home; the German hordes were slicing their way through Belgium leaving a trail of devastation and horror behind them.

A few days after my arrival in Paris, one of our Belgian dealers, a friend of my father, walked into our office, unshaven, unwashed, and exhausted. He was the first refugee we had seen. We were shocked at the stories he told of men and women herded together in the main squares of Belgian villages and shot; of towns and hamlets burned and sacked, of ruined crops; of the formidable German armies driving through Belgium, raping, pillaging, burning as they marched through the defence-less towns and villages.

He was one of the fortunate ones because he had a car of his own in which he had already packed the essentials for a long journey, including spare tins of gasoline, in readiness for emergency.

As the Germans entered one side of his village, he, with his wife and two children, had left by the other on their way to Paris, a trip which in normal times would have taken a day but which had taken them ten. Everywhere he had seen French and Belgian troops, sometimes in orderly but mostly in disorderly retreat.

Daily the news worsened. Louvain, that great medieval city with its incomparable library, town hall, and treasures of Gothic art, was sacked and in flames. The ravaging armies of Germany, undeterred by the condemnation of all countries, pressed forward with unrelenting vigour. The north of France was invaded. Refugees were crowding through Paris on their way south. Never a day passed that my father did not bring back one of our dealers and his family, refugees from the north, to lunch or dine at my mother's hospitable table. Each had tales to tell of horror and vandalism, of mass shootings of civilians, of burning villages and pillaged homes.

On August 30th, nearly two weeks after my return from Canada, my father decided that all the family should leave immediately for Scotland while he remained in Paris to look after the Company's interests. I refused to leave. I had not been sent over from Canada to abandon the duties assigned to me and retire to the comparative safety of Scotland. After many harrowing discussions, it was decided that my mother and sisters should go, and that I would remain with my father.

I was despatched to the British Consulate to try to secure accommodation on the overcrowded trains leaving for the coast.

On September 1st, came the news that the retreat of the British Expeditionary Force from Mons had taken an appalling toll of life. Thousands upon thousands of members of the small but highly trained expeditionary force, many of whom belonged to the regular army, had fought their first and last battle of the war.

When I called at the British Embassy on the following day, I received the news that the redoubtable General von Kluck was advancing on Paris by forced marches, that his outposts were already within thirty miles of the capital, and that the French government was leaving Paris for Bordeaux that same evening.

Panic had seized the people of Paris. Hundreds of thousands were leaving the capital for the long trek south, with such of their possessions as they could take with them loaded on carts, carriages, automobiles, trucks, pushcarts, baby carriages, or anything on wheels.

By the morning of September 3rd, all business was at a standstill.

I spent the day wandering through the city, fascinated by the excitement, the confusion, the fear, and the sorrow which had settled over Paris. In the courtyards of various ministries, great fires could be seen, where papers and documents of all kinds were being thrown from windows to be burned.

Towards evening, posters were rapidly being pasted on the hoardings at all the prominent places throughout Paris. They carried a proclamation by General Gallieni, the Commander of the Army of Paris. The message, short and tragic, consisted of but a few lines:

> The members of the Government of the Republic have left Paris to give a new impulse to the national defence.
>
> I have received a mandate to defend Paris against the invader. This mandate I shall carry out to the end.
>
> Paris, Sept. 3rd, 1914
> Military Governor of Paris,
> Commander of the Army of Paris,
> Gallieni

Here and there small groups of people gathered around to read the poster and then all would break out into animated conversation. None were strangers, all were as if bound together by a common tragedy. Many of the women and some of the men, on reading the simple words, "This mandate I shall carry out to the end," burst into sobs; others moved silently away, tears rolling down their tired, anxious faces.

The atmosphere throughout the city was charged with emotion. French flags could be seen hanging out from many balconies as a silent token of patriotism and defiance. Many thought, with good reason, that this might be the last time the tricolour would be allowed to fly from their homes.

I was at last successful in obtaining rail and boat tickets for my mother and sisters. On September 6th my father and I accompanied them to the Gare du Nord and later, as the time of separation came, we stood on the platform and watched the train pull out, with my reluctant mother and sisters waving tearfully to us from their carriage window.

Father and I then proceeded to the exit of the station to get a taxi to take us home. To our surprise, although we waited well over an hour, none was anywhere in sight. Finally, we started on the long walk home.

We had walked about a mile, when suddenly hundreds of taxicabs appeared, one following behind the other, each carrying five infantrymen with their rifles and equipment. These were followed by trucks and buses, all full of soldiers. What we were witnessing, on that afternoon, was one of the most important turning points in World War I.

Early that morning, every taxicab in Paris had been stopped by orders of General Gallieni, the passengers were asked to step down, and all the taxis were told to rendezvous at one of the central squares.

By 2:00 p.m., every vehicle was loaded with soldiers and despatched to the exposed flank of General von Kluck's army on the River Ourq near Meaux, forty miles from Paris. Over 6,000 men were thus rushed into battle. They played an important part in what later became known as the Miracle of the Marne, the battle which stopped the drive towards Paris, and rolled back the advancing German forces to defence positions along the Aisne.

The Germans had evidently overreached themselves. Vast areas of France had been overrun. The roads and fields were teeming with fleeing refugees. French resistance appeared to be crumbling all along the front. Both allied armies were falling back and had recrossed the Marne during the first days of September. But the army of von Kluck was exhausted by the speed of its advance. Von Kluck knew this, but he assumed that the French were so demoralized that no further resistance was possible, and that Paris was within his grasp. He had not foreseen Gallieni's sudden blow to his exposed flank.

By September 9th, the tide had turned. His exhausted troops were in full retreat. The allied forces had regained their morale. The myth of the invincibility of the German armies had been shattered.

After the successful Battle of the Marne, refugees began to return to Paris, although the government remained for some time in Bordeaux. Life took on, once more, a semblance of reality.

6

A Mission to Arras

THE PROBLEM MASSEY-HARRIS WAS FACING in France was one
of shortage of funds to carry on its operations, due to the moratorium which provided that collection of debts incurred prior to
August 2nd, 1914, could not be enforced by law.

My father, always a resourceful man, came to the conclusion
that persuasion and rapid means of locomotion were the only
solutions to our financial problems. Undeterred by the fact that
in 1914 the Massey-Harris Company owned no motorcars anywhere in the world, he purchased a Model T Ford. I was instructed to learn to drive, and thereafter to undertake a whirlwind tour of all our principal agents in France to endeavour
to extract from them, on a voluntary basis, some of the money
they owed us but which, owing to the moratorium, they didn't
have to pay. I am afraid what took place with my Model T Ford
hardly lived up to the whirlwind tour I was instructed to make.

The tires were my chief worry. I counted myself lucky if
I didn't experience more than six punctures a day, all of which
I had to repair myself. Pumping up tires with an ever-leaking
pump was another cause of irritation. Horses, pulling their
country carts in narrow winding lanes, invariably took fright at

the unaccustomed sight of a motor car, causing delays and abuse from irate drivers.

One real problem, especially in winter time after night-fall, was that when driving downhill or on slippery roads at a slow pace, the evil-smelling acetylene lights became so dim that I could see only a few feet ahead. The brightness of the headlights was related to the speed of travel.

All these difficulties were small compared to the problem of starting the engine on cold winter mornings. The first operation was to let the water out of the radiator and fill it up with hot water carried from the hotel kitchen. The next was to take the sparkplugs out and clean them with a toothbrush and gasoline which I always carried with me for this purpose. The third operation was to jack up the rear wheels. Then there was nothing left to do but crank, and crank, and crank until I and some of the interested and helpful onlookers who had gathered around were all but exhausted.

While these preliminaries were going on, the country folk who still travelled by horse-drawn carriages would stand around making rude jokes about modern means of locomotion. In-variably a smart aleck would call out that I should pour oats in the gasoline tank, a helpful suggestion that was always re-ceived with gales of laughter from the onlookers.

In spite of these handicaps, my collection campaign proved to be successful, probably because nearly all our agents had been mobilized and my dealings were almost exclusively with their wives, who responded to my youthful hard-luck stories of fin-ancial stringency more readily than their hard-boiled husbands would have done.

Many of the farmers, the moratorium notwithstanding, paid our agents on due date and in cash, usually in the form of silver five-franc pieces which were worth approximately $1.00 each in those days. Knowing the habits of the French peasants and country folk, I carried with me a large leather bag in which, if I were successful, the dealer's wife would deposit the pay-ment I was able to extract from her in five-franc silver pieces, which she usually kept secreted in her bedroom.

After having given her a receipt, I would carry my bag weighted down with silver coins to the local post office and exchange its contents for money orders which were despatched to my father's office. After a few months, the Company was back in funds again.

My next assignment was to travel to the various ports of France to expedite the unloading and reshipment of farm machinery received from Canada. Every port in France was suffering from a shortage of manpower and a congestion of military equipment which was shipped from England and, principally, from the United States.

Freighters, already in short supply, had to lie at anchor for days on end waiting for a place to berth and unload their goods.

Because the great majority of the farmers of France were mobilized, leaving only young boys, old men and women to carry on their farming operations, the demand for farm machinery was becoming very urgent, and speedy delivery was essential.

For a private firm to get its goods unloaded, put through customs, and reshipped to their destination in competition with military equipment, called for some ingenuity. I am sorry to recall that when persuasion failed, I resorted frequently—and not without success—to the evil practice of bribery which was not unknown in the ports of France in the early days of the war. Nor is it completely unheard of today.

On the eve of the Battle of the Marne, the German advance in the northeast of France cut through the Departments of Marne and the Meuse, reaching as far south as a line drawn roughly through Esternay, Fer-châmpenoise, Vitry-le-François, and Sermaize-les-Bains. Heavy fighting had taken place all along this line. Villages were captured and lost three or four times before the Miracle of the Marne compelled the Germans to abandon the whole area.

The countryside over which the contending armies had fought was completely devastated. The previous year's crop, in the process of being harvested when war was declared, was still lying out in the fields, irretrievably damaged. The homes of the peasants were burned or demolished by artillery fire. The livestock had been slaughtered, the farm machinery destroyed.

A few old people had straggled back to their villages after the German retreat, but without a home to live in, equipment to work with, or financial support, they could do little to help themselves. Instinct and the habits of a life-time had alone brought them back to live in the cellars of their houses, or under a lean-to which they had been able to build from the wreckage.

The British Society of Friends Relief Expedition in France stepped into the breach. They obtained the willing consent of the French government to their proposal that they should be allowed to supply the know-how, the manpower, the equipment, and the money to rehabilitate this once flourishing agricultural area, and get it back into production. Although most of the members of the Society were conscientious objectors who refused to take up arms for the defence of their country, they were honourable people who served Britain's cause in their own way, with enthusiasm, sacrifice, and devotion.

Their representative came one day to see my father with the proposal that they would purchase an important assortment of farm machinery, providing we could supply them with one or two people to instruct them in its operation, and to demonstrate how to repair and service the equipment.

I was chosen to supervise a small group of experts. After obtaining military authority to enter the army zone, I established my headquarters in the destroyed villages of Sermaize-les-Bains. I remained there until the crop was harvested in August.

It was fascinating work. I enjoyed my contacts with the Quakers, both men and women, who worked with untiring and intelligent devotion to help the French farmers get back on their feet.

It also gave me a great insight into the suffering this inhuman war had caused to these simple peasants who, knowing nothing of the issues involved, suddenly found themselves in the path of the invading armies.

By the late summer of 1915, the government had realized that the catastrophic drop in agricultural production was due to two facts: that vast areas of France's finest agricultural land were now behind German lines; and the mobilization of the farmers in the remaining areas had disrupted farm operations. They decided that something had to be done about it.

Among the many wise moves that were made, they proposed to give priority to the importation of farm machinery. But shortage of shipping, congestion in the ports, transportation difficulties, impeded the carrying out of this project with the thoroughness that had been envisaged.

The front line, after the retreat of the Marne, ran through the outskirts of Arras where, before the war, we had a branch office and distributing center.

Our records showed that when we last heard from Arras in the middle of August, 1914, our warehouse was full of farm machinery. What had happened to it since, none of us knew. We were pessimistic about it because, according to the military authorities, the front line was about 800 yards from our warehouse.

My father called on the Ministry of Supply and advised them there was a possibility that substantial quantities of farm machines in their original cases were stored at our Arras warehouse. He proposed that the military authorities should give us a permit to proceed to Arras on the understanding that if a reasonable number of machines were found to be still intact, the military would supply us with the manpower and the transportation to evacuate them. This was my fourth assignment.

Several months went by before the military headquarters in Paris finally sanctioned the project. On May 21st, 1916, I left for Arras accompanied by Dubocq, one of my father's foremen.

Owing to our warehouse's proximity to the front lines, we could work only at night, and as the walls facing the German lines were riddled with shell holes the military authorities would allow us to use only one shaded lantern to avoid alerting the enemy. The situation was not to the liking of Foreman Dubocq, who left me on the first day and returned to Paris. A few days afterwards I received a letter from my father, by military channels, urging me to return immediately as, according to Dubocq, the hazards involved were too great.

By this time, the work of the evacuation was well under way. I spent each night in the warehouse supervising the loading. So far all had gone well.

I was fairly comfortably installed in the basement of a house which had been only partly destroyed. A batman from a near-by military unit brought me daily rations and other necessities of life.

This was high adventure indeed. We were shipping out approximately fifteen tons of machinery every night. I couldn't bear the thought of leaving the job half done. Furthermore, I was just twenty-three, and loving every minute of it, so in spite of my father's letter, I remained at Arras until June 9th, when by two o'clock in the morning, we had shipped the last eleven tons, leaving behind in the warehouse only a few machines which had been so badly damaged that their evacuation was not worth-while.

We had a few casualties in the warehouse, and more on the road leading to the point of embarkation at the rear, but the military authorities appeared to feel that the operation had been worthwhile.

In 1938, the Canadian Corps held a reunion in Toronto, attended by veterans from all parts of Canada. In the Coli-seum building in which many of their activities took place, a replica of our shell-torn building of Arras was a principal fea-ture. A correspondent from the *Globe and Mail* wrote a long article on the subject, extracts of which I reproduce here:

> Over the door of the replica warehouse hangs a sign which reads "Machines Agricoles." It is a badge of recognition of an almost for-gotten exploit of twenty-two years ago which became a legend in the Canadian Corps.
>
> For months the old warehouse had been almost forgotten, and had been just another of the wayside hulks, roofless and wrecked, that lined the road as incoming and outgoing parties shuffled through the darkness behind the lines.
>
> Then one night it became a matter of headquarters importance. It contained hundreds of Canadian-made agricultural implements at a time when the French farmers were deprived of the manpower they needed, and the military government was hollering for food-stuffs.
>
> The warehouse was under almost constant fire. Sniper's bullets swished stealthily in the streets if life stirred. High explosives tossed bricks into the sky. Any indication of interest in the warehouse would have invited a bombardment from the Huns and would have destroyed the precious "machines agricoles." Lights were taboo.
>
> Along from Paris came a youthful expert on farm machinery.

The story of the evacuation was known all over the sector before long.

An artist went up when Arras was cleared towards the end of the war and painted a picture of the old warehouse. Two weeks ago, someone saw the picture, recalled the exploit, and suggested that the warehouse be rebuilt for the Corps reunion in Toronto.

To cut a long story short, James S. Duncan, now General Manager of the Massey-Harris Company Ltd. and late of the Royal Field Artillery which he left after the Armistice with the rank of Captain, will visit the French village in a few weeks and take a look at the wrecked, twisted warehouse. But he won't have to lead any salvage parties into the night. He will be able to light a fag in it if he feels like it.

After my return to Paris I sent a letter to Sir Lyman Melvin-Jones, outlining the action which had been taken. He replied by a charming letter of congratulations, somewhat marred, I must admit, by the last paragraph in which, coming back to reality, he said, "I have before me the stocksheet indicating the number of machines which were in the warehouse when you got there. Will you please explain why ten of these were left behind?" The German artillery could have explained this better than I.

7

I Join the Army

IT WAS IN ARRAS that my desire to give up the interesting and useful work in which I was engaged and join the army became pressing.

Letters were received from Sir Lyman strongly urging me to carry on the work I was doing, which he felt to be in the best interests of the war effort. Although I sympathized with his viewpoint, I rejected the suggestion. I reported to the British recruiting officer in Paris on July 1st, 1916 offering my services in any capacity.

Four days afterwards I received instructions to proceed to a recruiting office in London, from where I was posted to the Royal Garrison Artillery in Cornwall. Here, a distinctly authoritative sergeant put us through the elementary training which consisted almost exclusively of marching and forming fours. We had been issued no uniforms, and drilling in civilian clothes left much to be desired.

On the third day after my arrival the sergeant ordered me to accompany him to a large rectangular Nissen hut of the type used as a dormitory for sixty men, from which all the bunks had been cleared out. The sergeant pointed to a pail of water, an outsize scrubbing brush without a handle and a wooden palette with a generous heap of black soap, and said, "Scrub it clean, and report to me when you are finished."

After a few hours spent on my knees, still in my civilian clothes, scrubbing the floor of that barracks which, I am persuaded, had never been scrubbed since the commencement of the war, I began to wonder if I had not been a little hasty in giving up the work I had been doing in France in favour of the menial tasks I was now performing. These feelings were confirmed when, a few weeks later, I was put on a week's latrine fatigue.

I was willing—and indeed anxious—to serve, but I wished to do so in some useful capacity. I determined to work so hard at every job allotted to me that I would be singled out as soon as possible for some form of promotion. When this was accomplished I proposed to apply for a posting to a cadet school.

To my surprise I found out that competition for promotion in the British Expeditionary Force of 1916 was not as keen as I had imagined. A significant number of my fellow recruits preferred to stay in the ranks, arguing that they hadn't joined the army to take responsibility, only to fight the Huns. They were quite willing to do as they were told.

A few months after my arrival I received my first stripe—the very lowest form of noncommissioned rank, an acting supernumerary bombardier without pay! It wasn't much, but it was a beginning, for in December I was posted to "B" Reserve Brigade, Royal Horse Artillery Cadet School at the famous Lord's Cricket Grounds in St. John's Wood, London.

One of my most harrowing experiences at the cadet school was the daily riding lessons. I had never been on a horse, while many of my fellow cadets, brought up in the British Isles, were already accomplished riders. Furthermore, having never indulged in any sports, my physical condition was not such as to cause me to enjoy riding daily for two hours, bareback, and frequently in the rain.

On one memorable occasion, due either to the riding-master with his long whip or to my lack of horsemanship, my animal took fright, leaped over the wooden railing, and threw me off on a concrete sidewalk. This untoward incident resulted in a strained back and ten days in the hospital. Worse still, I who needed it most, got less training in horsemanship than the rest of my class.

Towards the end of the course, we were taken out on a ride through Hyde Park and put through various exercises by our commanding officer. Whether my horse was a wilful animal, or whether he recognized that I was unable to manage him, he disrupted our exercises by refusing to line up with the rest of the horses, and unheeding of my efforts, moved forward to the front alongside our infuriated Sergeant-Major. This humiliating performance caused unseemly amusement among my fellow cadets and awe-inspiring wrath on the part of the commanding officer who wasn't amused at all, as I gathered by the flow of barrackroom invective he showered on me.

I rode back through London to Lord's Cricket Grounds in a state of great despondency, feeling that in all probability I would be returned to the ranks. This pessimistic forecast proved to be illusory. In the spring of 1917 I received my commission as 2nd Lieutenant, was granted two weeks leave, and shortly afterwards was posted to "B" Battery, 180th Brigade of the 16th Irish Division. The brigade was then located in the ramparts of Ypres in preparation for an attack on the enemy which subsequently became known as the Third Battle of Ypres.

I spent the night in the wagon lines at Poperinghe with 2nd Lieutenant A. E. Freeman, a Canadian also posted to "B" Battery, who was subsequently to become a distinguished professor at M.I.T. The next day we were allocated two horses and a mounted batman each, and set out to report to our battery at the front.

Although I had had considerable experience of shell and rifle fire while in Arras during the previous year, my real baptism of fire came as we rode up the shell-torn highway of Ypres which the Germans kept under constant fire, and which was strewn with the wreckage of gun carriages and other equipment, together with wounded or dead horses which had not yet been attended to. It was soon brought home to me that being under shell fire when one is on foot and can readily throw oneself to the ground is one thing, but to be under shell fire on the back of a horse is quite another!

The Germans, recognizing that the unusual activity in the

area was indicative of an impending attack, kept the town of Ypres and all its approaches under constant shell fire.

Our batman led us through the rubble of the destroyed town to where the underground headquarters of "B" Battery was supposed to be. We were disconcerted to find nothing there but a huge crater. On the previous night "B" Battery headquarters had received a direct hit by a large-calibre shell which killed two of our officers who were in the mess at the time. We found our new headquarters some hundred feet away, and introduced ourselves to Major Stebbing, who commanded the battery, and who in turn introduced us to our fellow officers.

Shortly after my arrival at "B" Battery, Major Stebbing announced that I was to be put in charge of a party detailed to prepare an ammunition dump in No Man's Land, in a location which our battery was supposed to occupy during the initial stages of our advance. Each member of the party was to carry two eighteen-pounder shells and deposit them at a position located approximately halfway between our trenches and those occupied by the Germans. The operation was to be undertaken at 2:00 a.m. The sergeant who was in charge of the contingent of men laden with eighteen-pounder shells confided to me in a whisper that it looked to him as if we had been handed a suicide mission!

The prospects were not propitious. Our success depended entirely on our being able to cut the wire in front of our own trenches, scramble out into No Man's Land, and deposit our ammunition at the allotted spot, all this without attracting the attention of the Germans.

The mission was a complete failure. No sooner had we begun to scramble through our wire into No Man's Land, than the Germans sent up a stream of Very lights which illuminated our whole front and left those of us who were already over the parapet with a shell under each arm in full view of the enemy. We were recipients of a barrage of machine-gun fire. Those who were able to do so scrambled back to the protection of our trenches which were shortly subjected to intensive artillery fire.

We had lost any chance of carrying out our mission. Those of us who were left returned to our battery headquarters to report our failure.

The attack was to take place in the early morning of September 20th, 1917. The night before, Major Stebbing instructed me to take charge of a small group of signallers, and move up to the front, advance behind our attacking infantry, and lay telephone communications between the high ground which the infantry hoped to capture shortly after Zero Hour, and the new position to be occupied by our batteries as they moved forward.

We left on our mission at 2:00 a.m. It had been raining steadily for two days. The enemy shelling was intense.

It was impossible to move up to our front lines over the open fields which were pock-marked by craters, and half full of water. We had no choice but to follow what was left of the road, which was kept constantly under fire. Our progress was slow. The signallers who were with me were heavily loaded with their telephone reels and many fell by the wayside.

At dawn our infantry scrambled out of their trenches and under the protection of our massive artillery fire, captured the Frezenberg Ridge.

I followed closely behind them with what was left of my signalling party. We laid out our telephone wires between a German pillbox which I had selected on the Ridge, from which I could observe the movement of our advancing infantry, and our new but still unoccupied battery position. Undoubtedly the pillbox I had chosen afforded protection against shell fire when it was occupied by the Germans and facing in the right direction, but for our purposes it was facing the wrong way; and as the rear of the structure was open it afforded little protection against enemy shells of all calibres, which the German batteries were pouring onto the newly captured Frezenberg Ridge.

As so often happened with heavy shelling, no sooner had we established communications with our battery than our lines were cut by shell fire. As fast as our linemen repaired them, they were cut once more.

From my observation post I could watch through my field glasses the movement of our attacking forces, and of the German counter attacks. I sent back reports, scribbled in my notebook, to the battery by runners, since our telephone communications proved useless.

Although we had captured the Frezenberg Ridge, the high ground which was to have been our first day's objective remained in enemy hands. The movement of troops on our side and our battery positions were therefore in full view of the enemy's observation posts.

The clay soil of the Ypres salient, after three days of continuous rain, was so churned up by shell fire, by the advance of our infantry and vehicles of all kinds, that it was literally a sea of mud.

As night fell, I retraced my steps to our battery position through scenes of utter desolation. Attempts were being made to pick up the wounded lying in the rain-soaked fields, but the mud was so deep, and the going so slippery, that the weight of a wounded man on a stretcher caused the bearers to bog down. Four men had to be allotted to each stretcher, which slowed down the task of picking up the wounded.

As I slogged my way slowly back to our temporary battery positions, I passed an advance dressing station, the memory of which will remain with me always. Under a tarpaulin stretched over four poles, two young doctors, exhausted by their long hours of continuous work since the attack began, were dressing the wounded as they were brought up to them, one by one, by orderlies who deposited the stretchers on a table made up of six ammunition boxes. Two improvised lamps which swung from a temporary rafter lighted this blood-stained scene of horror, while row after row of wounded soldiers lay out on their stretchers in the rain, patiently waiting their turn to be attended to.

I arrived back at our forward battery position long after nightfall, soaked to the skin and exhausted.

I was met by a scene of tragic destruction. Three of our eighteen-pounders had received direct hits and were out of action. The temporary officers' mess which had been set up under a tarpaulin had received a direct hit and three of our officers, including Major Stebbing, had been seriously wounded.

Our kitchen equipment had been destroyed, and no fires could be lit in the streaming rain. The remnants of our officers and gunners sat around dejectedly on empty ammunition boxes, soaked to the skin, with nothing warm to drink and nothing to eat but the ever-present tins of bully beef.

On the following morning we were able to get one of our guns back into action, but our problem was to bring up the ammunition. Gun carriages would sink to their axles in the mud of Flanders. We finally got a limited number of rounds which were brought up to us around noon from the wagon lines, by horses carrying three shells on either side of their saddles. They slithered and floundered in the mud, sometimes up to their bellies, but we had secured a few rounds of ammunition to feed our two remaining guns.

The position was untenable. Towards evening we received orders to retire to a position where we were no longer under direct observation and where some sort of a shelter could be provided for our men.

On the following day, our last remaining officer was wounded. When Colonel Ward, commanding our brigade, came to visit what was left of our battery, I was the only officer remaining from the nine who had started the attack the morning before. After taking stock of the position, Colonel Ward instructed me to take charge of the battery until such time as reinforcements of guns and men could be sent to us. And so it came to pass that, just a few weeks after I had left the cadet school, I found myself in temporary charge of a battery.

In the following weeks we were taken out of the line, re-equipped and moved to a position near St. Léger, where we settled down to the routine of trench warfare, supporting our infantry in their attacks or raids, and laying down heavy bombardments on enemy trenches.

8

Retreat of the Fifth Army

IN DECEMBER, 1917, our batteries were removed to Ronssoy and our brigade headquarters, to which I had recently been transferred as Signalling Officer, to a quarry near Ste. Emilie. It was there that we received an intelligence bulletin despatched from Field Marshal Sir Douglas Haig's headquarters which informed us that owing to the cessation of the war on the Russian front, the great bulk of the German and Austrian divisions were being moved from the Eastern to the Western front and that a powerful offensive was to be expected.

By February, 1918, it became evident that the enemy offensive was in preparation. It was not estimated, however, that it would take place for three or four weeks. The adjutant of our brigade, Captain Miller, who was due for leave, left our headquarters at 12:30 a.m. on March 21st and I was appointed adjutant with the rank of acting captain.

The colonel suggested a nightcap to celebrate my new appointment. At 1:00 a.m. we retired to our respective dugouts. Three hours later all hell broke loose on our front! The enemy attack had begun.

A bombardment of great intensity accompanied by gas and high explosive shells of all calibres was opened up against us.

Our batteries, brigade and divisional headquarters, and all road centers as far back as St. Pol were engaged with gas and high velocity shells.

By 9:00 a.m. the Germans, equipped with gas masks and favoured by a heavy fog, overran our forward trenches, which had been all but obliterated, and were advancing towards our battery positions.

All telephone communications with our forward units had been cut by the bombardment. On my colonel's instructions I sent orders by runners to each of our batteries ordering them to retire to prearranged positions as soon as the teams I had sent up from the wagon lines reached them.

Most of our guns were saved, but some, from which our gunners had removed the breech-blocks, were surrounded by the rapidly advancing enemy infantry, and fell into their hands.

By early afternoon, the enemy infantry had reached the first line of our battery positions on practically the whole front of their attack. I was able to report to the colonel that many of our guns, after firing at the enemy over open sights, were able to extricate themselves and fall back to the positions which had been previously allocated to them.

The colonel and the remainder of his staff retired to the new headquarters, leaving two runners and myself with instructions to remain in contact with our batteries until they had recovered all remaining guns from our forward positions.

I remained in our dugout trying without success to contact our batteries. I posted one of the runners just outside the opening of our dugout, with instructions that he should warn me should any of the enemy infantry appear on the ridge of our quarry a few hundred feet from us.

The warning was not long in coming. A unit of enemy machine-gunners appeared over the crest and my two runners and I made a dash for it, leaving everything behind, including my tunic, on the arms of which my third star had been sewn only a few hours before.

We were suffering from splitting headaches due to the early morning gas attack, but no Olympic runners could have covered the space between our dugout and a stretch of high ground which screened us from the enemy in better time than we did. Our horses were waiting for us, and after laboriously extricating ourselves from the confusion of the retreating infantry units, we finally rejoined our depleted batteries which were already in action covering our infantry's line of retreat.

On the morning of March 23rd, orders were received to withdraw all our batteries by sections and proceed at once via Péronne to positions near Halle. As we marched through Péronne, we witnessed a contingent of men destroying the supplies of small arms, food, uniforms, and beverages which had been stored in this divisional supply centre.

Red wine was running down the gutters, barrels of beer were being split open, warehouses were on fire, and food and cigars were being handed out to all takers.

It was a rare sight to see our gunners jauntily smoking cigars as they rode through the main street. This was, of course, contrary to all discipline, but there are times in life when wise men overlook these misdemeanours, weighing them against the unusual circumstances which gave rise to them.

That evening there was a complete breakdown in communication. Our brigade was on its own. We knew neither the location of our infantry nor the position of the enemy.

For three days the retreat continued, and our brigade occupied one position after another. The enemy was still pursuing us vigorously and our losses were heavy.

By March 28th, the position over the entire front of the Fifth Army was deteriorating rapidly. The infantry in the line was made up of jaded remnants of the 16th Division: signallers, wounded who had to be evacuated from the hospitals provided they were still able to hold a rifle, cooks, batmen, and dismounted cavalrymen, a nondescript group known as "Carey's Forces." Our guns were positioned under cover of the Bois-de-Vaire in the vicinity of Amiens.

Our forward observation officers reported that there was now no infantry between us and the enemy on the front covered by our brigade. Towards evening a despatch rider brought me an order to report immediately to the divisional commander who was waiting in his car on the other side of the wood in which our guns were positioned.

On my arrival, the general, leaning out of the window of

his limousine, returned my salute and said, "Captain Duncan, orders have been received from corps headquarters that no further retreat is permissible. You must defend your guns over open sights and if this is not sufficient to hold the enemy you must fight them with your rifles. This," he added, "is the last stand. The enemy's advance must be arrested or we must die in the attempt." Having delivered himself of these brave words, he waved to his chauffeur, who drove him back to the comparative safety of divisional headquarters.

I called together the commanding officers of each battery and imparted the instructions I had received. With no infantry between the Germans and ourselves, and only a few rifles available, it looked like the end of the 180th Brigade. The choice lay between capture or death. The battery commanders listened to the orders with stoicism, then returned to their batteries on the edge of the wood to prepare for their defence, and to await the attack of the German infantry.

None came. The enemy was apparently as exhausted as we were. No attack took place the following day. Meanwhile, Australian infantry were moved up to occupy the line.

On April 4th, late in the evening, our brigade was at last taken out of action. We retired behind Amiens to recuperate, to refit, and to rest our men and horses.

At 11:00 p.m., after having done my rounds to see that men and horses had been suitably looked after, I crawled into my sleeping bag in anticipation of the first good night's sleep since the retreat had started two weeks before. I had barely settled down for the night when a despatch rider arrived from headquarters with instructions that we were to harness up and leave immediately on a forced march towards the Merville front where an attack on the Portuguese, who were in the line at the time, had been so successful that the front had been penetrated and the Portuguese were in full retreat.

With a good deal of grumbling, but with remarkable spirit under the circumstances, our men were awakened, our tired horses reharnessed, breakfast served. By 2:00 a.m., the Brigade was on the march once again.

The life of an adjutant of a brigade of artillery is an active and responsible one. I thoroughly enjoyed it. Under the colonel, the adjutant carries the responsibility for everything that takes place in each battery. Although, as captain, he carries a rank inferior to that of the battery commander, as mouthpiece of the colonel commanding a brigade, his authority goes unquestioned.

During the Battle of Arras, I was given a lesson in self-discipline and good manners by our colonel, a regular officer and a strict disciplinarian, which left a lasting impression on me.

Our brigade H.Q. was located in a spacious dugout forty feet below a slag heap of a coal mine, of which there were many in the area. As adjutant I was required to be available at all times both day and night to receive and send out messages to divisional headquarters, to our batteries, and to the front line trenches which we were covering. As the enemy was particularly active and our batteries were continuously being called on to open fire on various targets, I was confined to my subterranean quarters where my staff and office were installed for over two weeks without a break. I felt like a mole, eating, sleeping, and working forty feet below the surface.

On this particular occasion a massive attack on our lines had taken place after midnight and we fired until well into the morning, when our infantry counter-attacked.

Just before noon, Colonel Ward, our brigade commander, sent down a message saying that we were lunching above ground at 12:00 o'clock. As our colonel didn't like to be kept waiting, I handed over to my senior sergeant, and rushed upstairs just in time to sit down around an improvised table of ammunition boxes, over which the orderly had spread a small table cloth. The usual selection of cold bully beef was about to be served.

The temperature was over 80°. The table had been set up in the shade of a destroyed factory wall close to the opening of our dugout. I pulled up a camp stool, and just as I was about to sit down, Colonel Ward looked at me with obvious disfavour. "Haven't you forgotten something, Captain Duncan?" he asked.

Confused by lack of sleep and the stifling heat which had hit me as I emerged from my cool dugout, I couldn't think what I had forgotten—in fact I couldn't think of anything. After a few seconds of tongue-tied silence on my part, the colonel said in withering tones, "I believe what you have forgotten is that an officer does not sit down for lunch in his shirt sleeves!"

After a mumbled apology I went down the forty steps to my dugout, retrieved the missing tunic, and sat down at the table once again, properly dressed for lunch. Although resentful at the time, I came to realize on reflection that the colonel was quite right. It is so easy to slip into careless and slovenly ways when all around is going wrong, and yet these are the testing times when self-discipline is most required.

One of the first lessons I learned when I became adjutant of the brigade was that the happiest and most efficient batteries and those in which the men showed the finest spirit were always those in which the discipline was strictest, and where, regardless of the hardship of the moment, spit and polish was the order of the day.

Some of the lessons I learned during World War I applied with almost equal force to civilian life. When, in later years, I took over the management of our Argentine business, about half our employees reported to work each morning with a two- or sometimes three-day-old stubble. I called them all together two days after my arrival and told them that, eccentric as I might appear to be, the custom of shaving but twice a week was, in my opinion, a sign of lack of self-discipline, which could not be tolerated in our organization. I remained in charge of our business in Buenos Aires for three years and never saw an unshaven face in our office again. What is more, the staff liked it better that way, and I am sure their wives did also!

The happy and efficient organization is invariably the one where discipline prevails and where example is set by top management.

By October it was obvious to all of us that we were winning the war.

On November 11th, 1918, we received the following message from divisional headquarters, relaying one received from Army headquarters:

Interrupted message for Imperial Chancellor via German F.G.H.Q. ERZBERGER authorizes signature of Armistice conditions but requests modification certain points affecting food supply, to save part of Germany not being occupied, from starvation AAA London reports arrival German Emperor and Crown Prince HOLLAND AAA

Dutch Govt considering action AAA German wireless indicates Revolution spreading everywhere but little opposition or blood shed AAA Negotiations proceeding between Majority Socialists and Independent Socialists for formation of new Government including LIEBNECHT and HAASE AAA Republic declared at STUTTGART . . . message ends.

Although one of our officers and two of our men had been killed just before the cessation of hostilities, our brigade settled down to celebrate our victory. This could not be done without alcoholic beverages and we had none. The colonel suggested that I should proceed to Lille and, followed by a mess wagon and fortified by my knowledge of French, bring back by hook or by crook three barrels of beer!

On the way there we were halted by a sight which filled my heart with pride. All traffic was stopped to allow a brigade of the Royal Horse Artillery to ride through on their way to the occupation of Germany. The men were meticulously turned out. The harness was splendidly polished, the spotless brass shining in the rays of the sun; horses, gunners and vehicles were turned out as if on the parade ground at Woolwich.

If we were proud of them and cheered them as they went by, one can well imagine the feelings of the retreating Germans —tired, bedraggled, short of rations—when they saw this military turnout representing, in its own way, the might of the victorious British armies.

I returned to civilian life on March 13th, 1919 after finishing a career in the army which I had enjoyed and which in my opinion did more for me than any other experience in my life. The discipline, the spirit of camaraderie which existed in our armies, the responsibilities of an adjutant of a brigade of artillery, all of these served as a maturing process which stood me in good stead in the years to come.

I went through a demobilization unit in London, left immediately for Paris, and started work in the French Massey-Harris organization on the following day.

9
Nine Eventful Years

I WAS NEARLY TWENTY-SIX when I returned to civilian life and possessed a new self-confidence born of my war experience. Perhaps it was this that led me me to announce that I was not prepared to go back to the work I had been doing before I joined up and expected to be given a position of responsibility.

Whether the company officials—including my own father—were shocked by this ultimatum or not, I was quickly transferred to our headquarters in London and given the supervision of our operations in Spain, Italy, Tunisia, Algeria, and Morocco.

The next four years I spent most of my time in Italy and Spain, and acquired a fair knowledge of Italian and complete fluency in Spanish, skills which stood me in good stead in the years to come.

During the war, the territories under my supervision had been starved of agricultural equipment and our business in the post-war period increased very substantially. I was given a great deal of undeserved praise for results which were due much more to good fortune than to my own efforts.

I have subsequently observed that when economic conditions are good leaders in industry and commerce come in for a lot more praise than is their due, and conversely when the tide turns they are criticized far beyond their deserts. I have experienced both situations and know whereof I speak.

In 1922 our head office in Canada had been giving consideration to the desirability of opening a sales branch in Mexico. At Vincent Massey's recommendation it was arranged that I should be temporarily released from the European organization to carry out an investigation of conditions in Mexico. I spent several months in that country and concluded that the times were not ripe for expansion and that our existing arrangements should be continued. The political unrest which prevailed for many years after my visit amply justified my recommendations.

After my return from Mexico, I was temporarily seconded to make a study of the desirability of setting up manufacturing facilities in France.

Later I was instructed to undertake a sales survey in the Balkans and subsequently visited Damascus, Cairo, and Constantinople. While in Turkey I received a cable informing me that my father's health had deteriorated rapidly, and requesting that I should return immediately to Paris.

On my arrival I found my father was so ill that he was no longer able to attend to his affairs. I was called on to take over responsibility for the business, pending my father's recovery. I was subsequently appointed assistant manager, a promotion which brought ease to my father's mind and gave him great pleasure.

Following his doctors' instructions, Father left for his home on the Riviera in the hope that the more clement weather might hasten his recovery. This was not effective, however, and on January 23rd, 1925, he passed away.

The last letter I received from him was written from his home at Plage Cap Martin, the day before his death. It displayed the sense of humour which characterized him throughout his life.

"I am still very shaky," he wrote, "but sleep a little better. Doctors at sixty-five francs a visit are enough to drive anyone into good health or, if you include the drugs, into ruin!"

He was buried in the little cemetery at Mentone, high up on the rugged mountainside facing the Mediterranean. He had always expressed the desire that his last resting place should be in the soil of France which he loved so dearly, and in sight of the waters of the Mediterranean where he had spent so many happy days.

The board of directors of the Massey-Harris Company in Toronto sent me an extract of a minute which had been recorded at the time of my father's death. It read in part as follows:

> For thirty-four years with zeal and ability that characterized all his commercial relations, he contributed a thorough knowledge of the business under his charge, a mature judgement in all matters requiring consideration, a character of integrity and probity that brought honour to the Company.
>
> The present prosperous conditions of our business in France are in no small degree due to his personal efforts for he brought into his daily life the fruits of a long and interesting experience, an orderly mind, and an heroic spirit of duty and industry.

I was thirty-one years old when my father died. Pending a decision on his successor, I was made acting manager for France, Belgium and North Africa.

Before the beginning of World War I Father foresaw that France, an industrial country and strongly nationalistic, would follow a policy of favouring local manufacturers and raising customs duties against the importation of our farm machinery. He strongly urged headquarters to set up a manufacturing plant in France.

During the war these plans had to be shelved, but when peace was re-established, Father strongly urged that the establishment of a manufacturing plant in France be favourably considered. He repeated his recommendations in 1924 when the International Harvester Comany of Chicago, which had set up manufacturing facilities in France, was making serious inroads into our business.

This time he was successful. I was temporarily detached from our European headquarters in London to take an active part in drawing up final recommendations dealing with the pros and cons of manufacturing in France, and recommending a choice of location. My recommendations were accepted. In the spring of 1925, after a visit from Thomas Bradshaw, then our general manager, contracts were let for the erection of a factory in the vicinity of Lille.

This was an important decision. It was the first manufacturing plant to be established outside the North American continent, and was the forerunner of the network of factories which have since been established throughout the world.

Although Father had the satisfaction of knowing that at long last favourable consideration was given to manufacturing in France, and that the future of the business he had founded would be safeguarded, he did not live to see his plans come to fruition.

Six months after my father had passed away, I was appointed manager for France, Belgium, Holland, and North Africa. I was proud of the opportunity given to me to carry on where my father had left off.

Three years later, our parent company, having opened a plant in Germany, decided it was more logical that the European headquarters should be moved to the continent of Europe where the greatest developments were taking place. I was instructed to take over the European head office organization and install it in France. Following this move, our European general manager having retired, I was appointed joint European general manager with Cecil Milne, who was then Thomas Bradshaw's executive assistant in Toronto. Milne's responsibilities were to be confined to engineering and manufacturing. Mine were to be sales and finance.

I must confess to some disappointment in this arrangement. I had never been a believer in joint management and I regretted Thomas Bradshaw's decision to split the responsibility for the European office. However, Cecil Milne was a man of first class ability, and he and I settled down happily and effectively to handle our new responsibilities.

IO

Vincent Massey Enters Politics

I WILL RETURN NOW to the events which had taken place in
Canada during the war and the immediate post-war period.

Sir Lyman Melvin-Jones died in 1917. Probably the most
brilliant executive our Company ever had, he had ruled the
organization with an iron hand. Having an intimate knowledge
of every aspect of the business, he did not feel the need for
strong men around him, nor was the atmosphere he created
conducive to their development. The senior officials dated back
to the time of the amalgamation and had grown old in the
service of the Company.

Sir Lyman pinned his faith on Thomas Findley, a man in
his early forties, energetic, able, and of fine character. He was
confident that when the time came Findley would prove capable
of succeeding him and of carrying on the policies Sir Lyman
had pursued with such success.

Because of Sir Lyman's failure to develop a group of strong
executives of the right age, Thomas Findley, when he assumed
the presidency, found himself poorly supported, particularly
in view of the difficulties which he correctly believed would
assail the Company at the end of hostilities.

In the prime of life, only two years after Sir Lyman's death,

64

Thomas Findley fell victim to a peculiarly malignant form of cancer, the progress of which was slowed down but never arrested. By the middle of 1919, Findley faced, courageously, the harsh reality that his days were numbered.

He was obsessed by the thought that there was no one on his staff of sufficient experience or calibre to assume the leadership of the Company. I knew of his deep concern for the future, because I had been invited by him in the summer of 1919 to visit Canada and spend two weeks with his family. During that time he often spoke to me of his anxieties.

He was so ill when I arrived in Toronto that he was obliged to spend much of his time at home. His brilliant mental faculties were unimpaired and I spent many hours sitting by his bedside listening to the plans he had formulated for the development of the Company, plans which he would, he knew, not live to see carried out.

He told me, one day, in the strictest confidence, that his friend of many years, Thomas Bradshaw,[1] in whose ability and integrity he had the greatest confidence, had at last consented to join our Company and to accept the position of treasurer, on the understanding that he would in the course of time become general manager.

Findley had also arranged that after his death or resignation Vincent Massey, who had recently become a director and secretary of the Company, would succeed him as president. Vincent, together with his father, Chester Massey, who was honorary chairman, the Massey Foundation, and certain members of the Massey family, represented the controlling interest in the firm.

Unfortunately for the Company, Vincent Massey's brilliant qualifications did not run along business lines, nor had he ever been trained in any aspect of the farm-machinery industry. His inclinations and ambitions lay in other directions. He was a fine classical scholar, a graduate of Balliol College, Oxford, with second class honours in modern history, on which he lectured at the University of Toronto when he returned to Canada. It

[1] Thomas Bradshaw, partner of A. E. Ames & Co., investment bankers, and authority on municipal finance, became Toronto's Commissioner of Finance on the outbreak of World War I. Later when he resigned from Massey-Harris he headed North American Life.

was force of circumstances plus the responsibilities of ownership that brought him somewhat reluctantly into the service of the Company.

Thomas Bradshaw, a man of great ability, of proven financial standing, well and favourably known throughout Canada, was reluctant to give up his career in finance to enter an industry with which he was completely unfamiliar, and which, apparently, was headed for difficult times. I am persuaded he never would have made the sacrifice involved had it not been for his unwillingness to refuse the urgent request—almost a cry for help—from a lifelong friend who had a very short time to live.

By the fall of 1920, it was evident that the Company was heading into rough weather.

Thomas Findley's health was deteriorating rapidly. He knew that he was no longer able to carry on effectively. If he was to ensure his succession, action had to be taken without delay. Thomas Bradshaw was appointed general manager in November, 1920.

He was well equipped to deal with the financial buffeting which lay ahead of the Company. There were those, however, both within the organization and without, who questioned the appointment, because Bradshaw was neither an industrialist, a merchant, nor a farm-implement man, and it was the first time in the long history of the Company that an outsider had been appointed to a senior executive position. Having in mind the paucity of executive talent which existed within our Company at that time, I am satisfied that Thomas Findley made the best choice possible. Subsequent events justified Bradshaw's appointment.

Thomas Findley had taken me into his family when I first went out to Canada as a boy of seventeen. He had befriended me during my early days in Toronto, and later had helped me along the road. I looked on him with affectionate and respectful admiration. I was distressed and saddened when, towards the middle of 1921, Mrs. Findley wrote to tell me that her husband had expressed the wish to see me before he died, and I left immediately for Canada.

By that time he was confined to his bed. I spent many long hours sitting by his bedside. His mind was clear. He accepted his fate with the courage and fortitude he had displayed throughout his life, but he was saddened by the serious financial difficulties the Company was now encountering, and which he was no longer able to cope with.

He died in December, 1921, at the age of fifty-one. Vincent Massey was appointed president. One of his first moves was to nominate Thomas Bradshaw vice-president and chief executive officer of the Company. Vincent Massey's interests, in addition to presiding over the annual meetings, were largely directed towards public relations, in which he made an important contribution, as well as towards advertising, and contacts with the government which was often an exacting and controversial task. Bradshaw assumed control of the actual management of the affairs of the Company.

Vincent Massey and Thomas Bradshaw took over their new responsibilities at a time when the Company was experiencing the cataclysmic effects of the postwar agricultural depression of 1921-25. Gone was the concept that the Company was depression proof, because of the widespread nature of its operations.

It had always been assumed that a recession in one hemisphere would be offset by favourable conditions in another. In 1921-25, and again in the early '30's, farmers the world over were in trouble.

Canadian wheat prices fell from the wartime high of $2.45 to $0.81 a bushel, and farmers in most countries were no longer able either to purchase the new equipment they required or to pay for the machines they had bought in earlier years. The farm-implement industry was faced with a disastrous decline in demand and an alarming increase in its inventories and receivables.

When Vincent Massey took the chair at his first annual meeting, it was to announce that the operations of the Company in 1921 had resulted in sales of approximately $17 million, and a loss of approximately $1,400,000, a sum which would have been closer to $3 million had it not been that, in line with the less exacting accounting regulations at that time, the recovery of a war damage claim against Germany of $1,500,000 was credited to the 1921 operations.

Losses continued until 1924. Payment of dividends ceased

in 1922, and probably should not have been made in 1921. The proud record of profitable operations which the Company or its predecessors had enjoyed since 1847 had been shattered.

By the end of 1924, however, the worst was over. The implement industry was back on its feet. During the following years the Company enjoyed a period of unprecedented prosperity which went on gathering strength from year to year until 1929 when its turnover exceeded all previous records.

Then came the crash of 1930 which rocked the Company to its very foundations. But more of that later.

In 1924, Vincent Massey became involved on behalf of the Company in negotiations with Mackenzie King's Liberal government on the subject of tariff protection required by the implement industry. The government was under heavy pressure to reduce tariffs, and the Company felt that this would deal a crippling blow to its future.

As was the case with most manufacturing companies at the time, our organization was strongly Conservative. Vincent Massey as its representative took a very active part in championing that point of view.

Early in 1924, Mackenzie King brought down a budget in which, torn between free-trade pressures and protectionism, he yielded to the former, and farm-implement companies suffered along with many other manufacturers.

Vincent Massey addressed to Arthur Meighen, leader of the Conservative opposition, a letter which became a *cause célèbre* during the following election. In Vincent Massey's excellent memoirs, *What's Past Is Prologue*,[1] he referred to the incident in this way:

> We have always protested against any reduction in duty on agricultural implements, and far from regarding the duties as announced in the budget as satisfactory, we look upon them as having done a grave injury to the industry of which we form a part. I added, unwisely as it was to prove later on, the following heated paragraph. It is difficult to avoid a feeling of deep resentment at the actions of the government. We were assured by responsible Ministers up to the very last moment that nothing would be done to injure the farm implement industry. The whole attitude of the Cabinet in this matter

[1] *What's Past Is Prologue*, Vincent Massey. The Macmillan Company of Canada Ltd.

seems to reveal an even mixture of cynicism and hypocrisy. If the tariff changes would be of substantial value to the farmer, we would not complain, but you know the solution of the farmer's troubles must be found elsewhere.

In fairness to Vincent Massey and to the action he subsequently took, he was always more of a Liberal at heart than a Conservative. His interests, which in earlier years were centered in education and in art, were giving way progressively to the fascination of politics and the broader horizons of public life.

Mackenzie King was proposing to call a general election and, being a most astute politician, he was not unaware of the advantage of attracting to his party the Conservative president of a Conservative company whose directors and policies were opposed to tariff reductions. He therefore wrote to Vincent in August of 1925, asking him to come and see him in Ottawa. Vincent Massey in his memoirs describes what took place:

> I obeyed the summons with much interest, almost excitement. Would it lead to my entry into the political field? I discovered that it would. An election was in the offing. Would I contest a seat?
>
> Here opened a thrilling prospect. When you have talked and writ-about public affairs in theory, the chance of dealing with them in practice is nearly irresistible. I said "Yes" to the Prime Minister's invitation.

Vincent Massey suggested, however, to Mackenzie King that if he stood as a candidate for Parliament as a Liberal, he should be given ministerial rank. This Mackenzie King agreed to.

Back in Toronto, Vincent informed the board of directors that he had been asked to stand as a Liberal candidate and the board, surprising as it may appear, gave him formal permission to accept Mackenzie King's offer. Vincent Massey was appointed Minister without Portfolio while retaining his position as president and a director of the Massey-Harris Company.

No doubt the board was influenced in its decision by the fact that Vincent Massey represented a controlling interest in the Company, but when Lloyd Harris,[1] who had not been present at the meeting, and Mrs. Walter Massey[2] heard of what

---

[1] Son of Alenson Harris, founder of the Harris Company, and Conservative M.P. for Brantford.

[2] Widow of the former general manager and aunt, by marriage, of Vincent.

had taken place, they reacted violently. In the words of Vincent Massey, "Such an acrimonious debate took place among the shareholders over my standing for election as a member of the Mackenzie King government that it made it advisable for me to resign the Presidency and my Directorship, lest the situation should be prejudicial to the best interests of the Company."

At the same time he resigned his two other directorships, of the Canadian Bank of Commerce and the Mutual Life Assurance Company and, as he said in his book, "settled down to a period of politics which lay ahead. . . ."

He chose to fight the election in Durham County in which his home, *Batterwood*, was situated. The Liberal Party were on a poor wicket. The tariff was the main issue but the leadership of the party as a whole was listless and the voters lethargic. The result was a disaster for the Liberals.

Mackenzie King and eight of his ministers went down to defeat. The Liberals won only 101 seats against 116 Conservatives and twenty-four Progressives. Vincent Massey was embarrassed during the election by Arthur Meighen's proposal to make public the correspondence on the subject of the tariff exchanged a year earlier when he was president of our Company. This was not only somewhat abusive of the Liberal Cabinet but inconsistent with the speeches he was making in his riding. Had the letter been published it would have been most damaging to Vincent Massey and to the Liberal Party as a whole.

Fortunately Vincent's letter was marked "Private and Confidential," and Arthur Meighen agreed that it should not be published, although it was fairly generally noised around that a damaging letter had been written. In the light of the rout of the Liberal Party, Vincent Massey did very well in his own constituency, which he lost by 6,074 votes to 7,020 to the Conservative candidate, a majority against him of 946 votes.

On November 28, 1925, Vincent wrote me:

> The campaign was a most strenuous one and my own contest in Durham County particularly difficult because the Conservatives flattered me by making a personal attack on me, second only in violence and bitterness to that which was aimed at the Prime Minister.
>
> My defeat was due chiefly to the tidal wave of protectionist feeling which swept over the Province, but this wave of sentiment for extreme protection will, I believe, very soon recede.

I feel convinced that the extravagant measures which Meighen proposed are not in the interests of the country as a whole, not even taking the long view, in the interests of those who were most zealous in demanding them.

He attended one or two Cabinet meetings as Minister without Portfolio, but very soon after the results of the election were known, he laid down his responsibilities and unobtrusively withdrew from the Cabinet.

The door of business was now closed to Vincent Massey and his political future did not seem attractive. At this point Mackenzie King offered him the chance to become Canada's first diplomatic representative in the United States. After some hesitation, the offer was accepted.

Vincent Massey's entry into politics, which caused our Company serious embarrassment at the time, proved to be the first step in his distinguished career of public service. In 1926, he became Canada's Minister Plenipotentiary in Washington, and as such was the occupant of the first diplomatic post ever to be opened abroad. He was a forerunner in a foreign service which now comprises approximately 137 ambassadors and high commissioners representing Canada throughout the world.

The rest of his career, as High Commissioner to London, and as the first native-born Governor-General of his country, is now a part of Canadian history.

I was honoured by Vincent Massey's friendship for over fifty years. In my opinion he was the most distinguished and highly respected Canadian of his time. It is an opinion which is widely held throughout Canada.

When he was appointed to Washington in 1926, he felt that if he continued to hold his shares in Massey-Harris and to act as a trustee for the Massey Foundation, with its important interests in the Company's stock, he might become involved in a conflict of interest. He and his advisers therefore decided that the Massey holdings should be sold. What happened is recounted in his memoirs:

The price for both common and preferred stock had for some time been bid up briskly on the exchanges, and when it became rumoured that American interests were seeking to acquire control of the Company, an unprecedented speculation had driven the price of shares to an all time high. At this juncture, a Canadian syndicate was formed by Thomas Bradshaw of the Massey-Harris Company, and the Toronto financier, J. Harry Gundy, and they made an attractive offer for the block of stock determining control.

Through the National Trust Company, which conducted the negotiations, I decided to release to this syndicate my own Massey-Harris holdings and those of the corporation for which I was a Trustee. Newspapers, unfriendly to the government, and I cannot think friendly to myself, tried to make it appear that I had been ready to sell our Company to the American interests concerned and had been deflected only by the patriotic gesture of Messrs. Bradshaw and Gundy.

This was a willful misrepresentation of the facts. Had any offer from the United States far exceeded that of the Canadian syndicate I should then naturally have had to consider whether the best interests of those for whom I was a Trustee would be served by its acceptance. Such a decision would have neither been easy nor automatic, and I was glad that I was not called upon to make it.

Some difficulty arose over the form of the announcement in which the terms of our transaction would be made known to the public. A few hours before I was to leave for Washington, I went to the office of the National Trust Company to see the press statement that had been prepared by Bradshaw and his associates. His draft, as I thought it might do, sought to represent his syndicate as having saved an old Canadian firm from passing into American control. Rundle and I refused to accept it. The situation was not improved by the knowledge that my train was about to leave. I told Alice, who had been waiting elsewhere in the building, that she would have to go as far as New York City without me, and that I would try to join her there. She left with one or two members of her staff and was seen off at the station by a group of friends who were rather bewildered to find that the wife of the first Canadian Minister to the United States was going to Washington without her husband!

Meanwhile, following our refusal to sign the Bradshaw statement, Rundle of the National Trust and I had proceeded to draft our own, which, after much discussion, was finally initialled by Bradshaw. In this way the control of the Massey-Harris Company passed into new hands and the old firm ceased to be a family business exactly eighty years after its original establishment.

Control of the Massey-Harris Company was now in the hands of Bradshaw and Gundy, the latter taking over the new issue of preferred stock. The common was widely distributed;

and the family company which had played such an honourable and important role in the development of Canadian industry, and of her export trade, passed into the hands of the public.

Vincent's father, Chester Massey, chairman of the Company, never enjoyed robust health. I recall him as a frail, distinguished, very religious and kindly man. He never took an active part in the affairs of the Company. His fine, sensitive mind was not attuned to business and he was the first to say so.

On my frequent trips to Canada after World War I, when I was still in my twenties, Chester Massey always asked me to come and see him, sometimes in his office on King Street where I would find him reclining on a long couch reading reports. At other times he would invite me to his home on Jarvis Street for afternoon tea.

He was disappointed that none of his sons showed any compelling interest in the Company which had been founded by his father.

Raymond had given it a try, but after serving somewhat reluctantly one year's apprenticeship in the King Street plant, he decided the implement business was not for him, and he went over to England to take up professional acting.

To me Raymond's choice appeared excellent. Both he and Vincent had taken an active part in amateur theatricals in which they displayed unusual talent. As Raymond enjoyed independent means and had no taste for the implement business, I thought that his decision to follow a career of his liking was a very sensible one.

His father did not share these views. On one occasion, when I was having tea at his house, he told me of his disappointment, summing up his views in these words: "I would have been happy if my boys had shared your enthusiasm for the Company, but this was not to be. Vincent is a diplomat, and Raymond has become an actor. I have given Raymond's choice much thought and prayerful consideration, and I have finally come to the conclusion that he can serve his Lord and Master as faithfully on the stage as in any other walk of life. Please look him up occasionally, when you are in London, and see how he is getting along."

Raymond's father did not live to see him rise to a great heights in his chosen profession, in which he brought honour to his name and to his country. I have continued throughout my life to see something of Raymond Massey, one of the most charming of men, and I have never failed to applaud his outstanding success.

After Vincent Massey had been appointed to Washington but before he took over his office, he came to Paris, accompanied by his wife, Alice. His object was to invite me to resign from the Company and join him as First Secretary in Washington. He felt that my knowledge of foreign languages would be of assistance in his new post.

Although flattered by his choice I refused his offer. My interest lay in the Massey-Harris Company in those early days, as it has ever since.

I never regretted my choice.

II

The Great Depression

IN 1926, after the takeover, the Company appeared to be amply financed to meet the anticipated growing volume of business that lay ahead of it.

At the annual meeting in February of 1930, Joseph Shenstone retired from the presidency to become chairman of the board. He was succeeded by Thomas Bradshaw.

Bradshaw's appointment coincided with the early stages of the greatest period of depression that Canada and most countries throughout the world have experienced in our times. Grave economic distress of all kinds so affected the purchasing power of the wheat importing countries that unprecedented surpluses piled up in the hands of the exporting nations.

In Canada, wheat prices dropped below seventy cents a bushel in 1930 and fell progressively until in December, 1932, No. 1 Northern, Canada's top quality wheat, reached the unbelievable level of thirty-nine cents a bushel at the Lakehead, or about twenty-five cents on the farm, a price which in many cases did not even return the cost of harvesting operations.

As if this were not enough, the sorely tried farmers fell victims to a drought of unprecedented severity and duration. Leaving ruin in its wake, the drought spread throughout the wheatlands of western Canada and devastated agriculture in the Dakotas, Oklahoma, and parts of Kansas and Texas. The farmers in these areas became destitute. Many were only saved from starvation by government relief.

In the areas most severely affected, tens of thousands of Canadian and American farmers, destitute and discouraged by the persistent drought, and the dust storms which swept their topsoil into great drifts higher sometimes than their fences or outhouses, abandoned their land, their homes, and their equipment, and trekked to the west coast or the larger cities in search of a livelihood for their families and themselves.

Consternation spread throughout our Company and discouragement in our boardroom. Due to the impaired financial position of the farmers, accounts receivable increased alarmingly and these were matched by soaring bank loans and overdrafts. By August, 1930, manufacturing operations were radically curtailed and nearly fifty percent of our staff was laid off both in factories and offices.

From the highly successful peak operations of 1928 and '29, the Company suddenly found itself plunged into an unprecedented crisis and an alarming financial position. Nineteen-thirty closed with a loss of $2¼ million against a profit of $2.8 million in the previous year, a deterioration of over $5 million.

Thomas Bradshaw who, until the end of 1929, was widely and rightly acclaimed as being a wise, conservative, and dynamic leader, suddenly found himself criticized on all sides. In the fall of 1930, he was just as good a man as he had been in 1929, and none could have handled the crisis with greater dexterity than he, but Bradshaw became the victim of world events over which he had but little control. Following a difference of opinion with J. H. Gundy over the continuation of dividend payments on the preferred stock, which Bradshaw strongly opposed, he resigned from the Company.

To fill the vacancy, T. A. Russell, a member of our board since 1924 and a director of the Canadian Bank of Commerce, was appointed acting president with the primary responsibility of cutting down expenditures to a minimum, of collecting receivables, reducing inventories, and paying off the banks. This was a difficult assignment at a time when the Company, both at home and in most of its foreign branches, was in the throes of a gathering depression of unprecedented magnitude.

T. A. Russell was not a farm-implement man, but he brought with him an asset priceless at the time: the confidence of the Canadian Bank of Commerce.

The Company was rapidly reaching a state of insolvency. Had it not been for the generous and farsighted policy of the Canadian Bank of Commerce and the forbearance of our bond holders, the Company might not have been given time to work out its difficulties. In continuing to give the Company its confidence, and in lending us large sums of money during the years '31, '32, '33, and '34, the Canadian Bank of Commerce followed a policy which lived up to the highest traditions of Canadian banking. The bank appreciated the important role the Massey-Harris Company played in the economy of the country and placed its trust not in the financial position of the Company but in the honesty and ability of the senior executives of the organization.

While these events were taking place across the Atlantic, France and certain other European countries were not yet suffering from the extremes of depression which were afflicting North America, the Argentine, and several other countries. Our operations in France continued to be fairly buoyant and, although conditions were deteriorating, we were able to strengthen our competitive position, and to improve the quality and therefore the acceptance of our locally manufactured goods in both France and Germany.

I had been following at a distance the grievous events affecting our parent Company and, to mitigate their effects in Europe should these overtake us, we had launched a vigorous program of retrenchment which was reflected in improved operating results, and which prepared us for a deepening recession. This was my first experience of management during a depression. It was to stand me in good stead in years to come.

In Canada, Russell and the board, recognizing the need of stronger management to guide the Company through the crisis, were canvassing the situation and tossing around the pros and cons of appointing an executive from within the ranks of the Company or bringing in an outsider.

On February 3rd, 1931, I received from Vincent Massey, whose advice had been sought by Russell, a letter from which I extract the following paragraph:

> I have recommended that you should be brought over from Europe and appointed Chief Executive Officer of the Company, even if it were thought advisable to have associated with you, but junior to you, a man of managerial rank responsible for manufacturing operations.

Although I appreciated the compliment, and was never reluctant to accept a challenge, I was only thirty-eight at the time, and all my experience had been in the foreign field. I did not feel qualified to assume a position of such heavy responsibility under the difficult circumstances which were then affecting all our operations. I was, therefore, greatly relieved when I was told shortly afterwards that an appointment had been made, although it was with some foreboding that I heard that the candidate who had been chosen for the general managership was an outsider with no experience in the farm-implement industry, and one who, although evidently an able manufacturer, had never been connected with the problems of sales or finance.

In February of 1931 I received a letter from our president, inviting me to come to Toronto in early March. On my arrival there, Russell told me that my name had been considered for the general managership of the Company, but that owing to the nature of the crisis in which the Company was involved, and their unwillingness to withdraw me from Europe, which was at the time the only bright spot in the Company's operations, they had decided to bring in an outsider to fill the position.

"What is required to meet our problem," Russell told me, "is an outsider. A man experienced in manufacturing but one who has no ties of association or loyalty to the staff—a ruthless operator who will have no inhibitions about cutting down the organization regardless of long service, loyalty, or past contributions. In other words, a surgeon and not a doctor."

I assured the president that I was not disappointed at the decision the board had taken, and that I felt strongly, in view of the forecast worsening economic conditions in Europe, that it was desirable that I should remain at my post over there.

In the strictest of confidence, because the appointment had

not yet been ratified by the board, Russell told me of the choice they had made. "His name is Bertram W. Burtsell," said Russell. "He is an American from Niagara Falls, and has been superintendent of production for the Packard Motorcar Company, where he has proven himself to be a tough but effective operator. He is a city man," Russell added. "He knows nothing about agriculture, or the farm-implement business, and I am planning to send him over to Europe with you, just as soon as his appointment is ratified by the board, in the expectation that by spending three weeks in your company he will acquire some understanding of our business and the background of our Company before he returns to Canada to undertake the task for which we have hired him."

My confidence in inexperienced outsiders has always been limited, but, in this particular case, I realized that the special circumstances had probably justified the choice.

I left Toronto with B. W. Burtsell, on my return trip to France, with a feeling of some uneasiness at the thought that our Company's affairs were now in the hands of two men, both able no doubt, but one of whom had very limited, boardroom experience of the implement business, and the other of whom had no experience at all.

Although I could not imagine two people who, from the point of view of background, tastes and upbringing were more dissimilar, Burtsell and I got along famously. In many respects he was an interesting character, an extrovert, an amusing raconteur, a flashy dresser, a hypochondriac who kept talking about his health and his pills, his calories and his antibiotics. He had not enjoyed a sound education, he never read books, and had been brought up in the school of hard knocks, of which he was inordinately proud.

He had risen to a senior position in the manufacturing activities of the Packard Motorcar Company, where, in those days, a tough and somewhat ruthless approach to the workers was considered a necessary adjunct to success. He had never been abroad before and was inclined to look on Europeans and foreigners of all nationalities with patient but amused tolerance.

I made little progress in carrying out Russell's wish that I should indoctrinate my travelling companion. He was extraordinarily unreceptive. When I brought out reports of our European business, he invariably brushed them to one side, saying that his interest was not in papers and figures, but in people, and in the things he could see with his own eyes. He used to add that if *I* were satisfied that the figures were sound, *he* was perfectly satisfied to accept my judgement.

With the parent company hovering on the brink of disaster, I recognized that although Burtsell did not conform to the usual pattern of senior executive, his toughness, his single-minded dedication to cutting down the organization and to paying off our debts to the bank was not without its merit. In some respects I learned a lot from him.

The day after we arrived in Paris I took him to our head office. Within a few hours he had dismissed my colleague and co-general manager, Cecil Milne, a man of ability and experience, on the grounds that he did not believe in joint management. I was inclined to share his view in this, but certainly did not concur with the dismissal of Milne, who had much to offer our Company during the difficult times that lay ahead of us.

I was there and then appointed European general manager. Burtsell's methods were unusual and colourful. At our factory in northern France, after the briefest discussion with me about who might in time become redundant, he would ask me to call them into my office, and without preliminaries, without even asking them to sit down, he would address each of them as follows:

"Reach for your hat and coat my friend, and get yourself and your family on a boat returning to Canada. You are through with our Company. Good luck to you somewhere else. That's all. Thank you."

He went through our French and German factories like a tornado, damning everybody, telling the superintendents, engineers and inspectors in the most amazingly colourful language what he was going to do to them if the quality of the work in the factory, which he never took the trouble to examine, was not greatly improved. Then, taking me by the arm he would say, "Jimmy, let's get the hell out of here because if I stay any longer I may spoil the impression I have made."

Later, we travelled to England where he went through the same performance, leaving behind him a trail of people whose world had fallen in, and whose prospect of finding another job when they returned to North America was enough to worry the most courageous among them.

After we had completed our visit to England, he explained to me that his nerves were upset and that he required a few days of relaxation in Paris in my company. A good time was had by all.

I saw him off on the boat train for New York a few days afterwards. As it was pulling out of the station he said, "Jimmy, my boy, you are in full charge now, and good luck to you. I've put the fear of God into the organization, and have made everything easy for you."

These events took place in the spring of 1931. By that time we were beginning to feel the full effects of the depression. I decided to close our headquarters in Paris and move them to the north of France where I would be closer to the factory, or the smokestacks, as Burtsell used to call it.

Production was still our major concern, but as the depression worsened it became obvious that I would have to further curtail our staff, and cut salaries and expenses to offset the decline in our sales. The unorthodox methods of our general manager had simplified my task; everyone was expecting to be fired, and such modest measures as a decrease in salaries across the board, in which, of course, I participated, were looked on as a highly acceptable solution.

About that time I was fortunate to secure the services of W. K. Hyslop. I had known him as a competitor for many years when he was the successful representative of the International Harvester Company in Spain. Our friendship continued when he joined the Ford Motor Company as manager for Spain and subsequently for France.

Hyslop was ten years senior to me. He was a man of broad experience, an accomplished linguist, and a straight-shooter. He had been toughened by his experience with the Ford Motor Company which hired and fired senior officials with the greatest facility, and never allowed even a passing thought of appreciation for services rendered to interfere with what they considered to be the best interests of the business. Hyslop was a very successful manager of their Spanish company, but, like all others, he was required to sign a letter of resignation at the time of his appointment. One day he walked into his office in Barcelona early in the morning to find an unknown person sitting at his desk. "Your resignation was accepted in Detroit," the incumbent said, "and I arrived here last night to take over your functions."

Hyslop, who had the happy faculty of taking everything in his stride with remarkable equanimity, reached over the desk, removed some of his private papers from a couple of drawers, put on his hat and coat, shook hands with his successor, and left the premises.

A few months afterwards, while he was enjoying his new-found leisure in Paris, he ran across Big Bill Sorensen, Ford's right-hand man, who, when told what had happened, said that it was all a mistake. He appointed Hyslop immediately to the management of their French company.

Two years afterwards, Hyslop went through the same experience in Paris as he had in Spain. This time, having had his fill of Ford practices, he accepted my offer to join our organization. He was an experienced farm-implement man and a first-class executive. Shortly after he had joined us I was able to appoint him assistant general manager of our European operation.

Towards the end of July, Burtsell wrote me: "I was pleased to note what you said concerning having hired Hyslop. At the moment there is nothing which could make me feel better than to know that Hyslop could step into your shoes in the not too distant future and fill them as thoroughly as you can. I only wish that you were over here now."

Our European staff was responding splendidly to the Spartan measures I had imposed. Remarkable progress had been made in the quality and design of our product, both in Germany and France, and our staff and workers were in good spirits and looking forward to the future with confidence. Europe was a little island of success in the sombre picture of our world operations, but we were far from being out of the woods. Conditions were depressed and our staff reduced to the minimum.

To progress—indeed, to hold our own—everyone had to redouble their efforts and they did so willingly and to good purpose. As is often the case in times of great stress, enthusiasm was running high, and the spirit of the organization was excellent.

Every weekend for months on end our superintendent, chief engineer and sales manager would accompany me to various parts of France where we would follow the performance of our machinery in the fields, check the quality of our recent product, compare it with that of our competitors, and call on our agents and district travellers.

We left Lille by car after office hours every Friday, returning late on Sunday evening, and a point was always made that all should be on the job when the factory opened at 7:30 on Monday mornings. The message was not lost on our staff and our workers. They knew that their management was giving up every weekend in the service of the Company, and they responded accordingly.

We were undoubtedly setting a fast pace, but we were all young, anxious to make good, dedicated to the success of the European business, and I believe that our engineers and executives who undertook with me those weekly forays—if not their wives—enjoyed the exhilaration of it all. I know that I did.

I have always believed that a loyal, hard working, and dedicated staff can accomplish miracles. These attributes often mark the dividing line between success and failure. But these precious gifts cannot be bought or ordained. They must always flow from the example set by management. The price management has to pay in the sacrifice of leisure, and frequently of private life, is often a heavy and exacting one.

It was about this time that I experienced a set-back which to a great extent I had brought on myself.

In 1921, when travelling in Austria, I had met a charming Austrian girl, fair of face, intelligent, and kindly of disposition. She spoke only German in those days, but I was fluent in that language. Two years afterwards, we were married in Paris, and in due course set up a home in Purley on the outskirts of London.

She frequently accompanied me on my trips abroad, and we enjoyed each other's company, although she never developed a genuine interest in my career. Perhaps, naturally enough, she resented my devotion to business.

When I took over the management of our French company

after my father's death, we moved to Paris. Although she disliked my long and frequent absences, and deplored with me that no children had blessed our marriage, we lived happily in that great and interesting city.

The trouble arose when, after becoming general manager for Europe, I decided that it was essential that we should move to Lille. She was discouraged at the prospect of living in that unattractive manufacturing city where she knew no one. I did not blame her, but I was determined to protect the interests with which I had been entrusted, and I was persuaded that, as our main problem was centered at the time in design and manufacturing, it was essential that I should be close to the manufacturing plant.

I asked for patience until our Company had emerged from its difficulties. I then tried to meet the situation by arranging for my wife to spend a great deal of time in her native Austria. I should have known better. None of these solutions worked. In the course of time my wife asked me for a divorce, which I granted her.

It was largely my fault. I saw it coming when we moved to Lille. But I was captive of an inner force which drove me forward, and I couldn't bring myself to deviate from a course which I considered essential if I was to overcome the difficulties which were besetting our business on all sides. We were both victims of the recession of the early thirties, and of my belief that if I were to discharge my duties to our Company effectively, concentration and oneness of purpose were essential.

12

Memorable Years in the Argentine

IN CANADA, Russell and Burtsell were experiencing rough going throughout the year 1931. Sales dropped to approximately half of those of the previous year, and had it not been for an un-expected windfall of a six-million-dollar order for tractors from the U.S.S.R., world sales would not have exceeded $10 million, only a quarter of the figure reached two years before.

Factories in Canada and the U.S.A. were practically idle. Losses sustained in the year 1931 were over $4 million.

Towards the end of 1931 our business in the Argentine, one of our largest importing markets, was causing our parent Company great anxiety.

Sales had dropped to a negligible figure. Inventories had soared alarmingly. The condition of the farmers was such that they could neither purchase new machines nor pay for the old, and any moneys collected could not be transferred to Canada because of exchange difficulties.

Burtsell and Russell came to the conclusion that if I could be spared to go to the Argentine I might be able to straighten matters out. Burtsell was despatched to France to talk over the situation and to ascertain whether I felt Hyslop was ready to handle the European business during my temporary absence.

I have always loved a challenge and was confident of Hyslop's ability. Nor was I unaware of the advantages of the broadening experience which this appointment carried with it. I was then thirty-nine years of age.

I therefore agreed to go, with one proviso which was immediately granted, that I should be given full powers to take whatever action I considered necessary during my stay in South America. Three days afterwards, I was on my way to the Argentine.

Travel to South America in those days was exclusively by passenger ship. The journey from New York took three weeks, during which I employed my time making a close study of conditions in the Argentine in general, and of our business there in particular.

The business was evidently in a parlous condition. Economically, the Argentine had suffered greatly from the world depression. Cattle and wheat prices, the mainstay of the economy, had shrunk to unprecedented levels, and even at sacrifice prices found no ready outlet in their traditional importing markets.

The *estancieros* and the small *chacareros*, unlike our Canadian and American farmers, received no government aid in any form. It is interesting to note here that although the Argentine farmers went through years of desperate privation, their production costs had been cut to such low levels that when, in the course of time, wheat and cattle prices improved a little, they were able to operate with a modest profit. Their recovery was considerably more rapid than that of the Canadian and American farmers and cattlemen, who had been heavily subsidized by their governments.

Meanwhile, the poverty and destitution of many of the smaller *chacareros* was extreme. They were living in want, bereft of the most elementary requirements such as salt for their cooking or sugar for their *maté*, a species of tea, the universal drink of all Argentinian farmers.

I disembarked in Buenos Aires in the early spring of 1932. I sent my luggage to the Palace Hotel and went directly to our Argentine head office. I could hardly wait to get started on my new assignment.

J. R. Boyd, who had been in charge of our operations since

1925, was an Anglo-Argentinian, pleasant, knowledgeable, and popular with his staff, but he belonged to the old school, was easy going, and felt that the disasters which had overtaken the business were in the nature of an act of God, and that there was no solution to the present difficulties but to wait it out, and to gradually liquidate our inventories by price reductions. I realized during the first few moments of my interview with him that we were poles apart.

His ways were not my ways. I knew that I could not work through him, nor with him, and accomplish the things I had in mind. I asked for his immediate resignation.

I made a generous settlement with him. Somewhat unceremoniously and with some of Burtsell's unbecoming ruthlessness, I was installed in Boyd's corner office, and had taken charge of the business on the afternoon of the day on which I disembarked in Buenos Aires. I was living up to my reputation of being a man in a hurry.

I called for a conference of all our branch managers and senior personnel for the following morning. Some travelled from distant places overnight, but all were present when I opened the meeting at 8:00 a.m.

After being introduced to the senior officials, none of whom I knew, I gave them a rundown on what had taken place on the previous day, and explained that I had been sent to the Argentine to reorganize the business and to endeavour to set it back on its feet. I said that I had every confidence that with their help and co-operation this could be accomplished. At the same time, recognizing that none of these officials knew me other than by reputation, and that some of them out of loyalty to their past manager might be unprepared to give me their full co-operation, I said that I would accept the resignation of anyone who was not prepared to follow my leadership with loyalty and dedication. "I have nothing to offer you," I added, "but hard work, long hours, and sacrifice, but success will undoubtedly await us at the end of the road." No one stepped forward to resign.

We agreed on the program which, within two years, placed the Company in a position of leadership in the Argentine and Uruguay, and enabled us, after selling our entire inventory, other than tractors, to begin placing new orders with our factories in Canada.

The farm-implement industry, unlike drygoods or motorcars where models and styles change every year, should never look to price reductions as the answer to slow-moving stocks in time of recession, providing, of course, that these stocks are up-to-date and in good condition. The solution of slicing prices, which naturally springs to the mind of the inexperienced, is not the answer.

The remedy lies in salesmanship of a high order, enthusiasm, optimism, an imaginative approach, colourful advertising campaigns, and most important of all, the loyalty of an experienced, confident, hard working, and dedicated staff, all pulling together towards a clearly defined objective. This has been brought home to me and to those who worked with me during four depressions experienced under my management in France, the Argentine, and subsequently in Canada during the early '30's, and again in 1953, '54, and '55.

The customary measures of retrenchment were immediately taken. The office staff was substantially reduced, but the sales staff was increased. Machines that were shopworn by exposure were repainted.

A first class advertising program was undertaken, but more important than any of these measures, we embarked just as we had done in France on a program of field demonstrations, which were attended by hundreds and sometimes thousands of farmers.

These demonstrations were carefully organized a long time in advance. They were always held on weekends, when the farmers were free to attend the gatherings. Invitations were sent out personally to the farmers in the area in which our gathering was to take place.

In each case, an *asado* of vast proportions was served to all comers. The *asado* is an Argentine invention, and there were always *chacareros* in each area who were thoroughly competent and indeed expert in their preparation. The *asado* consists of the roasting of a whole ox, sheep, or chickens on a number of specially erected homemade outside grills, or revolving spits, placed at intervals in the field to avoid congestion. Barrels of red wine were set up on trestles and our guests helped themselves from the taps according to their thirst. The thirst of some of the local *chacareros* was awesome to contemplate.

The *asados* require none of the equipment usually associated with picnic luncheons or dinners. No plates or cutlery are required. From time immemorial the peons, workers on the cattle-raising haciendas, have been accustomed to felling a steer or calf for their evening meal, cooking their chosen portion over an improvised bonfire, and abandoning the rest. All of them carry well sharpened oversized pocket-knives, and, as the delicious aroma of well grilled beef permeates the atmosphere, they step up to the roasting fare, cut themselves the slice of their choice, and return time and time again to repeat this exercise and to refresh themselves with copious drafts from the wine barrels.

Before luncheon, and after the mandatory siesta later in the afternoon, demonstrations of our reaper-thresher and other machinery took place. Speeches were made, orders were booked where possible, and a good time was had by all.

It was a strenuous program. The dirt roads in the Argentine—and there were none other outside the cities—were so bad in those days (and probably still are) that, especially in bad weather, thirty or forty miles a day was about the limit of the distance one could travel by car. Sometimes, after heavy rains, the roads became impassable and many's the time some of my executives and myself had to spend the night in a car sunk to the axles in mud. Our vehicle would be extricated the following morning, for an exorbitant fee, by the farmers of the district who would ride out on horseback to places where the roads were particularly treacherous.

These weekly expeditions were rewarding, if exhausting. I used to leave Buenos Aires with four or five members of my staff after an early dinner on Friday night. We travelled by train or by car to the town nearest the area in which our machinery was to be demonstrated. We got up at dawn the following morning to reach the demonstration fields in time to see that everything was in order. We would repeat this performance on the Sunday, and rarely got home to Buenos Aires until late in the evening.

While our competitors in Buenos Aires spent their long

weekends at the country club playing golf or bridge and generally enjoying themselves, we carried out our demonstration
programs week after week and month after month.

The pace we set was a savage one, but when the organization
began to see the results flowing from it, they supported
the program whole-heartedly. Enthusiasm was running high
throughout the organization.

Our well advertised weekly demonstrations were widely
commented on in agricultural circles throughout the Argentine.
Our confidence in the future was catching; it was said in many
quarters that Massey-Harris was on the march. And we were.

Applications to join our staff, always an encouraging sign,
were received from many quarters.

During the outward journey to Argentina, one of my associates, Tom Carroll, spoke frequently to me of a small Italian firm
in the vicinity of Buenos Aires which had brought out the year
before a clumsy-looking model of reaper-thrasher, which, in
place of being pulled by fifteen to twenty horses, propelled itself with the aid of a powerful engine mounted on the chassis.
Their production, he told me, was insignificant—about fifteen
machines a year—but Tom Carroll had awakened my interest.
Shortly after our arrival in the Argentine, he and I called on
the Italian manufacturer, who was proud to show us his latest
model of self-propelled combine. We followed the machine in
the field, and it was obvious that it had many advantages which
the horse- or tractor-drawn machine did not possess.

Feeling strongly on the subject, I sent Tom Carroll back to
Toronto and arranged that he be given the facilities necessary to
build a self-propelled combine for the Argentine on the understanding that he would have a sample machine ready to be
tested in the Argentine harvest the following season.

Tom Carroll was a man after my own heart. Whatever he
undertook to do he did well and with despatch. He returned to
the Argentine with his machine in time to demonstrate it in the
harvest fields. We rented a large tract of land in an out-of-the-
way area, and surrounded it with guards to prevent our competitors from approaching it.

The machine was an immediate success. Those whom I had invited specially to follow its operations were enthusiastic about it. We placed an order with our Toronto headquarters to build a number for the following year.

I felt convinced that since this machine was enthusiastically received in a country where horses sold for between $5 and $7 each, it would be a winner in any other part of the world where wheat was grown.

What we were witnessing in this closely guarded field was the commencement of a new era in the affairs of our Company. No machine we have ever built did more to establish our reputation throughout the world. None made a greater contribution to our earning power, and none helped us more strongly to rehabilitate our business in the United States of America.

In the course of time all our competitors copied the self-propelled combine, but we had two or three years' lead over any of them. At a later period, approximately seventy-five percent of all the self-propelled combines operating in the United States and ninety percent of those operating in the United Kingdom were manufactured by our Company in a factory erected in Toronto for this purpose.

Ken Hyslop had been left in charge of our European business during my absence in the Argentine, but I was still responsible for it, and after spending a little more than a year in Buenos Aires, I returned to Europe on a short visit to look over the situation. I was so well pleased at the way in which Ken had handled our affairs during my absence that, with the concurrence of our head office, I appointed him European general manager in my stead.

There are few things which give one greater satisfaction in an organization than to watch a chosen understudy develop to a point where he is capable of carrying on unaided, and then passing on the full responsibility to him.

After making a quick tour of all our European branches to introduce Hyslop as my successor, I booked a passage on the first outgoing steamer for Buenos Aires, the S.S. *Julio Césare*.

It was a fortunate choice for it was on this liner that I first met the radiant, beautiful, and charming Spanish girl who, two years afterwards, was to become my wife. Her name was Victoria Martinez Alonso but she was known as Trini.

She was only twenty-two when we met on the boat, but had already risen to great distinction in Madrid's most successful repertory theatrical company. Together with the whole cast, she was on her way to South America for the winter season.

It was Winston Churchill who, referring to his marriage, said: "We met, we married, and we lived happily ever afterwards." This is exactly what came to pass in my case.

Many of Trini's friends—and mine—were pessimistic about the outcome of our proposed marriage, and I am persuaded that if we had submitted our intentions to a matrimonial consultant, which God forbid, he would have felt the same way about it.

We were, however, both civilized people with an international background, and had unbounded faith in each other.

What worried our friends was the dissimilarity of our backgrounds. Trini came from an old theatrical family; she had been on the stage since her early teens. She was well known and acclaimed in Madrid, Buenos Aires, and Montevideo; Hollywood was beckoning to her, and her future was secure in her chosen profession.

I, on the other hand, was an industrialist with a Scottish background, absorbed in and devoted to my business interests. I knew little of the arts and nothing of the theatre.

She was twenty-four, and I was forty one. She loved Spain, and particularly Andalucia where she was born. I was proposing to live in Canada, a country which she did not know and whose language she did not speak.

She was a Catholic, and I a Presbyterian. She spoke the pure Castillian of a trained artist. I spoke her language, but most inaccurately.

All these differences were lightly and gaily cast aside in the knowledge that the things which might have divided us were no match for the forces of love, mutual respect, and admiration which united us. Our optimism was rewarded. There are few who have lived a happier or more rewarding life than we.

It was shortly after my return to the Argentine that I

formed the opinion that conditions in the United States were on the mend. This deduction was obvious both to our competitors and myself, because we were receiving frequent and increasing orders to ship our surplus tractors to the United States market.

Tractors were not readily saleable in the Argentine during the depression because in that country, where horses abounded and were not only inexpensive to buy but fed themselves on the open pastures, the Argentine farmers had no option but to use them rather than to buy fuel for a tractor.

Just as a few years before I had prepared Hyslop to take over the management of our European business, so in the Argentine I had chosen Enrique Abaroa, a Spaniard from the Basque country and previously our branch manager in Rosario, to follow in my footsteps.

He was a man of outgoing personality and first-class ability. He was thoroughly grounded in the farm-implement business, popular with our staff, our customers and our competitors. I was therefore ready when, during the early days of 1935, I received a letter from our general manager, asking me to return to Canada as general sales manager.

On personal grounds, I was reluctant to leave the Argentine. I enjoyed living in Buenos Aires, I was basking in the sunshine of considerable commercial success, and enjoying the loyalty and friendship of an excellent staff.

Although reluctant to leave, I accepted the appointment which Burtsell was offering me with alacrity. It was another step forward, and time had not blunted my ambitions.

Twenty-five years earlier, as a raw and starry-eyed boy of seventeen, I had set sail for Canada determined to carve out a future for myself in this land of opportunity. Once again, at the age of forty-one, I was on my way to Canada. If, over the years, I had lost some of my sense of adventure, my enthusiasm and unbounded confidence in the future were still intact.

13

A Dramatic Reversal of Policy

I WAS APPROACHING MY FORTY-SECOND BIRTHDAY when I arrived in Canada to take up my new duties. I was confident from my experience in the Argentine that the corner had been turned in the United States, and that, after five years in the wilderness, our Company would be able to move forward towards the rebuilding of our organization which had been largely shattered by the measures of retrenchment that had been taken to save it from financial disaster.

My enthusiasm was shaken when I arrived in Toronto. Five years of disastrous operations and crippling losses had engendered, both in our management and our board of directors, feelings of profound discouragement.

I should have expected it. Few companies in Canada had lived through a more discouraging experience, and it was not yet over. Year after year was marked by declining sales and continued losses. Prospects for 1935 were brighter, but a substantial loss was forecast and realized.

Throughout the Company, massive and heavy-handed measures of retrenchment had been imposed. In the process of cutting down the organization, our business was blighted in many countries.

Europe and the Argentine had escaped the holocaust be-cause I had been fortunate enough to benefit from the manage-ment's confidence, and they had accepted my judgement concerning the retrenchments which could be made without permanent damage to our organization.

The qualities which had enabled our senior executives to carry out the needful retrenchments were not, unfortunately, those which were required to build up the business. An atmos-phere of gloom and defeatism hung over the organization.

I had hardly settled down in my new office when an incident took place which gave me great concern, and which I deeply regretted, because it shattered the bond of friendship which had existed between Burtsell and myself ever since he joined the Company. It happened this way.

Burtsell asked me to have lunch with him, saying that he had something of importance to discuss and preferred doing so in his suite at the hotel.

Accordingly we drove to the Royal York in his expensive-looking eight-cylinder Packard, of which he was inordinately proud. Lunch was served in his top-floor suite.

Toward the end of the meal, he unfolded his proposal in more or less these words: "Jimmy, my friend, I brought you from the Argentine to become sales manager, but my intention is that you should shortly take over my own responsibilities. My health is not as good as it should be and I don't intend to work at this job until they carry me out feet first.

"Now the policies which you and I are going to carry out are quite simple. I was hired to save this Company from bank-ruptcy and I have been successful in doing so. As a result of the retrenchments, the reductions in staff, and many other measures taken, the danger of financial disaster has now been eliminated.

"The board has already agreed to my recommendation that we don't belong in the United States and that we should cease to operate there."

Then he looked very hard at me, realizing, no doubt, what my feelings would be, and continued, "We also intend to close down the European business with the exception of England, which can stand on its own feet. We want no more factories abroad. We will then reduce our branches in Canada to three—one in the east, one in Ontario, and one in the west. The organization will be small, but it will be compact and will operate predominantly in Canada, and in some of our export markets like the Argentine and South Africa. It will be more suited to our reduced financial circumstances.

"This is the program," he continued, "which we have decided on, and which you and I are going to carry out, and we will have an enjoyable time working together on it."

I sat and listened to him in amazed and frozen silence.

"Well," he said with some irritation, "what's the matter with the program? What have you got to say about it?"

"In my book," I said with less than my usual diplomacy, "everything is wrong about it. I am satisfied in my own mind that the corner has been turned in the United States. The European business I know from my own personal experience is out of the woods and our competitive position there is strong. I am less knowledgeable about the Canadian business, but this much I do know—that it could not be successfully run with only three branches. We would be has-beens in the farm-implement business without the tractors which are manufactured in the United States."

Burtsell was a quick-tempered man, and this was too much for him. I could see his anger rising as I added, "Rather than be associated with a policy which means the dismemberment of this Company, in the future of which I believe and with which I have been associated all my life, and my father before me, I will immediately resign."

Burtsell jumped up from the table, dashed his dessert plate to the floor, where it broke to smithereens, and with his temper flaring, shouted at me sentences which I prefer to forget but which, divested of the four-letter words, were to the effect that I had let him down, that ever since he had joined the Company he had looked on me as his successor, and that on this very day when his intentions were about to be realized, I had refused to co-operate. "You have the goddamned nerve," he added, "to sit there calmly and tell me that you refuse to carry out my policies!" Thereupon, he stalked out of the room, banging the door behind him.

I finished my coffee, gathered up my hat and coat, and returned to the office.

The following morning, the president sent for me and

expressed his astonishment that on the second day of my arrival in Canada I had contrived to quarrel with the vice-president and general-manager, and had completely refused to carry out his policies. Russell went on to say that evidently I had climbed out on a limb which was about to be sawn off, but he asked me to explain to him why I felt obliged to act as I did.

"I had no option but to take a stand," I said, "against the implementation of a policy which I was convinced would destroy what generations of able people have built up." I restated my convictions that at least in the United States, the Argentine, and Europe, the depression had spent itself, and the time for rebuilding our shattered fortunes was at hand.

To my surprise, the president said that he had never been happy with the decision which had been taken by the board to close down the American operation. "Although our vice-president and general manager would probably not approve," he said, "I suggest that you should make a quick trip to the United States, re-examine the situation, and bring back your recommendations."

Burtsell had been so upset by the incident that he had left immediately for his home in Niagara Falls and did not return to the office for several weeks.

On my side, I headed for Racine, the head office of the United States company, that same afternoon, following discussions with the president.

In the process of retrenchment which had been so rigorously applied, the business in the United States had fallen on evil days. Engineering programs had been so curtailed that the equipment essential to the very existence of the organization had been denied them. The morale of the organization was at a very low ebb.

After a rapid visit to our plants and to each of our branches throughout the United States, I came to the conclusion that agricultural conditions generally were showing signs of improvement and if our organization were given the equipment it required, it could operate on a break-even and subsequently a profitable basis.

On my return to Toronto I presented my report to the president, who was sufficiently impressed with it that he asked me to review the Company's world-wide operations and prepare a budget for the year 1936.

Burtsell had not yet returned to the office. In May 1935 I was appointed assistant general manager.

In due course, I presented a budget to the president which showed that, without closing down any of our manufacturing plants or any of our branches at home or abroad, we could operate in 1936 with a substantially increased volume and with net losses which would not exceed $250,000.

I also showed him, with supporting figures, that if we followed the recommended policy of liquidating our business in the United States and in Europe and curtailing our operations in Canada we would, in the process, run into losses of many millions of dollars, besides which we would be destroying our chances of ever recovering our world-wide organization.

Russell was intrigued. He asked me whether, knowing that the board had already approved of the liquidation of the United States business, that two buildings at one of our plants were in the process of being torn down, that the Company had already lost some eighteen million dollars in the United States, and that in all probability the general manager would oppose my point-of view, I would be willing to present my proposals to a special meeting of our directors.

Determined as I was to do everything in my power to reverse a decision which, in my opinion, would be fatal to the future of the Company, I agreed.

Burtsell was recalled for the meeting. Russell was in the chair, and Harry Gundy, our most influential shareholder and director and the one who, through the holding of our preferred stock, had been the chief victim of the Company's financial disasters, watched the proceedings in stony silence.

Without preamble I was asked to state my case. I reviewed the Company's position both at home and abroad. I rejected the thought that we had come to the end of the road. I spoke of my faith in the future based on my knowledge of the business and my successful operations both in Europe and the Argentine, and I presented a detailed budget of operations for the ensuing year which I was prepared to stand behind.

As I concluded this presentation, I appealed to the board for patience, and asked them to give me an opportunity to prove whether I was right or wrong before deciding to pursue a policy which, in my judgement, would be fatal to the future of the Company.

There was an element of drama in the situation.

After a few moments, Burtsell got up and voiced his uncompromising disapproval of my recommendations, saying emphatically that if the board followed my proposals, which in his opinion would result in the bankruptcy of the Company, he would resign immediately.

Breaking the uncomfortable silence which hung over the meeting, Harry Gundy, always a man of courage and vision, turned to me and said, as closely as I can remember, "You have stated, Mr. Duncan, that you would undertake to operate the Company in 1936 with a loss not exceeding $250,000. I share your point of view that if we embark on a policy of liquidation, our losses will be very much greater. If you will agree that in the event of the losses next year exceeding $250,000 you will immediately resign from the Company, then I will recommend to the board that they give you an opportunity to prove your point."

I accepted the challenge. Russell favoured Gundy's proposal, as did all the directors with the exception of our general manager and one other, and the meeting broke up.

Burtsell left in a huff. He retained his title of vice-president for a few more months, but took no further part in the management of the Company. In November of 1935 the board appointed me general manager.

The record of the Company since 1930 had been disastrous, our net losses staggering:

1930	$2,247,000
1931	$4,043,000
1932	$3,827,000
1933	$3,305,000
1934	$2,209,000
1935	$1,420,000

These awesome losses did not dampen my confidence in our

recovery. I rejoiced in the opportunity of playing a leading role in the rebuilding of our Company, and I was buoyed up by the thought that with the co-operation of our staff, which I knew would not be lacking, I would be able to do so.

Since the death of Thomas Findley in 1921, the management of the Company had been in the hands of men of ability but without background or training in the farm-implement business. The appointment of one who had been born into the business, who had been successful in reversing the decisions which were stifling our organization, and who had played a leading and successful role in the Company's two largest export markets was received with enthusiasm by all the staff.

A feeling of renewed confidence in the future soon permeated the organization.

When 1936 was over, our turnover stood at $16.2 million, and our losses at $58,000. We had bettered our target both in sales and in forecast losses. Harry Gundy's challenge had been successfully met.

In 1937 I was elected to the board and subsequently was appointed vice-president and general manager. I was grateful for the opportunity which had been given me to lead our Company out of the wilderness. While I had no illusions of the difficulties still facing us, I accepted this further promotion with confidence.

The problems which the Company faced were indeed challenging. Among these, the most important were: the shortage of working capital and, owing to our past record, no immediate means of raising new funds; a line of tractors which, owing to past restrictive polices, were now outdated; the reluctance of the American banks to grant us essential short-term credit; and the understandable discouragement previously prevalent throughout the organization and not yet entirely overcome.

In assuming the management of the Company I determined that if policies had been pursued in recent years with which I disagreed, I would never refer to them. There would be no post mortems, no criticism of my predecessors.

Who was I to judge what I might have done under similar circumstances? I was happy to give them the benefit of the doubt. Besides, I have never had much use for men who, in the vain hope of valorizing their own services, try to lessen the contributions of those who preceded them.

To bring it down to the lowest denominator, it is a useless pastime. If one does good work it will always be recognized and to endeavour to diminish the contribution of others only diminishes oneself.

I spoke along these lines to our staff. No criticism of the past could be countenanced. The order of the day was "eyes front," to use military parlance. The past was behind us—let it rest. The future was our concern, and if we all worked together as a team and set our sights high enough, we could make it great.

Step by step our difficulties were met and at least partially overcome. Our improved line of equipment was giving a good account of itself. Our sales were increasing slowly but surely both at home and abroad. Confidence in the future of the Company, self-assurance, and job security had lifted the morale of the organization. We were on the way.

Even our American banks, which had taken a jaundiced view of our situation, were becoming more friendly.

One of my most difficult and distasteful tasks during the years immediately following my appointment as general manager was that of obtaining from reluctant bankers short-term loans essential to our American business.

Five banks in New York shared these loans. The amount involved was not very large, but our credit was at its lowest possible ebb, based on our past performance in the United States.

All we had to offer our bankers was faith and confidence in the future, and this hardly seemed sufficient to some of them!

After one of these particularly harrowing meetings, George Moore, now chairman of the First National City Bank, took me to one side saying, "Difficult as I know your American company's position is, I am confident that under your management you are going to work things out. Operating, however, as you have been obliged to do, is to say the least, cumbersome. I am prepared to back you with a larger line of credit, and if one of the other banks wishes to go along for a smaller figure, this will greatly simplify the present proceedings."

George Moore's confidence in our future at a time when confidence in us was a scarce commodity was gratefully received, and an adequate line of credit was opened by the First National City Bank and the Irving Trust.

From that time until my retirement from the Company in 1956, the First National City Bank remained our principal New York bankers. George Moore, whose confidence in us was amply justified by subsequent events, remains to this day one of my closest friends.

One of the factors which assisted in reducing our losses in 1936 was the courageous, if unpopular, decision to increase sales prices which were sadly out of line with costs. Over the years, the farm-machinery industry headed the list for unpopularity throughout western Canada. Tariffs and politics had played their important role in a situation which became aggravated during the years of the depression by lower farm-produce prices, poor crops, drought, dust-bowl conditions—all of which had reduced many farmers to dire poverty.

That in 1936 we and other manufacturers in the United States and Canada found it necessary to increase selling prices worsened the situation, and gave rise to an outcry which, in turn, led to an all-embracing parliamentary enquiry into every aspect of the price structure of the implement business.

Supported by three members of my staff, I gave evidence before the Implement Price Enquiry of 1937. Over a period of approximately two weeks I was subjected to probing and exhaustive questioning by members of both parties in the House.

We came out of the enquiry with flying colours, and I personally derived considerable benefit from it. It had been necessary for me to go into all the various aspects of our organization dating back to the latter years of the past century. Moreover it provided me with an excellent opportunity of becoming well known to Cabinet Ministers, leaders of the opposition, and to an important group of members of Parliament which included those who were members of the committee as well as numerous other Senators and members of Parliament whose interest had been aroused by the wide-spread publicity given to the hearings.

Certain members of Parliament, particularly those from the western provinces, did their best to trip me up in their endeavours to produce evidence that we were overcharging the western farmers, but we had an ironclad case.

One day I met Charles Dunning, then Minister of Finance,

in the corridor of the House of Commons, close to where we were holding our hearing.

"Congratulations," he said. "I hear you are holding your own end up at the enquiry."

I asked him where his information came from, and he replied that Bill Fraser,[1] the member from Trenton, had dropped into his office that morning and said, "Charlie, come down and sit in at the enquiry for a few minutes. You'll get a kick out of hearing a two-bit western M.P. trying to take on a hundred-thousand-dollar executive!"

This was, in fact, unfair criticism because many of the western M.P.'s were very well informed and kept me on my toes.

The enquiry served a useful purpose in clearing up many of the incorrect impressions under which the western farmers were labouring.

Early in 1937 it became evident that crop conditions in the west were again going to be disastrous, bringing another serious setback to our Company.

During the harvest I undertook an extensive tour of the prairie provinces to try to form an accurate impression of existing conditions and prospects for the future.

It would be difficult to exaggerate the tragedy which the prolonged drought had brought to the farmers in the provinces of Saskatchewan and Alberta.

Day after day we motored through areas where tens of thousands of acres of parched land had not even a semblance of a crop. Men and machines were idle. The small lakes in the area which we visited had been dried up, river beds were overgrown with scrub weeds. Gaunt, gnarled, and leafless trees were dying for lack of moisture.

Patches of Russian thistle, growing here and there, were being gathered up to serve as fodder for the few remaining cattle.

Everywhere the farmers were on relief, plagued by enforced idleness, despondent, discouraged and unable to make any contribution to the maintenance of their families.

[1] W. A. Fraser, M.P.

It was during this trip to the west that I first met H. H. Bloom. He was then the manager of our Saskatchewan branch. I watched him in action for a couple of days and was so impressed by his ability, his enthusiasm, and particularly by his profound knowledge of the implement business, that shortly afterwards I brought him to Toronto as assistant Canadian sales manager. His promotion thereafterwards was to be rapid.

I returned to Toronto from the western provinces distressed and disconcerted by what I had seen, but I was unable to share the pessimism of many both in the east and the west who felt that large areas of the prairie provinces would never return to the fertility of the past.

I gave a number of interviews to the western and Toronto press in which I expressed my confidence that these years of drought which had scourged vast areas of the prairie provinces were a passing phase and that life-giving rains would return once again. In the fullness of time—perhaps even sooner than we expected—the west would come into its own once again.

Many disagreed with my forecast and did not hesitate to say that I was overly optimistic. My expectations, however, were justified more rapidly than I had hoped. In 1938 the western crops showed the largest yield of any since 1932, and in 1939 the wheat and barley crops were the second largest in the history of Canada till that time.

At the annual meeting for the year ending November 30th, 1937, I was able to report that despite the unfavourable crop conditions experienced in large parts of the Canadian west, our world sales had shown an increase of forty percent compared with the previous year, and our net profits, after all reserves and charges, exceeded one million dollars.

This was the first profitable year the Company had experienced since 1929. We were now on our way to full recovery. The spectre of insolvency, which had cast a shadow over our operations and slowed down our progress, was no longer with us.

Models of large and smaller self-propelled combines had been successfully tested in the Canadian and American harvest fields. Our line of machinery had been updated. The organization had regained its esprit de corps, its drive, and its enthusiasm, and we all looked forward to the future with confidence and justifiable optimism.

There was a good deal to be optimistic about. The profitable year of 1937 was a forerunner of a long period of unbroken growth and prosperity which characterized the next nineteen years during which I presided over the destinies of the Company.

Throughout this period I travelled intensively. I have always believed that it was essential for me to be in close touch with our far-flung organization, to get my information first-hand, to discuss the Company's local problems on the spot.

I made it my business to ensure that all our organizations were acquainted with our objectives and the role they were called on to play within a world-wide concept and I endeavoured to bring to them a sense of belonging, and something of my own enthusiasm and faith in the future.

My aim was to keep the organization uncomplicated, uncluttered by unnecessary red tape and a profusion of organizational charts.

When an organization is closely knit, and manned by experienced people, many of those costly and time-consuming appendages so dear to the heart of the professional organizational experts become unnecessary and redundant!

14

The War Is Upon Us

No one could have travelled in Germany during the years
1937, '38, and '39 without becoming acutely conscious of the
increasing dominance of the Nazi Party, of the fearsome growth
of militarism, and the unquestioning and frightening enthusiasm of Germany's arrogant youth for Hitler and the things
he stood for.

We all realized that owing to the international nature of our
Company we would be among the first to suffer from an outbreak of hostilities. Accordingly I followed the unfolding events
with the closest attention.

Nineteen thirty-eight was a year of tension, of compromise,
and growing defeatism in England and France and of triumphant and aggressive progress in Hitler's Germany. The mould
was being shaped for the tragic events which were to engage
us all in the fall of 1939.

I was now firmly convinced that war in Europe was inevitable. I arranged to set up a committee of top-flight executives
to examine the steps which should be taken throughout our
organization to prepare our Company to play an active role in
defence production should we be called on to do so, and to plan

the measures to be taken at once to protect our regular operations in the event of war restrictions being applied.

A mission headed by our chief engineer, Guy Bevan, was sent to England to study that country's industrial preparedness. Some felt that such steps were premature, but they proved to be a godsend, for when war broke out on September 3rd, 1939, our Company was ready to take appropriate action.

Four days after the declaration of hostilities I went to Ottawa, accompanied by two of our senior officials, and outlined to the Hon. C. D. Howe who was to achieve such success and fame as Canada's minister in charge of war production, and to General Andrew G. L. McNaughton who was to take Canada's troops overseas, preparations we had made for the contingency of war, and our readiness to place all our facilities at the government's disposal.

In December, we obtained our first war contracts. One of them was from the Department of Munitions and Supplies for wings and spars for the Avro-Anson Mosquito aircraft, and the other was for the production of shells, which was the first contract awarded in Canada by the British purchasing mission.

Among the measures of preparedness for the coming conflict was my decision in 1938 to transfer W. K. Hyslop from Europe to the United States to take over senior responsibility for our rapidly expanding American business.

Hyslop was a top-flight executive. He had always shown strong qualities of leadership although his approach to his problems was more detached and unemotional than was usually to be found among our senior executives. He was a tower of strength, first as general manager and then as president of our American company, and would have qualified in time for the senior executive position in our organization had it not been for the unfortunate fact that instead of being ten years younger than I was, he was ten years older. He had long since made up his mind that he would retire before he was sixty-five to devote his declining years to golf, fishing and hunting, in all of which he excelled.

When I use the words "declining years," I am speaking metaphorically, because he is now over eighty-seven, is an expert fisherman, shoots big game in Africa, hunts wild turkeys in Mexico, snow geese in northern Ontario, mallards and prairie chickens in Alberta, ducks and quail in the United States, and from what I see of him, he will continue to do so for many years to come.

S. S. Voss succeeded Hyslop as European general manager of our Company in 1938. He was a European in the broadest sense of the word. A Latvian citizen, a nonpractising Jew, born in Russia, his French, English, German, Russian, and Hungarian were word perfect. He had been with us since he was a boy.

His keen and resourceful brain marked him out for promotion at an early age, and he successively occupied senior executive positions in Germany, England, Hungary, and France. He was a great asset to our Company. His interests were centered in our business. He was without religious, racial, or political prejudices. His administrative and organizational ability was of a high order and his sense of loyalty to the organization was unequalled. When I appointed him in succession to Hyslop in 1938, I insisted that in the event of the outbreak of hostilities he was to pass on his responsibilities to a chosen executive on the French staff and proceed immediately to Canada where his services would be invaluable to us, and where, as a Jew, he would be removed from the dangers of Nazi occupation of France.

Unfortunately, when France was overrun, his keen sense of responsibility and loyalty to the business counselled him to overlook my instructions and remain at his post. In the early days of the German occupation all went well, but soon the German authorities in the war zone insisted that, being a Jew, he should resign and hand over his responsibilities to a French managing director.

Voss still felt that his presence in France was essential and, although he worked unofficially from Nantes, close to the free zone, he continued indirectly to manage the affairs of the Company.

He had arranged for his family to escape across the dividing line between the German zone of occupation and the free zone. In the course of time, they found their way to London where we looked after them. But Voss elected to stay behind a little longer. This was his undoing.

Anti-Jewish activity in France was stepped up, and soon

Voss was put under arrest in Nantes. Our French staff, who were devoted to him, and some of whom were connected with the underground, endeavoured to arrange his escape. He refused their help, however, fearing to compromise them and clinging to the belief that, not being a German or a practising Jew and having never been connected with politics or played any role in national or international affairs, he would remain unharmed.

His overconfidence was not rewarded. He was transferred to Frèsnes, a fortress prison at Vincennes, near Paris. Massey-Harris spent considerable sums of money in various ways through intermediaries in attempts to secure the release of Voss from Frèsnes prison, but without success. A few weeks afterwards he was shipped to Germany in a cattle truck with hundreds of French Jews. He was now beyond human help.

On his arrival in Germany, he was consigned to Auschwitz where, being beyond the age for heavy manual labour, he was incinerated.

When, shortly after D-Day, the British government flew me over to Paris, General Vanier, Canadian Ambassador to France, sent a car to meet me at the airport. I drove directly to our Paris office. On my arrival, I was handed a letter written by my old friend Voss from the Frèsnes prison, on the night when instructions had been issued that they were to entrain for Germany. It was a sad little letter, dignified, courageous, uncomplaining, resigned.

He had accepted his cruel fate, expressed his regret that he could no longer look after the Company's interests, and asked me to care for his wife and children. He sent messages to one or two of his close friends, and expressed the hope that our Company, which he loved so well, would continue to prosper.

In the late fall of 1939, large orders for agricultural equipment were received from the United Kingdom, which had embarked on a policy of increased agricultural production as a protection against probable import difficulties. We were able to meet their requirements in the shortest possible time, owing to the stockpiles of raw materials we had accumulated following the recommendations of our war preparedness committee.

During Canada's splendid wheat harvest, the largest ever

recorded up to that time, our self-propelled combines met with spectacular success throughout the prairie provinces. The few we were able to send to the United States were equally well received.

Although none of our competitors at that time followed our lead in the design and production of self-propelled combines, we were so confident of the role this outstanding machine would be called on to play that we engineered and tooled up for production of new and improved models.

In view of the uncertainties of a war economy, this was a courageous decision to take, but it stood us in good stead when, under war restrictions, all new designs and engineering projects were frozen.

Our forehandedness gave us an advantage over our competitors and laid the foundation for our leadership in self-propelled combines in Canada, the United States and later in the United Kingdom. The dominant position we held in the sale of these machines, together with the unequalled publicity value of the Harvest Brigade in the United States, which I shall refer to later, played an important and, indeed, major role in the rapid development of our United States business. It was a decisive factor in the increased earning power of our Company.

With the outbreak of war all our assets in Germany were written off. It was the second time in my experience that Germany at war had taken over our organization. But worse was still to come. When the "phony war" came to an end and the victorious German armies overran one country after another, we found ourselves obliged to write down all our assets on the continent of Europe and in North Africa to $1.00. Our relatively small operations in England were now all that was left of our large and prosperous European business.

In the first week of April, 1940, I left for California on a business trip. My wife accompanied me.

We arrived in Stockton, our first port-of-call, to find that several calls had come in for me from Ottawa, requesting that I should return them immediately. I did so as soon as we were in our room. The operator informed me that the Hon. Norman Rogers, Minister of Defence, was on the line.

"I am speaking on behalf of the Prime Minister and my-self," he said. "You must have seen in the press that the gov-ernment is being attacked on its management of the British Commonwealth Air Training Plan. In many respects, it is our biggest contribution to the common war effort. The Prime Minister and I would be most grateful to you if you would con-sider joining us in Ottawa to help get this mammoth air training plan off the ground."

"We are making progress," Norman Rogers went on, "but not fast enough to meet public demand, which fails to under-stand why at this stage of the war more pilots and observers are not being sent over to England. We feel that you can help us."

My immediate reaction was negative. I told Norman Rogers that I could not consider his suggestion as I was too involved with the pressing responsibilities of our growing organization which was preparing to play a major role in the supply of war equipment both in the United States and Canada, and that I was seriously concerned over the deteriorating health of our presi-dent. "Apart from these reasons," I said, "I feel myself un-qualified to assume a major responsibility in a field which is completely unfamiliar to me."

The Minister was disappointed and said so.

When I hung up, my wife took me to task. She thought I had been too hasty in turning down Norman Rogers' request. As usual, she was right. When a country is at war, a contribu-tion to the war effort must take primacy over any other con-sideration.

I put in a call to the Minister, and when Rogers came on the line I told him that I would be in Ottawa the following morning to discuss his proposals.

On my arrival there, I went directly to the Minister of Defence's office, where the Prime Minister and C. D. Howe, the Minister of Munitions and Supplies, joined us.

The Rt. Hon. Mackenzie King explained the importance and extreme urgency of training young airmen for the defence of the Commonwealth, the vast expenditures involved, the number of training centers to be opened throughout Canada, and he went on to say that he felt this major contribution to our war effort was insufficiently understood by the Canadian public.

"We require a man," he continued, "of recognized organizational ability, well known to the public, and capable of expressing our objectives in language all can understand. We have considered several candidates and believe that you are the best qualified to undertake the task."

With reluctance and serious misgivings, I accepted for a period of three months, but balked at the proposal of the Prime Minister that, to carry out my duties effectively, I should have to become Acting Deputy Minister of Defence for Air. This I did not wish to do. I was prepared to offer my services at no cost to the government, but I felt that to assume the title of Acting Deputy Minister of Defence for Air was too formal, perhaps too restrictive, and carried with it the implication of greater permanency than I was prepared to consider at the time.

Rogers explained, however, that as Deputy Minister I would be senior to the commanding officers of the Air Force and that without this rank I would find it difficult to operate successfully. I agreed, therefore, to accept the post subject to the approval of my president.

It looked, however, as if fate had decreed that I should not take on this responsibility because, when I tried to get in touch with Russell, I found he was in hospital in Boston, where he had suffered another heart attack.

I informed the Prime Minister of this development, and withdrew my acceptance subject to a decision by our board of directors in Toronto.

The following morning, having returned to Toronto, I found that C. D. Howe and Norman Rogers had already been in touch with three of our leading directors. The board expressed the unanimous opinion that in these difficult times I had no option but to accept the Prime Minister's request.

Thus I found myself launched on one of the most dynamic experiences in my career.

The three fighting services were at that time grouped together under the Minister of Defence. Each service was headed by a Deputy Minister. I was in charge, under the Minister of Defence, of all activities of the Air Force, with special emphasis on the British Commonwealth Air Training Plan. My appointment was apparently well received by the press from coast to coast.

The British Commonwealth Air Training Plan was big business indeed. I found myself presiding over, or attending, a multiplicity of meetings dealing with staff matters, purchasing, forward planning, relations with the Commonwealth high commissioners, the British government, and, last but not least, the press. Like many of my colleagues I had most of my meals served at my desk, worked sixteen hours a day, and loved every minute of it.

Shortly after my arrival in Ottawa, events in Europe became daily more alarming. France was invaded and the Maginot Line bypassed; German armour in its plenitude of power drove through France to the channel ports, undeterred by a routed enemy or the pitiable plight of the hordes of terrified refugees fleeing before them. An atmosphere of tragedy hung over the Ottawa scene, but it stimulated rather than discouraged the unremitting and vigorous toil of all concerned.

Occasionally, in the late evening, those of us responsible for the armed services would be summoned to the Prime Minister's office to discuss the steps which were to be taken to accelerate our assistance to Britain. It was during one of these meetings that our hopes were raised by the news that the British Expeditionary Force was being evacuated from the harbour and beaches of Dunkirk.

On June 10th, 1940, a great tragedy befell us. Norman Rogers, the brilliant and popular Minister of Defence, who had recently returned from a conference in London with the British leaders, was killed in a plane crash on his way to Toronto to address a gathering. He was greatly missed and deeply mourned.

To me it was a great blow. I had been looking forward to working with Norman Rogers. He was a man of great charm and fine background. Only forty-six at the time of his death, he had much to offer to the war effort and to his country.

I found myself on my own only a few weeks after my arrival in Ottawa, a Deputy Minister without a Minister. Shortly afterwards, Colonel Ralston, then Minister of Finance, took over the additional responsibility for Defence.

At a meeting of the Air Council on June 17th, a secret

and confidential message was handed to me announcing the imminent fall of France. England was now on her own, undaunted and undismayed.

On the radio especially brought into my office for the occasion, I listened to Churchill's message of determination, of defiance, and of unbounded faith in the future.

> We shall fight in France, we shall fight in the seas and the oceans, we shall fight with growing confidence and growing strength in the air, we shall defend our Island whatever the cost may be.

While I was still listening to Churchill's message, a note was handed to me asking me to attend a meeting at 11:30 p.m. in the Prime Minister's office.

News had come through of the first raid on England, in which nearly a thousand planes took part and 182 were shot down. It was obvious that the Battle of Britain was about to begin. The object of our meeting was to discuss how best we could help that beleaguered country.

The Canadian public, in their natural and generous desire to see our Air Force take a more active part in the defence of Britain, had already been calling on the government to discard the long-range training program and send our fighting airmen overseas at once. This was an emotional plea, but the group in the Prime Minister's office decided that we should send a message to the Air Ministry in London outlining the alternatives and requesting that they should tell us what we should do to be of greatest assistance.

The reply was not long in coming. Britain asked for two squadrons which we sent overseas at once. She asked for fighter and bomber aircraft, and although this left our coastline inadequately defended, we despatched them on the first outgoing steamer. But Britain said most categorically that we could best help her cause by carrying on with the British Commonwealth Air Training Plan and doing so with the utmost vigour and energy.

In other words, although Britain was then fighting for her very existence over the skies of England, she had the fortitude and the vision to refuse our proffered help of a few hundred airmen immediately, so that in the fullness of time we should build up the training plan which would enable us to send her tens of thousands of airmen during the years '41, '42, and '43.

Our air training plan was in serious trouble, however, because the United Kingdom was obliged to suspend indefinitely the supply of training aircraft and instruments she had contracted to send to us as her contribution to the joint effort.

C. D. Howe, the Minister of Trade and Commerce, and I, accompanied by an air officer in charge of supply, left immediately for Washington to discuss our problem with Arthur B. Purvis, head of the British Purchasing Council. I had met Arthur Purvis in Canada prior to the war.

Born in England in 1890, he became associated with Imperial Chemicals and was sent out to Canada where he became president and managing director of Canadian Industries at the early age of thirty-four. Much sought after, he became a director of many of Canada's most important enterprises. He was popularly supposed to be Canada's highest paid executive.

He gave it all up when war broke out, and at Britain's request, became Chairman of the British Purchasing Council in Washington. His influence in the United States from the President downwards was very great. None played a more important role than he during the early stages of the war.

He was still only fifty-one years of age when he flew to London to discuss the co-ordination of various independent British missions to Washington. While on his return journey his plane crashed during takeoff at Prestwick, Scotland, and he was killed, leaving a void which was never adequately filled.

He was kindness itself to C. D. Howe and me during our visit. Through his agency we were able to get from U.S. sources the planes and other materials that Britain could not supply.

In view of the extreme urgency of the situation all the objectives of the air training plan were revised upwards. All flying fields which were to be developed in 1940 and '41 were now to be completed in 1940. The thousands of buildings which were to be erected in connection with our various training establishments were to be completed by the end of the year. Over 5,000 additional airmen were to be taken into our manning depots.

On June 17th, 1940, Minister of National Defence Ralston telephoned Mackenzie King that he and Minister of Defence for Air Charles G. Power—known universally as Chubby —had been discussing methods whereby the strength of the

Defence Department could be increased. The suggestion was made that I should take his place as Minister of National Defence for Air, while he should become Associate Joint Minister of Defence. A week later, Mackenzie King offered me a seat in his Cabinet.

The Prime Minister said that he could arrange for a safe constituency either in Kingston or in Waterloo, or in a French-speaking riding which Chubby Power had volunteered to select for me. "All you have to do," Mackenzie King added, "is make a couple of speeches. You will be elected without any trouble, and will immediately be brought into my Cabinet to carry on your work in connection with the Air Force and the British Commonwealth Air Training Plan."

It was a tempting offer. Becoming a Minister of an important war department only five years after I had taken up residence in Canada, and while I was still carrying not a Canadian but a British passport, would have constituted somewhat of a record in our country's political history. I asked the Prime Minister, however, to give me a few days to think it over.

I was completely bilingual. The air training plan, so criticized a few months previously but now better understood by the public, would, I knew, be one of the most popular features of Canada's war effort before many months had elapsed. I would have been immensely proud to have been associated with it as Minister for Air; but the more I thought about it, the more I felt I would be unwise to accept this tempting offer.

Some of my reasons for refusing were selfish. Others were not. I felt very strongly that as Acting Deputy Minister in charge of the air training plan and a "dollar-a-year" man, I could devote myself more completely to the work at hand than I could as a Minister of the Crown. I was independent. I was able to choose my own staff, and had been able to surround myself with an outstanding team chosen from the business world— men such as Terry Sheard of the National Trust; George Black who subsequently became president of Canadian Breweries; John Martin, the able and incisive public relations officer of my own Company; Norman Smith, now editor of the *Ottawa Journal*, whose fine newspaper background was invaluable to me; H. G. Colebrook, the experienced director of the Robert Simpson Company; and H. G. Norman, a partner in Price Waterhouse, who did Trojan work in connection with the financial aspects of the plan.

As a Minister my choice of staff would have been restricted. I would have been hampered by frequent Cabinet meetings, and by the time-consuming necessity of sitting in the House.

If I joined the Liberal Cabinet, I would be obliged to resign from the Massey-Harris Company, at a time when, owing to the precarious health of our president, my services were required. Did I have the right to leave the Company at this juncture? Was it fair for me to do so after the directors had so generously allowed me to place my services at the government's disposal for a limited period only?

The training plan was now well staffed and organized, and progressing smoothly towards well defined objectives. Our Company, on the other hand, was deeply involved in war production both in Canada and the United States. Was it in the common interest that I should choose this time to step down from the leadership?

These and other questions beset me as I travelled to Toronto to discuss Mackenzie King's proposal with our ailing president and our board of directors. They were very generous, but while unwilling to influence my judgement, they were perturbed at the thought of my severing my connection, even temporarily, with the Company, particularly in view of our president's failing health.

The interview helped to clarify my own thoughts. I decided to advise the Prime Minister that I could not accept his invitation, but would be happy to continue my work as Acting Deputy Minister for Air.

While waiting for an afternoon appointment with the Prime Minister to inform him of my decision, I went to see Ralston, Chubby Power, and Angus MacDonald. They gave me sound advice, which as I recall it was along these lines: "You have never been in politics before. It's a rough game in which appreciation for past services is infrequently considered. You happen to be the 'white-haired boy' at the time in the Chief's estimation, because you have been successful with the air training plan, and because you are a Toronto industrialist. You would be a desirable addition to the Cabinet under existing circumstances. We would like to see you join us, but before giving up your permanent work with Massey-Harris, you must realize that if anything ever goes wrong in the months or years to come, the Chief would not hesitate one moment to throw you into the discard."

Ralston added, "But join us all the same. We must all live dangerously during these anxious times!"

All this wasn't very encouraging, but I had already made up my mind, fortified by the thought that although I felt myself quite able to handle the Ministry of Defence for Air during the war, I was equally confident that I did not have the suitable qualifications to become a successful Cabinet Minister in times of peace.

On December 29th, 1940, the Massey-Harris Company suffered a grievous loss in the death of its president. T. A. Russell had guided the Company's destinies through trying years in the early thirties and his contribution to the Company's affairs during these very difficult periods will long be remembered.

With the passing of the president our board felt very strongly that I should now return to the organization. I shared their views, but it was with considerable reluctance that I advised the Prime Minister that I wished to retire from my position with the Air Force at the end of January, 1941.

I did so with a clear conscience, however, because thanks to the co-operation of all those who were working with me, the objectives which had been laid down by the government when I first entered its service had been not only attained but considerably surpassed.

The organization was working smoothly. Chubby Power, now Minister of Air, released from his onerous duties with the Defence Department, was now devoting his full time to the Air Force. Air crews were being turned out and sent to England in ever-increasing numbers. The Canadian public understood our long-term objectives, and were apparently satisfied with the progress we were making.

Chubby Power gave a dinner to mark my retirement from the Air Force. It was attended by members of the government, British government representatives, members of the Air Council, and my own staff.

The Privy Council conferred on me the honorary rank of Air Commodore, and an honorary membership in the Air Council of which I had been vice-president.

In a press release at the time of my return to civilian life, the Prime Minister was generous enough to say: "Mr. Duncan has well and truly served the British Empire in its time of greatest need."

Mackenzie King was always an enigma to me. He befriended me, gave dinners at his home for Trini and myself, offered me a seat in his Cabinet—but somehow I never felt close to him.

An able and distinguished politician, whose understanding of how to keep himself and his party in power was remarkable, he lacked, in my opinion, some of those basic qualities which are the stuff out of which great war leaders are made. I felt, during the period of hostilities, that his actions were always tempered and adjusted to policies which in his judgement were best for the Liberal Party.

In his home he was a good host and an interesting conversationalist. As is customary in France and in several other Continental countries, when he had several guests to dinner he sat, not at the end, but in the center of his table, which greatly facilitated conversation. It is a seating arrangement we frequently adopt in our own home.

King's veneration for his mother, whose portrait hung in his sitting-room with a light burning below it, casting a religious glow on the picture, was always just a little embarrassing to me.

There was never any doubt when he was in power about who was running the Cabinet or the country. He had many admirers, but few friends. His least endearing quality was his lack of loyalty to those who worked for him.

Ralston had served Mackenzie King with unequalled devotion before and during the war years, first as Minister of Finance and then as Minister of Defence. His long hours of work, his heavy travel schedule, had undermined his health.

Originally he had gallantly supported his chief's non-conscription policy. He felt that, so long as sufficient troops could be obtained for voluntary service overseas, no change in policy was required. However, when towards the end of hostilities reinforcements were no longer sufficient to support the army overseas, he came out strongly for conscription.

Mackenzie King did not hesitate to throw him over and did so unceremoniously. Many of us felt at the time, as no doubt Ralston did, that the conscription issue was determined not so much by what was best for the war effort, as by what was best for the unity of the Liberal Party.

Throughout my stay in Ottawa, I worked very closely with C. D. Howe, who was already a towering figure in Canada.

I recall the consternation in Ottawa when the news was flashed across the country that the *Northern Prince* on which Mr. Howe was travelling to England had been torpedoed and sunk. He was accompanied by my friend and neighbour in Bayview E. P. Taylor, W. C. Woodward of Vancouver, and Gordon Scott of Montreal. Soon the glad tidings were received that they had been picked up on the high seas and all were safe and sound excepting Gordon Scott, who had drowned under distressing circumstances just as salvation was at hand.

I was in daily contact with John McConnell,[1] the Montreal industrialist who later became the publisher of the *Montreal Star*. At the beginning of the war, McConnell made a donation to Britain of one million dollars for the purchase of Spitfires. Later he undertook the task of organizing the civilian ferry crews who flew our planes and frequently our air crews across the Atlantic to Britain. Many of these pilots were patriotic Americans, anxious to join in the war effort.

John McConnell, who had amassed a great fortune through the operation of his various enterprises and who was by long odds the most generous supporter in Montreal of all good charitable and educational causes, was by any yardstick a great Canadian. He and I got along splendidly both while I was in office in Ottawa and subsequently.

He had only one idiosyncracy that I knew of. He could talk more and at greater length on the long distance telephone than any other man I have ever met, either before or since. I will say this for him—what he had to say was always worth while.

Another man whom I saw a great deal of was that great but

---

[1] John Wilson McConnell, industrialist, financier, newspaper publisher and philanthropist.

modest figure to whom all humanity owes a debt of gratitude, Sir Frederick Banting, the co-discoverer of insulin, who at the outbreak of the war had joined the services with the rank of major and was associated with the National Research Council.

His fertile and inventive mind and his tireless energy were entirely devoted to the development of scientific research largely in connection with air services.

One day Banting came to my office in a despondent mood and told me something of the valuable projects which he and others in the National Research Council had been working on, but which, because they had not yet been proven, were refused financial support by the Treasury. He had great confidence that many of his projects could make a valuable contribution to the war effort and he was frustrated by the thought that the bureaucratic unwillingness to supply the funds necessary to bring these projects to the testing stage was slowing up the war effort.

Calling on the generosity of many of my wealthy friends, who were unable to get into the active service of their country for one reason or another but were anxious to make a contribution to the war effort, I undertook to raise a fund to enable Fred Banting and the National Research Council to work on projects they believed in but which were still unproven. I concluded an agreement with the government that whenever a project that had been worked out under the auspices of the fund was subsequently adopted by the government, all expenses involved would be paid back into the fund.

Such was the spirit and patriotism which characterized those early war years and the generosity of the few friends whom I approached that in the shortest possible time I gathered together over $1,800,000.

My friend, John David Eaton of Toronto, Bob Stanley, the leading figure in the International Nickel Co., Samuel Bronfman of Seagram, James Y. Murdoch of Noranda, and John McConnell were among the largest contributors.

After Fred Banting's tragic and untimely death while flying across Newfoundland on his way to England, I arranged to have the fund named after him, and I had the satisfaction of knowing that so many of the projects worked on had been adopted by the government that the Sir Frederick Banting Fund was practically intact at the end of hostilities.

In the more leisurely prewar days, Fred Banting had taken up painting and often accompanied A. Y. Jackson, a distinguished member of the Group of Seven, on his painting expeditions to northern Ontario or Quebec.

We were living in Bayview at the time and I had returned from Ottawa on Christmas Eve to spend the day with my family.

In the afternoon the doorbell rang, and when the housemaid went to open it, Fred handed her a framed picture, but declined to come in. I went to the front door just in time to see his retreating figure as he turned out of my driveway onto the main road. I ran after him, but he had already reached his car and driven away. It was the last time I saw him before his tragic death.

Fred's gift of his own painting was his modest way of saying "thank you" for the assistance I had been able to provide, not for him but for the great work he was doing in the National Research Council. His picture is among my most prized possessions, and is hanging in my hall today.

It is a painting of St. Tite des Caps, Quebec, and was painted in 1937. On the back it is inscribed:—"To James Duncan, in appreciation of what you are doing for Canada's war effort. F. G. Banting, Xmas, 1940."

Throughout my term of office in the Air Force I kept in very close contact with the press and greatly enjoyed my frequent and sometimes daily meetings with them.

On many occasions, for purposes of background, I gave the press representatives off-the-record information about our problems, our progress, and our failures. I cannot recall one occasion when any of them broke my confidence.

I have had a lot to do with the press, and it has been my invariable experience that its members are a first-class group of men and women who, if one is willing to co-operate with them, understanding that they also have a job to do, will invariably respond in a like manner. I cannot recall any incident when I was misquoted. Those who claim to be misquoted are mostly to blame themselves for saying things they later regret, or for saying them in a muddled and confusing manner.

15

Back in the Fold

ON JANUARY 20TH, 1941, I was unanimously elected to the presidency of our Company. I had reached the goal towards which I had been working for over thirty years.

I accepted my appointment with modesty, I hope, but with a sense of elation. I had been given the opportunity of leading our Company through its wartime endeavours and then onwards towards the objectives which I had long since formulated in my own mind.

I recognized the weight of responsibility which had been placed upon my shoulders, but I carried it lightly, because I knew where we were going and had faith in the ability and devotion of my fellow workers to help us get there.

I have always believed as an article of faith that if one aims at a clearly defined objective and is supported by a disciplined, experienced, and hard-working staff, dedicated to the job in hand, happy in their work, loyal, and confident in the future, success become almost automatic. This proved to be so in our case.

At the time of my appointment, I made it clear to the board that while I intended to devote myself whole-heartedly to the interests of the Company, I felt very strongly that a leader in business, especially in wartime, owes something to his country and his community, and that I proposed to devote a portion of my time to public service.

The board, led by Harry Gundy who was a great supporter of public causes, agreed generously and whole-heartedly.

Accordingly, I accepted the presidency of the Board of Trade, a governorship of the University of Toronto, and several directorships including that of the Canadian Bank of Commerce and Canada Cement. Others were to follow later.

During my absence in Ottawa, the Company had become to an important degree involved in defence production. At the same time the requirements for farm machinery in Canada, the United States, and particularly in the United Kingdom were taxing our plants to capacity.

I was particularly proud of the initiative and the resourcefulness displayed by our engineering and manufacturing executives who, although trained in the less exacting field of farm-implement production, did not hesitate to undertake important war defence programs requiring skills and disciplines of an entirely different order.

Under the leadership of E. G. Burgess, we became one of Canada's, and subsequently one of the United States', important and highly successful producers of aircraft assemblies, tanks, shells, howitzers, personnel carriers, ambulances, and a great diversity of other military equipment. This fine tribute to our organization gave me great confidence in our ability to meet the challenge of the future.

We had not gone outside to seek special skills, but relied on the fund of talent which existed within the ranks of our organization. Our leaders and our workers had risen to the challenge of new ways and new skills, and had done so with outstanding success.

In 1941 and '42 we suffered the loss of three influential directors. One of these was George Allen, K.C., of Winnipeg, "the grand old man of the west." Another was E. R. Wood, an outstanding investment banker. One of our ablest directors, he had been a tower of strength to the Company during our financial difficulties and he rejoiced at our recovery and shared my optimism concerning the future. I greatly missed his wise counsel at our meetings.

Our third loss was George W. McLaughlin. He had been on our board since 1926. It was entirely through an inexplicable misunderstanding that George McLaughlin had been asked to accept the nomination to our board. The then president, J. N. Shenstone and the vice-president, Thomas Bradshaw, had intended to invite his brother, R. S. McLaughlin, who was in many respects more prominent. George McLaughlin, however, was a man of outstanding ability, judgement, and personality, and he made an excellent director.

Our Company was progressing rapidly. Its future now seemed assured and I was looking around for men of stature to fill the ranks of our depleted board. After the tragic death of Arthur Purvis, who had been head of the British purchasing commission, Churchill and Beaverbrook, with their opposite numbers in the United States, set up the Combined Production and Resource Board in Washington. Bill Batt represented the U.S.A., Rab Sinclair the United Kingdom, and E. P. Taylor became member for Canada.

Eddie Taylor was at that time president of Canadian Breweries. We were neighbours in Bayview; I saw a lot of him and enjoyed his friendship. He was far from being as well known or as wealthy in those days as he is now. In fact, he wasn't wealthy at all, but he was already turning over in his fertile mind the many speculative moves which, in his opinion, would lead him to financial eminence in the postwar period—and so they did.

Col. W. Eric Phillips, prominent in the glass industry and at this time in government service as president of Research Enterprises, was making a worthwhile contribution to the war effort.

Although I did not know these men as well as I should have, it seemed to me at the time that both would add strength to our board. With the consent of our directors I invited them to join us. Both readily accepted.

Whether I made a mistake in doing so is a matter of opinion. If I did, it was my own mistake. No one prompted me to do so. Some of our directors, in fact, had reservations about their appointments.

One thing is certain: if I had not invited them to join our board I would have saved myself a lot of headaches in the years to come.

During the honeymoon period, everything in the garden was lovely, but as the years succeeded one another, it was gradually borne in on me that Taylor's and Phillips' approach to the Company's affairs differed greatly from mine and from that of our other directors. There was nothing wrong about this. Both were men of ability and experience, and if we approached our problems from a different angle, this was largely due to a difference in background and objectives.

To me, the Massey-Harris Company was more than a business. It was something more intimate, more personal. I had been brought up in it. I felt a strong sense of responsibility to its traditions, to its shareholders, and to my fellow workers. I was proud of our Company's Canadian background, of the role we had played in Canada's pioneering days both as manufacturers and exporters. My ambition to see our Company succeed and take its place among the great international organizations of the day knew no bounds. I felt a deep sense of loyalty to the memory of those past leaders of our Company who had brought me into it and set my feet on the first rungs of the ladder which had led me to my present position of authority.

I believed fervently, as did my predecessors, Sir Lyman Melvin-Jones, Thomas Findley, Bradshaw, Russell, that if management pursued a conservative financial policy, built up adequate reserves, and devoted itself single-mindedly to the growth and development of the organization, the shareholders' interests would be automatically cared for.

I had never been particularly knowledgeable or indeed interested in the techniques of the stock market.

There was no good reason why Eric Phillips or Eddie Taylor should share my sentimental attachment to the Company. To them it was, no doubt, just another investment. They shared my desire to see the Company grow, but for different reasons. It soon became evident that their long-term objective was gradually to accumulate an important shareholding through contracting bank loans for this purpose, in order to influence both the composition of our board and its managerial policies.

Above: My father, James S. Duncan, Sr.

Right: A picture taken when I was an artillery captain in France, 1917.

Below: My family—Trini, Jimmie, Maruja and Rosa Maria—in 1947.

Harry Ferguson and I signing the merger agreement, 1953.

The warehouse at Arras from which the implements were recovered at night, a hundred yards from the German lines. The reproduction was built for the Canadian Corps reunion in Toronto, 1938.

A 1951 photograph of me with
a self-propelled combine.

E. G. Burgess, general manager of the
United States company, and I, in a
World War II tank made in our U.S. plants.

The Spanish Ambassador Rafael Cavestany visiting
the Massey Harris farm near Toronto, 1955.

Below: Princess Margaret on a tour of the Queenston-Chippewa power development.

Left below: Visitors to Hydro's St. Lawrence power plant: Herbert Hoover, 1957; Harry S. Truman, 1958.

Right: Opening of the sluice gates at the St. Lawrence Hydro plant. From left to right: Governor Averell Harriman of New York, Premier Leslie M. Frost of Ontario, myself, and Robert Moses, New York State Power Authority.

Above: The Queen and Prince Philip taking their leave after Her Majesty had unveiled the international boundary marker at the St. Lawrence power plant in 1959. Vice-President and Mrs. Nixon and my wife are in the background.

Left: Vice-President Richard M. Nixon and I watching Prince Philip sign the guest book. In the background is Governor Nelson Rockefeller of New York.

Above: an inspection of new entrants into the British Commonwealth Air Training Plan. At the time I was acting Deputy Minister for Air.

Right: Three honorary graduates at Dartmouth College, New Hampshire, 1957. From left to right: Rt. Hon. John G. Diefenbaker, Prime Minister of Canada; myself; Sidney E. Smith, retired President of the University of Toronto and Secretary of State for External Affairs.

A merry group at Cyrus Eaton's luncheon for
Nikita Khrushchev in New York. From left to right:
Khrushchev, the interpreter, myself, and Eaton.

Directors of the Dollar-Sterling Trade Board and
its British affiliate, the Dollar Exports Council,
in conference. From left: R. R. D. (now Sir Ronald)
McIntosh, executive secretary of the Council;
myself; Sir Cecil Weir, chairman of the Council;
A. G. S. Griffin, secretary of the Board.

I was less concerned over this than I should have been, but in those early days of our association I was confident in my ability to safeguard the independence of the Company.

While all three of us clearly recognized the sharp differences which divided us, our personal relationships were intimate and friendly.

As the war progressed the demand for strategic raw materials was such that civilian industries had to be severely restricted.

The Hon. C. D. Howe invited me to Ottawa one day and asked me to draw up recommendations covering the allocation of raw materials to the Canadian farm-implement industry affecting their sales at home and abroad. It was unusual that I should be asked to submit a plan restricting our own and our competitors' operations, but C. D. Howe knew that I would not take advantage of the situation. In the course of time my recommendations were adopted, including the proviso that no restriction should be imposed on Britain's requirements for farm machinery as these were essential to the success of that country's intensive food-production program.

As a result of these restrictive measures, the 1942 and 1943 manufacturing programs for farm machinery were seriously hampered. Our war production, however, was correspondingly increased, and our Company in 1942 went through a period of great expansion.

We required more manufacturing space. Our old plants were enlarged and rearranged. New ones were built, others were acquired.

The quality of our highly diversified defence production was given full marks in both Ottawa and Washington, and the exactitude with which we met our scheduled dates of delivery were gratefully acknowledged at a time when being on schedule was of primary importance.

As the months went by, I found myself obliged to take on a number of additional activities which in my estimation at least could not well be refused while our country was at war. Among these was a membership in the National Research Council, which I accepted at the suggestion of the Hon. C. D. Howe, and later on, again on his recommendation, I took over the chairmanship of the newly formed Combined Agricultural and Food Machinery Committee of UNRRA in Washington.

Nineteen forty-four heralded for me a period of intensive travel in the United States, Canada, and Europe for the purpose of reorienting our organization towards peacetime operations.

Demands were still being made on my time for activities connected with the program of a country at war. Gradually, however, I began to withdraw from my many outside commitments; this was indeed forced by my frequent absences from Canada throughout the year.

With a view to strengthening our organization to meet the challenge of the postwar era I announced the appointment of six vice-presidents, each one to carry full responsibility for the operations of his respective department. This plan left me more free to devote myself to the formulation of overall policy at home and abroad.

At the same time I appointed W. K. Hyslop president of our American company. I became chairman of the board.

All of these men were thoroughly experienced farm-implement executives, and most of them had spent their whole business lives with our Company. All were men of proven ability. Most had gone through the searing experience of the early thirties, all had played their respective parts in the upward surge of our Company since 1935, the successful conversion of our organization from peace to war production. They were well equipped, each in his own field, to chart and steer a successful course throughout the post-war period.

All recognized that there was nothing static about these arrangements, and that, as the organization progressed, as we recaptured the markets which had been lost to us during the war, further changes would be required. This is always so in the case of a well run and progressive organization.

Organizational patterns cannot remain frozen. They have to be rearranged from time to time to meet changing conditions.

Although our self-propelled combines which we had designed when I was in the Argentine and introduced to the North American market after I became general manager, were now in full production for the British market, we were unable to undertake their manufacture in large quantities either for

Canada or the United States, owing to governmental restrictions on the availability of raw materials.

Our organization in Racine came up with an imaginative proposal which I endorsed enthusiastically and which we laid before the authorities in Washington who gave it their blessing. Our proposal was that, given adequate supplies of raw materials, we would manufacture in Canada five hundred self-propelled combines which would be shipped to the southern states and incorporated in a Harvest Brigade. This Brigade would commence operations in the South and work its way through the harvest fields as the crops ripened, going as far north as the prairie provinces in Canada.

We gave the government an undertaking that we would thresh a minimum of one million acres of wheat during the 1944 season, and we were able to establish to their satisfaction that more wheat could be harvested by our revolutionary self-propelled combines, powered by one engine and operated by only one man, for a lesser expenditure of raw materials and manpower than by any other method.

The operation was launched in Texas and the five hundred machines incorporated into the Brigade harvested one million, five hundred thousand acres of grain by the time they had completed their task in western Canada. This was fifty percent more than we had undertaken to thresh.

This harvesting exploit was one of the most spectacular achievements that had ever taken place in the harvest fields of North America.

16

Safeguarding our International Position

THE WAR WAS NOW MOVING to a close, and our Company's activities were rapidly shifting from a war to a peacetime economy. We were well prepared for the move. All our factories were gearing up for full production of farm equipment.

Based in no small measure on the success of our self-propelled combine in the United States and the prominence it had given our organization, we had set our sights high. The role we were prepared to play in the United States of America after the war was vastly greater than in the past.

The recently modified organizational set-up was working smoothly. Enthusiasm and optimism were running high.

My major preoccupation first centered on our post-war plans for our European organization. The United Kingdom was the only country with which we had been able to maintain contact throughout the war. We were without news of any kind about our Continental organization.

Were our factories still in existence? Had our sales organization been disbanded? Had our resources been confiscated? These and other questions could be answered only when the countries concerned were set free.

It looked as if we would not have too long to wait. Events

were moving fast. Rome was captured on June 4th; two days later, allied forces under the leadership of General Eisenhower crossed the Channel in an Armada of over four thousand ships and established bridge-heads on the coast of Normandy. On June 20th, the U.S.S.R. opened her summer offensive and in July, under constant pounding of the British and American forces, the German front collapsed in France. On August 26th, our troops entered Paris.

By September all of France was liberated. I immediately set the wheels in motion to obtain an air passage to London and entry permits to France, Belgium, and North Africa. As president of Massey-Harris Company, I was unable to obtain such documents under then existing circumstances, but as chairman of the Combined Agricultural and Food Machinery Committee of UNRRA I could. By special arrangement with BOAC, I was allocated a seat with high priority on a Boeing leaving Baltimore for Ireland and England in early September.

My first concern was for Britain, in which we had operated successfully for sixty-seven years, and where we were now enjoying a large and profitable business. The question uppermost in my mind was whether, when peace was once more established, Britain, drained of her dollar resources, would be able to continue to import farm equipment from the United States and Canada.

I was so pessimistic on this score that I recommended to our board before my departure that if it became evident Britain was planning to curtail the importation of farm machinery from North America we should give consideration to undertaking manufacturing operations in that country.

I pointed out that in all probability Britain's decision would be followed by the sterling area bloc and by other dollar-short countries. What was at stake, therefore, was not only our British business but our exports to all the so-called soft currency countries.

Under the leadership of Eric Phillips and E. P. Taylor, this suggestion was strongly opposed. They could see no merit in investing capital in England of whose recovery they had the gravest of doubts, when the American and Canadian market requirements would probably exceed the productive capacity of our plants. They strongly recommended that we should concentrate our efforts on North America and limit our capital expenditures to the United States and to Canada.

This short-term view left me unimpressed. I proceeded to England with an open mind on what our future policy should be. My first visit in London was to the Rt. Hon. R. S. Hudson, the able and forthright Minister of Agriculture. It was a discouraging one. After expressing his appreciation of the contribution our Company had made to British agriculture throughout the war, he said, without equivocation and with almost brutal frankness, that if we wished to safeguard our important position in the British agricultural industry we should have to undertake manufacturing operations in Britain.

"In view of our expected dollar stringency," he said, "I am recommending to my government that we should restrict our imports from North America, and stimulate local production. You are our largest supplier of harvesting equipment, and I hope you will decide to manufacture here. If you do, we will assist you in every possible way."

During the next few days I discussed the situation with various members of the British government, including Anthony Eden, Foreign Secretary Sir Andrew Rae Duncan, Minister of Supply, Sir John Wood, the Permanent Undersecretary of the Board of Trade. None was as forthright as the Minister of Agriculture but all felt that some degree of import restrictions on goods from North America would have to be imposed.

Vincent Massey, then Canadian High Commissioner, shared this point of view as did many other prominent industrialists and importers.

With members of our British management, I visited a number of our competitors, some of whom were local manufacturers. Those who weren't were pessimistic about the future. Those who were talked of increasing their manufacturing capacity.

I had become convinced that we must set up manufacturing operations in the United Kingdom. Confident of my ability to break down the resistance of a reluctant board, I sent for several members of our Canadian engineering and manufacturing departments and, upon their arrival, instructed them to take all the preliminary steps preparatory to manufacturing operations in England. These involved building sample machines of six different types in common use in Britain, using British materials and labour, to be ready for exhaustive tests during the coming spring and harvest season. They were also to make a selection of a few suitable manufacturing sites, and secure options on scarce raw materials and machine tools.

All this was put in hand at once so that a final decision on operations in Britain could be taken on my return the following summer. In the event of a favourable decision, the preliminary steps taken would advance our program by fully twelve months. With the growing activity of our various British competitors, every day counted.

From London I flew to North Africa, to confer with what was left of our organization there, then over to France in a military plane.

As we approached Le Bourget, the signs of devastation became more numerous, and as we circled to make a landing I was able to appreciate the completeness of the destruction of the airport. Its buildings were a mass of rubble, the hangars destroyed. Here and there Nazi planes, with the hated swastika cross on their wings, were strewn around the airport where they had been shot down or destroyed on the ground.

Our Canadian Ambassador, General Vanier[1], who had been informed of my arrival, sent a car to the airport to meet me. He had returned to his post in Paris just two days before I arrived.

I drove through the streets of the city, glad to recognize the familiar landmarks, largely unchanged and undamaged by the long years of occupation. What immediately captured my attention was the almost complete absence of all motor traffic, other than American army vehicles. There were a few horse cabs, and bicycles in great numbers. Some of these were equipped with a hooded trailer capable of accommodating one passenger, probably very uncomfortably. Everywhere one saw hand-carts pulled by men or women. Occasionally a car chugged its way through the streets equipped with a monstrous-looking coal or wood burner.

The city itself was, generally speaking, undamaged. There were traces everywhere of the fighting which had taken place

[1] Subsequently the Rt. Hon. Georges Vanier, Governor-General of Canada

during the last few days of the German occupation; many buildings had been damaged by machine-gun fire and windows here
and there were broken, but no devastation of a serious nature
was in evidence anywhere in the parts of the city I visited.

In some respects France had suffered economically less than
I had expected. In other respects, she had suffered more.

She had suffered less because her agriculture, other than in
the areas where fighting had taken place, had remained undis-
turbed. Throughout the zone of occupation, there was a ready
market for the products of the soil at inflated prices. Her industries had operated on a high level of activity. Full employment at high wages was fairly general.

She had suffered more than I had imagined because, in addition to her 1,500,000 prisoners of war, the taking of hostages
and the mass levy of French workers had swelled this figure to
nearly 3,000,000.

Her communications had been largely destroyed. For three
months before D-Day, the bombing of the R.A.F., the American Air Force, and the R.C.A.F. had been so effective that
practically no means of communication was available to the
civilian population. Such communications services as had not
been destroyed before D-Day were mostly wrecked afterwards
by the British and American forces, the underground French
fighters, or by the devastation the Germans left during their
hurried retreat.

During my short stay in Paris, few trains were in circulation throughout France. The telegraph service was practically
non-existent, the telephones were not working, and even the
great network of canals over which an important percentage of
France's freight travelled was damaged through the blowing up
of sluice gates and embankments. Four thousand bridges had
been dynamited, 450 of these railroad bridges over important
rivers or through mountain passes.

Coal mining was hampered by a shortage of pit props, available only in the south of France. Factories intact and fully
equipped were unable to operate because raw materials were not
available.

Food was plentiful and great surpluses were piling up in the
areas where it was produced, but in the large centers where food
is consumed the people were on very short rations.

During my stay in Paris, no public buildings, hotels, or private houses were heated. Hot water was unavailable. And this was in October.

Electricity was turned on for a few hours each day in certain districts only. The prospects of a cold winter faced the people of Paris, but they were taking everything in good spirits. To be free once again made up for a lot of hardship.

De Gaulle, who in France's darkest hour had refused to acknowledge defeat, was immensely popular. His government, which represented many parties and political views, was made up of men who, in most cases, had fought for the great cause of liberation. An outstanding exception in de Gaulle's Cabinet was Maurice Thorez, the Communist leader, who had spent the war in Russia.

De Gaulle stood for law and order, for participation in the war on the side of the Allies, for the punishment of those who had been traitors to the French cause, and for rewards and honour to those who, in the underground or abroad, had assisted in the defence of the homeland.

At the time of my stay in Paris, he was at his most difficult. He refused to receive the British ambassador until a month after Duff Cooper arrived. His relations with the U.S.A. were at the lowest ebb. Here he was not entirely to blame because the U.S.A. had failed to recognize de Gaulle or his government until two months after Paris had been liberated. His susceptibilities and arrogance, I was told, were unbelievable.

I spent a few hours with Gaston Palewski, the head of de Gaulle's *Cabinet Civile*. At his suggestion I called on General Koenig, the military commander of Paris, and on Hervé Alphand, then Director of Economic Affairs at the Ministry of Foreign Affairs.

"Our great problem," Palewski said, "is one of transportation and communications. Our railways are paralyzed, our ports in many cases are completely destroyed, especially where the Germans had established pockets of resistance. Of the 360,000 railway cars available when the war started, only 31,000 are left, and it is reported that only 1,200 of our six thousand locomotives can be located. All the others have been destroyed or sent to Germany. In their retreat, the Germans requisitioned everything on wheels—horse-drawn carts and carriages, motorcars, trucks, and hand-carts. I am optimistic, however, about the viability of the de Gaulle government and the General's ability to address himself successfully to the dual tasks of internal pacification and reconstruction. Both of these," he added, "can only be achieved if sufficient American aid is forthcoming"—a factor which has long been forgotten by France's government.

General Vanier was kind enough to put me up at the Hotel Vendôme, where he and Mrs. Vanier were staying. On the morning after my arrival he took me to the Embassy's temporary offices at 62 rue du Faubourg St. Honoré, in front of the British Embassy, where I met the senior personnel of the Embassy.

Food in Paris was scarce and, unbelievable as it may seem, wine had disappeared from the market. On the evening of my arrival, after a brief visit to our office, I dined informally with General and Mrs. Vanier, all of us wearing heavy coats to protect us from the cold. We partook of a very frugal meal prepared with military rations and washed down with water.

Our ambassador placed a government car at my disposal throughout my entire stay in France. The next morning I drove to our Company's headquarters.

There I learned that after the German controller of the farm-implement industry insisted on the dismissal of our European general manager, S. S. Voss, because he was a Jew, Lamard, one of our senior executives, was promoted to managing director of our French business. He in turn appointed Jean Roy, the ablest and most experienced among our French executives.

They had both been young commercial travellers for my father. When I succeeded him and opened up several new branches, I had made both of these men branch managers.

Throughout the war both officials, cut off from any contact with the rest of the Company and harassed by the German authorities, discharged their responsibilities with an ability and loyalty to the Company worthy of the greatest praise.

I was greatly encouraged and surprised to find that until D-Day our business in France had operated almost normally. Our factory was intact, sufficient allotments of raw materials had been obtained and our finances were in good order. As was the case with many other industries, the Germans had been so sure of their final victory, and so confident that France would become a satellite, that they were careful to avoid unnecessary destruction of property or damaging interference with the operations of commercial organizations.

In the car which General Vanier had allotted to me, we all travelled to our factory in the north of France. It took us the best part of the following day to get there, because roads and bridges were so badly damaged it was frequently impossible to move through the towns and smaller cities, especially those close to the railway tracks, where the rubble of destroyed buildings blocked our way.

Again I was surprised, on my arrival in Lille, to find our factory operating with about five hundred men, and with no serious damage to buildings or equipment. Twenty-six bombs had fallen on our property but none of them on our buildings.

The neighbours on either side of us were less fortunate; their plants were seriously damaged.

Our Paris management had been skilful in countering German requests that we should engage in war work. Throughout the hostilities, only farm machinery was manufactured in our plant.

Contrary to what I had feared, our working capital was intact.

Our management both in France and in Belgium were strongly of the opinion that when the war was over there would be a very strong demand for our product, as well as a swing away from horse-drawn equipment towards mechanization. They expressed the hope that I would be able to give consideration to the manufacturing of a tractor and tractor equipment in France as soon as conditions had become normal once again.

17

A Crucial Decision

DURING THOSE MOMENTOUS MONTHS that led up to the cessation of hostilities, my major preoccupation was increasingly centered in the growing inability of countries in the soft-currency areas to purchase their requirements in the hard currencies of North America. Here was a major threat to our Company's future.

Historically, our Canadian and American plants had supplied farm machinery to nearly every country throughout the world where wheat was grown and harvested. For many years our sales to the export markets substantially exceeded those of our home trade. I was determined that every reasonable step should be taken to maintain our historical position in the world's export markets.

Our position was complicated by the fact that the stepped-up demand for farm machinery in the United States and Canada was such as to tax severely our financial and organizational resources. It was principally for this reason that the majority of our directors and many of our senior officials, whose experience had been confined to North American operations, were reluctant to follow my recommendation that our export trade should be preserved at all cost.

I was convinced that our future demanded both expansion in North America and increased participation in the export markets. I was persuaded that with energy, imagination, and strong leadership both these objectives could be attained.

I was well aware that the pioneering spirit, which had inspired the early leaders of our Company to expand their operations throughout the world, had withered under the difficulties experienced abroad following World War I, the great depression, and the economic and political perplexities which now confronted England, France, Germany, and many other countries in which we had operated successfully in prewar days. All of this strengthened the feeling in the minds of many that our best interests would be served by concentrating our efforts on the North American market.

The argument went along these lines: "Why risk our capital in these semi-bankrupt and politically unstable countries when an important and profitable postwar demand awaits us right on our doorstep here in North America?"

I had faith in the recovery of Britain and the continent of Europe. I knew something of the pent-up demand which existed there, and I knew from personal experience that our Company's position in the export markets was one of our greatest assets. We held a privileged position which was shared by only one of our North American competitors, the International Harvester Company.

To operate successfully in foreign lands, it is essential to have a staff who possess an intimate knowledge of the national language and customs, tastes and prejudices, and the pattern of trade.

I had not been brought up, trained, nurtured in our foreign business, and then risen to the presidency of our Company to become the instrument of a policy which would restrict our operations to North America and a few remaining countries whose access to dollars would enable them to purchase their requirements in the United States and in Canada. Our pre-eminence in world exports was an asset which had taken generations to build up. I was determined that it should be preserved.

Ten years before, I had offered to resign rather than carry out B. W. Burtsell's still more radical policy of restricting our manufacturing operations to Canada alone. This time I was in a much stronger position.

In spite of my urgent recommendation, the board, led by E. P. Taylor and Eric Phillips, remained adamant in their opposition to investing Canadian funds in the rehabilitation of our continental European plants in France and Germany. However, I was successful in obtaining the board's authority to undertake manufacturing operations in Britain, but only on the understanding that a maximum of $500,000 would be transferred from Canada for this purpose.

This restriction, naturally, would force us to display considerable ingenuity if a manufacturing operation of world-wide dimensions was to be established in England, but I accepted it in good heart, convinced of the rightness of my policy. I went at once to the United Kingdom where I arrived on September 4th, 1945. I reached our headquarters in Manchester to find that the team of experts I had brought over from Canada the previous year had made great progress.

A highly suitable wartime factory had been selected in Manchester, our sample machines built with British raw materials had been tested and found satisfactory, the raw materials and machine tools had been spoken for, and all that was required was my final stamp of approval.

Before taking the last step I went to see Tom Williams, the Minister of Agriculture, to ascertain whether the Attlee government's point of view on the importation of farm machinery was similar to that of the Churchill government. Williams was just as adamant about imports from other countries as his predecessor, Hudson, had been. Then, at the Board of Trade in conference with Sir John Wood, I was given assurance that in three weeks' to a month's time all formalities would be completed, including authority to commence manufacturing operations in Manchester.

I then went to see Sir Stafford Cripps, the President of the Board of Trade, and urged on him that, in view of our willingness to set up manufacturing operations in England, we should be granted import permits for important quantities of machines, assemblies, and spare parts from Canada for 1946, '47, '48, and that we also be granted high priority status which would enable us to secure raw materials, machine tools, and specialized labour within the shortest possible time. My request was granted. It ensured important production for our Canadian and American plants up to 1948. At the same time, it enabled us to get into production in our British plant with a minimum of delay.

As I left for Canada I was satisfied that our new venture was off to a good start and in capable hands. My optimism was rewarded. By the end of 1946, our Manchester plant was in full operation, and several thousand units of various types had already been supplied to the United Kingdom and the continent of Europe.

The speed with which we reached the production stage was due in large measure to our forehandedness in testing implements made in Britain during the previous year, but the remarkable performance was mainly the result of the all-out efforts and organizational ability of the Canadian executives whom I had sent over twelve months earlier to plan and organize every detail of the establishment of manufacturing facilities in the United Kingdom.

In setting up these facilities, we had both safeguarded our important local market in Britain, and had taken the first step towards supplying the continent of Europe and other countries in the sterling area which could no longer purchase their requirements from America.

In my opinion, the decision to commence manufacturing operations in Britain in 1945 is second in importance only to that which resulted in the reversal of the board's decision to liquidate the American business on my return from the Argentine in 1935. Had we not undertaken manufacturing operations in the United Kingdom we would have lost our British business, the majority of our traditional export markets, and the possibility of purchasing Harry Ferguson's organization. Indeed we would have been today only a small organization operating predominately in North America.

18

A Fresh Start in Germany

My MIND NOW AT REST about our manufacturing project in England, I turned my attention to the continent of Europe.

There was no particular problem requiring immediate attention in France. I had already sent W. K. Hyslop, whose experience as our European general manager was to prove invaluable, for a period of three months to supervise our manufacturing operations and direct such changes in our organization as were required. Under his leadership great progress had already been made, and our factory was returning to normal operations.

No news of any kind had been received from Germany since the declaration of war, however. I decided to go there to see what was left, if anything, of our pre-war organization, and what steps could be taken to renew our operations.

Having been granted official status before my departure from Canada, I received a military permit to visit Holland, Germany, Belgium, Denmark, and France, and on September 21st, 1945, accompanied by George Thomas who, before the war, had been our managing director in Germany, set off from London in a military Dakota en route to Holland. We were on our way to the headquarters of Lieutenant-General Guy G.

Simonds, the Commander-in-Chief of the Canadian First Army, who was to provide us with all the necessary facilities for travel in Germany.

We arrived at his headquarters, in the Chateau den Brant at Apeldoorn, in time for lunch. I found General Simonds, whom I had not met before, a most attractive officer in his early forties, energetic, intelligent, with fine qualities of leadership, who looked every inch a commanding officer. He placed a car at our disposal with a driver and a staff officer. By early afternoon we were on our way to Bad Salzufen, the Canadian military headquarters in Germany.

A few hours later, we crossed the German frontier. My first impression of Germany was one of destruction, desolation, drabness, poverty. Many of the men on the streets were still in uniform, without any insignia of rank. They were unkempt, unshaven, dispirited, and generally bedraggled looking.

Towards evening we arrived at the Canadian section, first echelon, at Bad Salzufen. Colonel H. O. Moran, who subsequently became ambassador to Turkey and later to Japan, and all his staff were awaiting us for dinner.

Early the next morning, we left for our plant at Westhoven in the outskirts of Cologne. We travelled through the famous Ruhr Valley, passing through many cities renowned in the days gone by for their industrial production, but more famous now through the communiqués of the R.A.F., R.C.A.F. and A.A.F. —Dortmund, Bochum, Duisberg, Dusseldorf, Essen.

It would not be correct to say these cities were flattened. They were gutted out! Shattered walls were standing everywhere, surrounding charred and empty spaces, or a tangled and twisted mass of girders. The buildings had in part fallen into the streets, and a pathway was being cleared so that one car could get through slowly. Wherever I looked, I never saw an undamaged building.

At about 11:30 in the morning we arrived on the banks of the Rhine. Never before had I seen a more dramatic picture of destruction than that which confronted us as we rounded the bend of a great avenue of destroyed buildings and saw the wreckage of the bridges on the Rhine, facing Cologne.

Here was a mass of metal work with one span sticking up in the air, as high as a four-storey building, while the other span was protruding from the swift flowing waters. Beyond this was a suspension bridge, now only a tangled mass of wreckage, and beyond that again another blown-up bridge. One segment was standing there in midstream, the other had been carried several hundred yards downstream.

We threaded our way slowly and laboriously across a temporary military bridge, following army trucks, jeeps, hand-carts piled with household goods, women with children in their arms or pushing a baby carriage heaped high with all that was left of their possessions, old men with knapsacks on their backs, young women carrying bundles in each hand.

Before us lay the ancient city of Cologne which I knew so well. The two spires of the great cathedral were still standing, but around its venerable structure, as far as the eye could see, all was a tumbled mass of roofless buildings, burned, charred, wrecked, and destroyed.

It was growing late in the afternoon and the military authorities advised us that we would find no food or accommodation of any kind in Cologne. They directed us to Bonn, where we spent the night at the military headquarters.

Early the next morning we set out to visit our factory. From what we had seen of the almost total devastation of Cologne, we feared that our factory would be seriously damaged; but we were hardly prepared for the total destruction which confronted us on our arrival. There was nothing left but a silent and abandoned mass of debris.

Here and there, under the fallen masonry, one could see the outline of a damaged machine tool, but, ironically, about the only thing left standing was a large bronze plate, fixed to a shattered wall at the entrance of the plant, which carried, when translated, the words, "Erected to the memory of our glorious dead, our Massey-Harris fellow workers, who died defending their fatherland." Who could say, after that, that we are not an international organization!

When we drove into the neighbouring village, to see if we could locate any of our previous employees, we were told that the superintendent of the plant was still alive but that he had moved to another area. We were given the address.

From him we learned the details of the tragedy that had overtaken our organization. Our plant had been destroyed by the British Bomber Command. It had been rebuilt and turned over to the manufacture of war equipment; when ready to operate it had been destroyed once again. Our organization was completely dispersed.

Some sections had been shipped to Wels, which was then a part of the greater Reich, but had since become once again a part of Austria. Another element of our business had been transferred to an area which was now situated in the Russian zone.

In pre-war days we had purchased our castings from a large foundry located in the Cologne area. When this plant was destroyed in 1944, we lost all our patterns, our moulding machines and equipment.

It all looked rather hopeless; but I was determined that at least a start should be made towards rebuilding the business which, at one time, was a valuable asset to our Company, and would, I was persuaded, become a still more valuable one in the future.

When we visited the British industrial commission in Dusseldorf and Berlin, we found them very forthcoming. Certain essential raw materials were allocated to us and permits were granted enabling us to requisition the essential machine tools from other German plants.

Our pre-war superintendent, still our only contact with our previous organization, volunteered to gather together a few of our old workers to clear out a bay in our plant, to undertake certain essential repairs, and to make a start on the manufacture of spare parts and horse-drawn mowers. As a result of these minimal measures, a triumph of ingenuity and hard work, our German organization was able to take the first halting steps which very gradually led us to full-scale manufacturing by the time I left the Company ten years later. It has continued to grow ever since.

I made a quick survey of conditions in Berlin which used to be our headquarters, and where we owned a very large office building, and also in Denmark, Belgium, and France. Then I returned to Canada, feeling that we had gone about as far as possible, under the existing circumstances, to prepare for the better days I confidently believed lay ahead of us on the continent of Europe.

This brought to an end a year in which much had been accomplished. For the first time in the history of our Company our turnover had substantially exceeded one hundred million dollars. Our manufacturing facilities had been greatly enlarged and modernized, a new and highly mechanized foundry had been brought into operation, our traditional export business had been safeguarded, and we were now geared to take advantage of the unprecedented demand we had reason to believe would take place over the next few years.

19

A Move Towards Possible American Control

ONE DAY in 1943 Eddie Taylor had told me of his growing confidence in the future of our Company. He asked me whether I would have any objection to his accumulating a substantial holding of our common stock. I saw no objection to this, and told him so. There were others on our board who were substantial shareholders.

Later, in 1946, Eddie Taylor told me that Eric Phillips and he had accumulated 20,000 shares of common stock.

Before the end of that same year, I became aware that important purchases of our stock were being made. On investigation, I was given to understand that these were being purchased by Phillips and Taylor, on behalf of Victor Emmanuel, an able and influential American industrialist, president of a large American organization which had been formed by integrating a number of important American companies whose interests ranged all the way from broadcasting stations to aircraft engines and household equipment.

Among its other possessions, this organization had acquired a small but successful farm-machinery manufacturing company.

I was shocked and disappointed when I became aware that, without consulting me, these two directors had apparently been actively assisting an American group to obtain an influential stake in our Company.

A few months later, while I was in England, I received a note from Taylor telling me that Phillips and he were in Paris. They would like to meet me there to visit our French plant, and then to go with them to Brussels.

I felt that our friends had something on their minds they wanted to discuss, and I was not surprised when, half way through dinner at the Asti restaurant in Brussels, Phillips explained, with some hesitation, that the Victor Emmanuel group had accumulated an important shareholding in our Company. This was no news to me.

"Victor Emmanuel," Eric said, "is greatly impressed with our organization, and its progressive management, and is anxious to open conversations leading toward some sort of amalgamation between his Company and ours." He went on to point out that his group had also substantially increased its holdings and that, between their shares and those of Victor Emmanuel, they could establish a working control over the Company. They explained that Victor Emmanuel's interest was contingent on my continuing as president and senior executive officer, and that if I were willing to go along with these proposals, I would also be nominated to the vice-presidency of Victor Emmanuel's company. Substantial financial advantages would accrue to me when the deal was concluded.

Their proposals from the very beginning were distasteful to me. It was only too obvious that, however dolled-up the proposition was, the ultimate result would be that the control of our Canadian company would probably pass into American hands.

I was not a Canadian citizen in the sense that Phillips or Taylor were, because I had only become one when my British passport was exchanged for a Canadian one, when I was Deputy Minister of Defence for Air in Ottawa; but I was the head of a company as Canadian as the maple leaf, and I intended it to remain so.

Our organization had grown up with Canada. We were among the first of her early industrialists, and we had pioneered in the development of her export trade. I was the successor to a long line of Canadian presidents, many of whom were great figures in their time. I did not fancy myself in the role of one who, for whatever benefits I might derive from it, would become a party to the possible Americanization of our Company.

Phillips wanted a quick answer. He believed in striking the iron while it was hot, and he was anxious to conclude a deal without delay.

I played for time. Then, while returning on the *Queen Elizabeth* to New York, I sent Taylor a wireless that I had decided against their proposal.

Subsequently, at the request of Emmanuel, Taylor and Phillips, none of whom would willingly take "no" for an answer, I visited a number of the American company's manufacturing and other facilities. My answer to their proposal was still in the negative.

At a later date, when Victor Emmanuel finally became convinced that I would not go along with the proposal, he decided to sell the shares he had been accumulating with the assistance of Taylor and Phillips. This important bloc was purchased by these two gentlemen, and perhaps some of their colleagues. As a result their group became the dominant shareholders in our Company.

This was, I believe, the turning point in my relations with Taylor and Phillips. They never forgave me for having thwarted their plans. It was probably at this point that they decided that, by increasing their holdings and influencing the composition of our board, they would make it more difficult for me to oppose their plans in the future.

In this assumption they were correct. A beginning had already been made in this direction when, towards the end of 1946, Phillips and Taylor asked that, in view of their important holdings, they should be represented on the board by three members of their own choosing, and that in order to make way for these appointees, two of our present directors should not be re-elected. I discussed this matter with some of our directors who liked the proposal no more than I did, but felt that in view of the standing of the proposed candidates it was not worth making an issue of it.

All the candidates were friends of mine; they were John S. D. Tory, Joe Simard, and Harry Carmichael. As things worked out, Joe Simard took little interest in the organization, and attended only a few meetings; John Tory assured me that, although he recognized his nomination was not of my choosing, he would neither represent any faction on our board, nor would he be influenced by any considerations other than those he believed to be in the best interests of the Company.

In the course of time John Tory became one of my best friends and most loyal supporters, as well as one of our ablest, most conscientious and dedicated directors. My intimate friendship with and admiration for John lasted until his untimely death in 1965.

On another occasion, I met Taylor and Phillips in the Ritz Carlton Hotel in Montreal, where I was staying. In the course of conversation, Eric made the surprising suggestion that J. H. Gundy should be asked to resign from our board. He added that since Gundy was in his suite in the hotel, it might be very timely for me to approach him on the subject before returning to Toronto that evening.

This was an outrageous suggestion which I refused to carry out. Harry Gundy had been closely associated with our Company ever since 1928 when he and Thomas Bradshaw bought out the Massey family interests. At one time, Gundy virtually controlled the Company. He was largely responsible for my appointment as general manager in 1935.

A great Canadian in every sense of the word, Gundy was a leading financier, one of our most public-spirited citizens, and a ready and effective champion of good causes. I admired his integrity, courage, and sound judgement.

Faced with my opposition, the matter was dropped, and Harry Gundy remained on our board as one of our most valued directors until his premature death.

These moves were obviously only the thin edge of the wedge. By the end of 1948, out of a total of sixteen directors, nine either belonged to the Taylor group or their appointment had been influenced by them.

Although I realized what was taking place, I was probably less concerned over these moves than I should have been, because our Company was progressing greatly, and I was firmly in the saddle.

I knew from experience, as most senior executives do, that so long as a business is prospering, and its president is in good health, and in good standing with the public and his staff, his position is all but impregnable. It is only when his health fails him and difficult times are being experienced that he becomes vulnerable. This time, so far as I was concerned, had not yet come.

Two days before our annual meeting on March 26th, 1947, the following news items appeared in the Toronto press;

> Rumours are in circulation on the street that E. P. Taylor's financial group is about to acquire control of Massey-Harris.[1]

> Will the Taylor group acquire Massey-Harris tomorrow?[2]

The Taylor group referred to was Argus, which had been formed the previous year by Taylor, who became its president, and Phillips, its chairman.

This was the situation in 1947, the year in which the Company celebrated its hundredth birthday. Our sales and profits rose to an all-time high, notwithstanding that profits were being unfavourably affected by our very conservative policy of building up tax-paid inventory and contingency reserves. Experience had taught us that our industry was subject to ever-recurring swings between prosperity and recession, and I was determined to safeguard our Company against losses which might be incurred through unduly heavy inventories and other untoward factors which invariably accompanied periods of recession.

We had become the world leader in the sale of self-propelled combines. We had outgrown the plant in which we were building these machines, and a new one had been built and brought into production in record time.

It was about this time that a delegation of workers from Racine, Wisconsin, made me a presentation which gave me great pleasure. It was a fine reproduction of one of our self-propelled combines, skilfully made in our plant, gold-plated, and accurate to the smallest detail. On a plate affixed to it, the following words were inscribed:

---

[1] *The Telegram*
[2] *The Star*

To James S. Duncan, whose faith in the American company made possible its existence today.

From the men and women of Massey-Harris, Racine, who take pride in having vindicated your confidence and trust.

Our plants in the United States were modernized, re-equipped, and converted to handle our ever-increasing require-ments.

Economic conditions on the continent of Europe and in Great Britain were improving greatly. The success of our manu-facturing operations in England was such that our directors began to take a more favourable view of European develop-ment. They were still adamant against investing Canadian capital on the continent of Europe, but they now looked with favour on my proposals to raise money in Britain to expand our operations there.

I was particularly gratified by the progress being made in Germany. It was modest, because we were hampered by lack of capital; but we had made an interesting tie-up with a refugee from East Germany, expert in the manufacture of roller chain, and later with a manufacturer of straw presses, both of which helped enlarge our operations.

In 1947, at the request of C. D. Howe (now Rt. Hon.), I joined a trade and good-will mission to Africa headed by the Hon. James McKinnon, Minister of Trade and Commerce. This suited me very well because I was due for a visit to many of the countries in which we had important interests. While in South Africa, I met General Smuts and his outstanding finance minister, Hofmeyer, for the first time. I saw a lot more of these distinguished men during subsequent visits to South Africa.

I have met many great leaders, particularly during and immediately after the war, but only Winston Churchill left a greater impression on me than Jan Christiaan Smuts. His sim-plicity, his brilliant and wide-ranging mind, his courage, and his judgement marked him out among the great leaders of our time. On each occasion when I left him, I felt I had been in the presence of greatness, and came away understanding why Win-ston Churchill leaned so heavily on him for advice and counsel.

In South Africa negotiations were undertaken by which our company became associated with, and subsequently made a sub-stantial investment in the capital stock of the South African

Farm Implement Manufacturing Company of Vereeniging. The arrangement provided us with a strong manufacturing base in this important agricultural country.

Nineteen forty-eight was also a busy and successful year. Our operations in England were so successful that it became imperative that we should open a new factory. The site chosen was at Kilmarnock in Scotland. The manufacture of self-propelled combines was undertaken there.

Our world-wide sales during 1948 amounted to $143.8 million, an increase of no less than 71.6% over 1947. Our profits, after paying out $8.6 million in income tax, were slightly over $9 million.

We did well in all our markets, but our star performer was the United States where our sales were twelve times greater than they had been only nine years before, and eighty-two percent greater than the previous year.

Although our board was now whole-heartedly behind the British operation, they continued to be less than enthusiastic over the policy I was championing for developing our interests on the continent of Europe. They continued their refusal to agree to the transfer of any Canadian funds to these areas.

Yet it was obvious to me that an expansion of our operations in France and Germany was essential. There probably was no country in the world I knew better than France, and I realized that she was standing on the threshold of a great expansion of her agricultural-implement industry. France was going through an evolution from horse-drawn equipment to tractors and tractor equipment. I knew that we had to participate in these important developments or lose our standing in the great French market.

To do this we had to increase our factory capacity and build tractors and tractor-drawn equipment. Both projects required fresh capital. I flew over to France, and after several interviews with Baumgartner, the Chairman of the Bank of France, I was successful in convincing him that if a small tractor replaced a team of horses or a span of oxen the change would have an important effect on the agricultural economy of France. Baumgartner granted our Company a twenty-year franc loan on the understanding that we would undertake the rehabilitation of our

French plant and the manufacture of a small tractor along the lines described, with its corresponding equipment.

This proved to be a turning point in the history of our Continental business. Over the following years our production increased very greatly. Having established ourselves in the confidence of the Bank of France, we were able to negotiate further long-term loans with which we further increased our plant and undertook the manufacture of self-propelled combines.

Within a few years, our operations in France became so important and profitable that they played a significant role in the affairs of our organization as a whole.

During these same years, we were actively addressing ourselves to the development of our German business. It had become evident that here, also, additional manufacturing space was required. Negotiations were entered into with a view to securing a new factory at Eschwege, in the beginning for the manufacture of straw and hay presses, later for the new small combine which was to become very popular in Germany and other Continental countries.

By 1955, manufacturing space in Westhoven had increased to 163,000 square feet, and Eschwege to 297,000, and negotiations were undertaken for manufacturing space in Cassel.

20

Differences Over Dividends

In 1949, a serious difference arose between the Taylor group and myself. This time it was over the payment of dividends.

I had agreed to an increase in the regular dividend, but I objected vigorously to Col. Phillips' suggestion that an extra dividend of $1 per share should be paid out.

I felt strongly that, being engaged in a development program including the building of numerous branches in the United States and rapid expansion in the United Kingdom, we should preserve our resources and remain as liquid as possible. The Taylor group, which had probably incurred very substantial bank loans in order to purchase large blocs of our stock, felt that the receipt of substantial dividends was a major consideration.

At all events I failed to convince them that the payment of an extra dividend during our period of expansion was not in the Company's best interests. With reluctance, but in order to maintain harmony on the board, I agreed not to oppose their wishes.

I did not have long to wait for the proof that concessions and compromise do not pay off. One would have thought that after the generous increase in dividends paid out in the previous year, the Taylor group would not, like Oliver Twist, be asking for more. In this I was mistaken.

Once again, the year 1950 constituted a new record for our Company both in turnover and in profits. I was well aware, however, that we and the industry as a whole in North America were enjoying a period of unusual abundance, further stimulated by the tensions resulting from the outbreak of hostilities in Korea.

Prospects for 1951 and 1952 were apparently excellent, but experience had taught me that a cycle of abundance and prosperity based on exceptionally favourable circumstances is invariably followed by periods of declining sales, increasing inventories and receivables, greater competition, and lesser profits.

I felt very strongly that in view of our need for working capital to finance our expansion, our substantial funded debt, and the necessity of preserving our liquidity, it behooved us in these abnormally prosperous times to follow a conservative policy. I was a voice crying in the wilderness.

Great pressure was brought to bear on me not only to agree, but to recommend to the board that we should raise our dividends on the common stock, and that in addition we should add an extra $3 per share for the current year. This involved a total dividend payment of approximately $7.3 million, against dividends of approximately $1.5 million in 1948, and $3.19 million in 1949.

In other words, it was proposed that, although our profits had been increased by only $1.3 million over the previous year, our dividends should be increased by $4.2 million. To me, this made no sense at all.

When the matter was brought before the board, I explained my point of view and refused to recommend the proposal.

Senator G. P. Campbell, K. C., who had recently joined our board on the recommendation of Eric Phillips, and who had little background in the affairs of the Company, was asked to present the case for increased dividends, plus the additional $3 per share. He did so with such talent and effect that, as I had expected, the board disregarded my warning, and voted for the payment of the higher dividend package as recommended by Taylor and Phillips.

This was the first time since I had been elected to the presidency of the Company that I had been overruled at a board meeting. The handwriting on the wall was clear for all to see.

In 1950 only three of our directors had been on the board during the difficult days of the thirties. None of the others had experienced a period of recession with a consequent shrinkage of sales and profits.

The directors elected on the recommendation of the Taylor group were now in a majority both on our board and our executive committee, of which Eric Phillips was chairman.

I seriously considered resigning over the issue, since I was persuaded that the action taken was contrary to the best interests of the Company. If I failed to do so, it was because I felt more strongly than ever that my restraining influence, such as it was, my understanding of the business, and my more conservative approach to dividend payments and to protective reserves were more necessary now than ever. Besides, although my views on dividends went unheeded, no attempt had so far ever been made to interfere with the commercial activities of the business, and I had plans in hand for further expansion which I wished to carry out.

I believe still that I took the right decision. If I had resigned at that time there would in all probability have been no purchase of the Ferguson company which so notably increased the importance and profitability of our organization in subsequent years.

In 1950, my colleagues invited me to a dinner which had been organized to mark the fortieth anniversary of my service with the Company. Senior executives from various parts of the world were present, and, after dinner, a portrait of myself painted by Cleeve Horne was unveiled. It is now hanging above the mantelshelf in my library at *Somerset House*, where it brings back valued memories of those senior executives who played such an important role in the building of our Company. But what really touched my heart was the presentation of a fine, leather-covered book, signed by fourteen thousand of our employees from all over the world.

In 1950, also, my good friend, Kenneth Hyslop, decided to

retire. He had sought to do so two years earlier and had only stayed on at my urgent request. H. H. Bloom succeeded him to the presidency of the American company. As executive vice-president he was thoroughly familiar with the organization, and all recognized that in his ground-roots experience in the farm-implement business of North America, he had no peer in our Company.

During 1951, the Company—and I personally—suffered a grievous loss in the death of one of our most valued directors, J. H. Gundy, C.B.E., LL.D. He had been ill for some time and he passed away on November 10th, after having served on our board since 1928.

He had lived through the great depression, and it had been his influence which had enabled me to reverse the board's decision to liquidate the American business.

In all matters he placed the interests of the Company before his own. He was always on the side of progress, and while he was gratified by the notable developments which had taken place since 1939, he shared my view that it was unrealistic to expect that the favourable conditions under which we were operating would continue indefinitely. He agreed whole-heartedly with my conservative if unsuccessful approach to the husbanding of our Company's resources in order to protect our future.

In 1948 I had formed an executive committee which included a number of our most influential directors. It was suggested in 1950 that Eric Phillips should become chairman of this committee and, as such, a salaried officer of the Company.

In view of the important, if not controlling, interest the Taylor group now enjoyed, it was logical that their representative should become chairman of the executive committee. I agreed without demur to this appointment.

From then on, I saw to it that Phillips was closely informed on all important aspects of the organization. I made a special point of seeing that no decisions were taken unless he and I were in full agreement. Although I recognized that this was another step towards the group taking control, the arrangement worked out very well. With the one exception of his continued insistence on paying out larger dividends than I considered desirable or prudent, we never had a difference of opinion on the policies to be pursued by the organization or the personnel appointed to carry these out.

In the fall of 1952 it became clearly evident that we had entered a new phase of the business cycle. The long inflationary trends were giving way to deflationary policies, and more cautious purchasing was taking place. In addition, lack of moisture was making itself felt in large areas of the United States and Canada. That fall, the recession set in which was to last until the fall of 1956.

Those companies whose business was largely centered in the American market were the most seriously affected. This continued to be the case throughout the years of the recession. Our North American sales which had been steadily climbing since 1939 registered a decline in 1952 of 8.4%.

Our world operations, however, reached a new record level of $293 million, which showed an increase over the previous year's operations of approximately sixteen percent.

For the first time in the history of our Company our sales were drawing a little closer, at least within measuring distance, of those of Deere & Co., who occupied the second place among all the farm-implement companies of the world. They were first-class operators and were managed and controlled by men who had spent their lives in the business. In 1952, however, their sales declined by twelve percent, whereas ours had increased by sixteen percent.

This disparity arose in part from the fundamental difference between the operations of both companies. They were dominant in the great United States market, whereas much of our strength lay in the export markets of the world. Deere & Co., however, always operated much more profitably than we did, and they still do.

Such was the severity of the recession which showed up in the fall of 1952 that their profits declined by no less than thirty-one percent.

The turn in the tide which most experienced farm-implement manufacturers had foreseen, and which I had warned against so unsuccessfully during our dividend controversies, had come to pass and we entered a period of recession with a shortage of self-generated capital and with a pattern of dividend payments which in my opinion was disproportionate to our earning power.

Our Company had a very clear appreciation of our position in the United States. We had secured an advantage over our American competitors because we had been more agile in preparing for the post-war period, more forehanded in building new plants, and new sales outlets, more aggressive in obtaining scarce raw materials, and more fortunate in having correctly appraised the merits of the self-propelled combine. All of this gave us a substantial head-start over our competitors after the war.

Yet we saw very clearly that in a highly competitive buyers' market, our position in the United States might well be reversed.

The older, more solidly entrenched organizations, with their larger network of strong, experienced and financially sound dealers and their built-in replacement-part income, could make life very difficult for our younger and less solidly established organization.

This was a challenge which our executives and I had long expected and we were prepared to meet it. We were confident that by stepping up our enginering and pressing forward with even greater vigour we would be able to hold our own, and if we temporarily lost some of our newly gained advantages in the American market, we would regain them again in a few years' time, and resume the upward trend.

This assurance, insofar as I was concerned, was not merely a matter of optimism, but was based on my confidence in the ability and fighting spirit of our organization.

During the following year, the recession deepened, particularly in the United States. Farm-produce prices were falling, manufacturing costs were increasing, and drought conditions were spreading over many important agricultural areas. Our sales in North America dropped approximately twenty percent, while our world-wide sales showed an increase of fifteen percent.

More important, however, was our decline in net earnings. These had slipped from $13.1 million in 1951 to $10.8 million in 1952, and $7.3 million in 1953.

This was due to factors always present during a recession

and accentuated in our case because we were carrying a lot of sail in an endeavour to hold our own, particularly in the increasingly competitive United States market.

The downward trend in farm-commodity prices and other adverse factors affecting the industry didn't, in the opinion of our competitors or ourselves, bear the earmarks of the kind of depression we had gone through in the early thirties. It was generally agreed that the situation would probably right itself within two or three years. It went to prove, however, that the optimists were mistaken and that the balance of rise and fall in consumer demand was still with us, a pattern which reasserted itself with damaging results in 1970.

Nineteen fifty-three turned out to be the most eventful year in our long history, for in it we purchased the Harry Ferguson organization, an amalgamation of interests which was correctly described at the time as the most important event in the farm-implement industry since the incorporation of the International Harvester Company in 1902 which united five of the largest independent farm-machinery organizations in the United States.

The bringing together of our two renowned organizations had the outstanding advantage that our lines were, in the main, complementary rather than competitive.

The negotiations which led up to the purchase of the Ferguson organization were so important to the future of our company that I have incorporated a detailed relation of them in the following chapter which, contrary to my usual practice, I recorded at the time.

21

The Curious Story of Harry Ferguson

THROUGHOUT THE YEARS, many steps were taken which led our Company from its small beginnings to the position of leadership which it occupies today. None of these, however, had a more profound effect on our destinies, or made a greater contribution to the growth, prestige, and future prosperity of our organization than the agreement I entered into with Harry Ferguson to purchase all the assets of his world-wide company on the afternoon of August 4th, 1953 in the garden of his home in Stowe-on-the-Wold.

Harry Ferguson was a colourful Irishman, loveable, able, eccentric, self-centered, mercurial, a visionary with more than a touch of genius.

He oscillated between exaggerated bursts of friendship and admiration and unreasonable hostility and invective. He had few friends because he quarrelled with nearly all of them, and yet he was sentimental to a degree, and when in the right mood, kind, friendly, and generous. At times he appeared to be quite uninterested in money. On other occasions he would drive a hard bargain.

His quarrels with his many associates both in England and America were legendary.

He was an inventor of note. As a young man, he designed his own aircraft, but his life's work was devoted to the improvement of mechanized farming.

Towards the end of his career, he became interested in the automotive field and worked on a special type of four-wheel drive car which, in his opinion, was going to revolutionize the industry. In this expectation he was disappointed.

Harry Ferguson felt, with sound reason, that the tractors being built in the late twenties, which depended on their dead weight for traction, were unnecessarily heavy, unwieldy and costly. He experimented with and finally developed a tractor which was light in weight, and which ensured its traction by the transfer of the weight and pull of the mounted implement to the tractor through an ingenious hydraulic system.

Although this was a notable break-through in the tractor industry it was not recognized as such in the early days, and notwithstanding Ferguson's ability and his powers of persuasion he was unable to introduce his tractor successfully in the United Kingdom.

Discouraged and without money, he decided to give up the struggle in Britain and shipped an experimental tractor with a set of mounted implements to Detroit in the hope of interesting Henry Ford in its manufacture.

Harry Ferguson was much too complicated a man to look on his invention, as other industrialists would, as an important step forward in tractor design. He chose to look on it as an instrument designed to decrease the cost of agricultural production, a decisive answer to the problem of feeding the hungry masses of the underdeveloped countries, and a priceless weapon to stem the spread of inflation and Communism throughout the world.

I have never been quite able to decide whether this fervent belief in the contribution his tractor was supposed to make towards the betterment of mankind was entirely genuine, or whether it was the brilliant concept of a master salesman! No doubt it was a little of both because no one ever exceeded Harry Ferguson in his idealism, nor in his ability to promote an idea successfully.

Harry Ferguson's visit to Henry Ford was the turning point in his career. It enabled him to make a splendid contribution to the development of agricultural and industrial tractors which ensured him a lasting place in the annals of the farm-implement industry. It also resulted in his making a very substantial fortune in a surprisingly short lapse of time.

Harry Ferguson's altruism never got in the way of his ability to make money!

Ferguson, the inventor, the supersalesman, the promotional expert, sold Henry Ford on the proposition that by taking up the manufacture of the Ferguson tractor he would not only vastly extend his already mammoth manufacturing activities, but he would at the same time be making a significant contribution to the advancement of mankind. According to Ferguson, his invention would be a sort of super-Model T in the tractor field, and avalanches of orders for tractors and their mounted equipment would flow in from all parts of the world.

Henry Ford was ripe for this approach. He also was somewhat of a dreamer and the concept of lightening the load of mankind appealed to him. Equally important, he was still smarting from the comparative failure of his American-designed Fordson tractor, in which he had sunk a considerable sum of money. He recognized the merits of Ferguson's design, instructed his engineers to make such modifications as were considered necessary to adapt it to mass-production methods, and entered into a gentleman's agreement with Ferguson, whereby Ford undertook the manufacture but not the sale of the Ferguson tractor, under the name of Ford-Ferguson.

Sorenson, Ford's tough but able right-hand man, did not share his chief's enthusiasm for this arrangement, but this was immaterial because Henry Ford's word was law, and his decisions final.

To Ferguson's credit, the tractor he was offering Ford constituted a remarkable advance in design; and even if he did get somewhat carried away with his enthusiasm, and his forecasts of mammoth sales were never realized, his tractor eventually— long after he and the Ford Company had quarrelled—occupied a leading position in the industry. The hydraulic system, which was the core of Ferguson's invention, has influenced the design of tractors of all makes ever since.

Having arranged for the manufacture of his tractor, Ferguson addressed himself to the problem of setting up a sales organization and of securing the co-operation of various American manufacturers to produce a full line of farm implements to be mounted on the Ford-Ferguson tractor.

Fired by Ferguson's enthusiasm, the magic of the Ford name, and the alluring prospects of fantastically large sales, manufacturers in many parts of the United States vied with each other to tool up for and supply the necessary equipment at rock-bottom prices.

Between the genius of this Irishman, the Ford Company's unsurpassed manufacturing ability, and the glamour of the Ford name, the Ford-Ferguson tractor with its mounted equipment became the most talked-of newcomer in the farm-implement field. The progress it made at the expense of the old-line companies, while falling far short of Ferguson's enthusiastic forecasts, was nevertheless impressive. Harry Ferguson, between the distribution of the tractors and the farm equipment which went with them, wound up with a very considerable fortune.

Sorenson, however, claimed that Ford lost money on every tractor built and when Henry Ford died at the age of eighty-two on April 7, 1947, the Ford Company was quick to implement a decision, taken in November, 1946, to discontinue its unprofitable association with Harry Ferguson. Ford ceased manufacturing the Ford-Ferguson tractor in July, 1947.

Then, using as a vehicle the Dearborn Motors, a company which it had incorporated in November, 1946, Ford undertook the manufacture and distribution of a tractor similar to that designed by Ferguson.

This was a shattering blow to Ferguson. Eight years of collaboration with Henry Ford, during which it is estimated that approximately 500,000 tractors were manufactured and sold, had come to an end.

If Harry Ferguson was anything, he was a fighter. Ford had infringed some of his patents. He promptly instituted legal proceedings against the company for infringement of patents and loss of business in a suit for damages of $251 million, one of the largest suits ever filed in the United States courts. There was a settlement of the suit with a consent decree.

Meanwhile Ferguson, ever resourceful, returned to England, and, following the pattern of his association with Ford, made arrangements for the Standard Motor Car Company of Coventry to manufacture his tractor in Britain. At the same time he entered into contracts with various British manufacturers to supply the necessary mounted equipment.

He was determined, however, that he would not retire from the American market and decided either to manufacture his tractor in the United States or to arrange to have it manufactured there by another company.

With this objective in view, on a visit to the States, Ferguson arranged for a meeting with one of our vice-presidents, J. M. Tucker, in November of 1947. His purpose was to ascertain whether our Company would be interested in manufacturing the Ferguson tractor for his American organization.

Although Ferguson had lost upwards of eighty percent of his sales organization to the Ford Company, he was convinced that as soon as the original model of Ferguson tractor reappeared on the American market, the purchasers would desert the Ford company *en masse*, and rally to his standard.

During the course of this interview, it was suggested that Ferguson and I should get together in Detroit prior to his return to England to discuss the proposal. Although I was not enamoured of the plan to build Ferguson tractors in the United States in competition with the Ford Company, I met Harry Ferguson in Detroit, and sat in at a talk and demonstrations of his tractor which he handled with consummate skill.

This was the first time I had met Ferguson. I liked him, and we got along splendidly together.

After my return to Toronto, I discussed the situation fully with our board, which agreed with me that our best interests would not be served by accepting Ferguson's proposals. We never had any cause to regret this decision.

I wrote Ferguson to this effect, and on December 30th, 1947, I received a very nice letter from him in which he said that he was sorry we would not be working together but that his company had formed a high opinion of me and my associates whom they had met.

We had closed the door on our relationship with Harry

Ferguson, but as it turned out it was to be opened again later, under circumstances which were very much more advantageous to our Company. Before that, however, I had turned down a second proposal that we undertake, in our plant in Scotland, the manufacture of a small combine which he had designed for his tractor and which, in his opinion, was going to revolutionize harvesting.

None of us shared Ferguson's enthusiasm for his combine. Furthermore, our manufacturing capacity at the time was fully engaged in the production of our own self-propelled combine, which, immensely popular in Britain, accounted for an overwhelming proportion of all combines sold in that market.

By 1952, business had slackened off a little, and in order to bolster production in our Scottish plant, we decided to approach Eric Botwood, Ferguson's general manager, to see whether he was still interested in our building Ferguson's small mounted combine to be marketed not by us but by their own organization. Botwood reacted very enthusiastically, and we agreed to sign a contract for the manufacture of this machine the following week, at their head office in Coventry.

I was in England at the time. When I returned to Coventry for the contract signing, I was met by a flustered Eric Botwood who told me that, much to his chagrin, negotiations which were to be completed that day had been cancelled out-of-hand by Mr. Ferguson, following a long distance call from Ireland where he was recovering from an operation.

Botwood went on to tell me, what was no news, that Ferguson was a very arbitrary man and that, although he held the position of general manager, his own authority was strictly limited. He added that Ferguson, although still convalescing, had returned from Ireland to meet me and hoped that I would accept his invitation to lunch at his home at Stowe-on-the-Wold. Ferguson's Rolls Royce, in fact, was waiting in front of the office to drive me to his home.

Harry Ferguson and his very charming wife met me on the steps of their home, *Abbottswood*, and gave me a heart-warming welcome.

After an excellent lunch, served in the best British tradition by a butler of impeccable manners, Ferguson proposed that we have coffee in a little tea-house in a corner of his garden, as he wished to lay before me a proposal in which he thought I would be interested.

Knowing something of Ferguson's vivid imagination, his ability and his salesmanship, I was prepared for some unusual approach, but certainly not for the one he made!

"I hope you were not disappointed," he said, "that I cancelled the negotiations which, without consulting me, my general manager had entered into with your staff and yourself. These proposals," he went on, "were of such minor interest in relation to the larger issues I have in mind that I felt I had no option other than to call them off."

I assured him that I was not concerned over the cancellation of these proposals, and asked him to proceed.

"Although I have only had the pleasure of meeting you once," he said, "I have followed your career with a great deal of interest over many years, and I have observed the truly remarkable progress the Massey-Harris Company has made in its world-wide business ever since you assumed its leadership in 1933. I have been particularly impressed," he continued, "with the vision you displayed towards the end of the war in opening up factories in Britain and particularly with the dominant position your Company now occupies in the self-propelled combine business throughout the world. Like myself," he added, "you are a dedicated person, and have an exceptional grasp of the export business, and I have set my heart on becoming associated with you."

This was both unexpected and embarrassing. I interrupted him by asking him what he meant by becoming associated with me.

"I was coming to that," he said. "I have a good staff who have served me well, but they lack calibre; few of them speak any foreign languages; they are too insular in their approach; and as I am getting old and time is running out, I have invited you to join me today in order to make you a proposal which, no doubt, may surprise you."

"My main interest," he went on, "is the development of my business throughout the world, and bringing to the farmers of the underdeveloped countries the advantages which my tractor and mounted equipment alone can give them, and I have come to the conclusion that this could best be achieved by you giving up your connection as chairman and president of the Massey-Harris Company and joining me as an equal partner in my business. If you do this then you will become a wealthier man than you are at present, and I would hand over to you the exclusive management of the business, while I would devote myself to the design of new products which will greatly add to the value of the Ferguson line. I no longer have the health to worry about the financial and commercial end of my business. The strain is too great, and furthermore I have a deep and abiding interest in the development of a four-wheel-drive car which, in my opinion, will become as prominent in the automotive industry as my Ferguson tractor has in the farm-implement field.

"If you will, therefore, accept a fifty-percent partnership in my world-wide business without any financial commitment on your part, I will also make an agreement with you that when my four-wheel-drive car has been suitably engineered, this new and valuable asset will be included in our partnership!"

With characteristic eagerness and enthusiasm he ended his monologue by saying, "I know how attached you are to a company with which you and your father have been connected all your lives, but I feel that the partnership I am offering you will hold much greater opportunities. You can write your own ticket, you can name your own conditions. I'll accept them right now. All I wish is that you should become my partner and that together we should spread the Ferguson products far and wide throughout the world."

I found Ferguson's proposal embarrassing. He was so sure that his offer was irresistible and that I was going to jump at it. It was necessary, however, to meet the situation head on, so I told him, after expressing my appreciation of his confidence and the kind things he had said, that there were no considerations, either monetary or otherwise, that would cause me voluntarily to give up my association with the Massey-Harris Company which had been my life's work since I was a boy of sixteen.

Ferguson was not a man who liked to be thwarted in his proposals, and showing a certain amount of well-mannered irritation at my refusal, he got up from his chair saying, "Well I think you are making a great mistake which you will probably regret all your life, but let's forget about it and take a walk around the garden."

This we proceeded to do. His conversation was always interesting although I felt at times that his unbounded confidence in the things he was doing and in the contribution he was making to agriculture and to humanity as a whole was not entirely warranted.

"I have solved the tractor problems of the world," he said. "I have solved the problems of ploughing, tillage, and seeding. There are two aspects of agriculture I have not yet solved, but I will do so very shortly—the problem of transportation by mounted truck, and that of harvesting by mounted combines. Models are already tested for both of these, and are now awaiting production."

And then he turned to me and said, "Mr. Duncan, let's go back to the tea-house and sit down again."

When we were duly installed and I had lit my pipe, he said, "Have you really made up your mind that you will not accept my offer of a partnership under any circumstances whatsoever?"

I replied in the affirmative.

"Well then," he said, "I still intend to endeavour to retain your services and therefore I am prepared to sell my company to yours."

This was quite another proposition! I expressed my interest in his new proposal and asked him to elaborate on it.

He proposed that the first step should be that we purchase his American organization, Harry Ferguson, Inc., with headquarters in Detroit. At the same time, he would enter into an agreement with us to sell us progressively, year by year, an interest in his British business so that at the end of ten or fifteen years, we would have ownership of his organization.

This was an amusing example of Ferguson's conflict between altruism and business acumen. His British and world-wide operations, with headquarters in Coventry, highly successful, although not a very large money-earner, were somewhat depressed at that time. And he was fully aware of the fact that Harry Ferguson, Inc. was rapidly becoming somewhat of a problem child.

It was a good try, but I told him categorically that I doubted very much whether our board would be interested in purchasing his American business which I looked on as being more of a liability than an asset. Nor would we be interested in a gradual purchase of his British business over which, in the meantime, we would not have any direct control.

He countered with the suggestion that if I would go along with his proposal to purchase the American organization, he would offer me the senior executive management of the British business also, providing that I felt this responsibility, added to my present ones, would not be too burdensome.

I thanked him for the suggestion but told him that even under these circumstances I could not see my way clear to recommend his proposal to our board.

He then asked me if I would go as far as to visit the American headquarters in Detroit. I agreed to do this, and he promptly dictated a letter to his American headquarters asking them to place all their information at my disposal, without reservation, during my forthcoming visit.

After my return to Canada, I arranged to call on Harry Ferguson, Inc. in Detroit together with a number of the officials of our Company. We had an interesting conversation with Horace d'Angelo, the president of the U.S. organization, and one or two of his directors, including their chief engineer, and the vice-president in charge of purchasing.

Although there were undoubtedly certain attractive features about Ferguson's American organization, our visit amply confirmed our views that the company was making heavy weather, and the undesirability of purchasing this portion of the Ferguson organization was clearly established in our minds.

Their sales volume was slipping, their distributors were demanding credit, and the gross margin on the tractor assembly operation in Detroit was causing anxiety.

I discussed our conclusions with the board on my return to Toronto. Our directors unanimously concurred with the views we had arrived at and I wrote Harry Ferguson to this effect.

Shortly afterwards I received a letter from him in which he expressed regret that we were not interested in his American company and urged me to return to England to discuss what he termed "a broader proposition." I assumed that this might be the purchase of his entire organization, because I had by this time come to the conclusion that Harry Ferguson, who was growing old and tired, was becoming seriously concerned over the future of his enterprise, and his ability to lead it.

After full discussion with our board, an evaluation was placed on the assets of both companies and I was given *carte blanche* to negotiate a deal with Ferguson. This full authority was essential because during my previous conversations with him in England he had made it clear that he would deal only with me.

"I have only had one partner in my life," he said, "and that was Henry Ford. I will only have one other, and that is yourself. So I won't deal with your directors, nor your legal people, until you and I have come to an agreement. After that your directors and my own officials and our legal advisors can work out the details."

Before leaving Canada, I received another letter from Ferguson asking me to bring my wife, and inviting us to stay with him at *Abbottswood*, his home at Stowe-on-the-Wold. Again he impressed on me the need for keeping our negotiations strictly confidential and discussing them with no one in his organization nor with any of our competitors in Great Britain.

We flew to London on August 3rd. Ferguson's Rolls Royce was waiting for us at the airport, but before leaving I telephoned to him that I was proposing to bring with me the comptroller of our Company, Harry Metcalf. He replied that this would be quite satisfactory, because on his side he had sent for the president of the American organization, d'Angelo, to sit in with us during our conversations.

After lunch we were joined by d'Angelo and Harry Metcalf and we all moved out to the little tea-house in the garden.

Ferguson said that he had given much thought to the future of his company. Because he was getting old, and wanted to retire from his business activities and devote his time in a more leisurely fashion to the design of his four-wheel-drive car, he had reluctantly decided that, since I would not join him as a partner, he would sell his company to Massey-Harris, lock, stock and barrel.

He accepted without question the value which we had placed on his assets and our offer to allocate to him approximately 1,800,000 shares of our Company's common stock in compensation for his sale to us of all his world-wide assets. He took note of this and other stipulations on the back of an envelope; then, after a few moments' reflection, he said that our terms were satisfactory to him subject to two minor points on which he would like to secure my agreement before concluding the deal.

The first was that it would be very much more acceptable to him if our arrangements could be referred to in the press both in Canada and in England as an amalgamation rather than a straight purchase. I agreed immediately that this interpretation would be entirely satisfactory to us.

"My second point," he then said with a good deal of emotion, "is not one which I will insist on, but would hope that you will grant me. I am a proud man," he went on, "and I would feel better about our arrangements if you would grant me an honourable title in the new organization during the transition period only."

I replied that his request appeared to me to be entirely reasonable, particularly since he would become our largest individual shareholder, and I suggested to him that, as I carried the dual title of chairman and president, and as the chairmanship in the U.S.A. and Canada, unlike what is the case in England, is usually regarded as a more or less honorary title, I would be delighted to relinquish it to him for a period not exceeding five years, on the understanding that, as president, I was the senior executive officer of the Company, and that his functions and responsibilities would be limited to taking the chair at our annual meetings in Toronto.

There followed an embarrassing scene when Ferguson, pulling out his pocket handkerchief, wiped away the tears which were falling profusely and said, "This generous gesture on your part is more than I had any right to expect, and what you have done goes to confirm the feeling that I have had for several years that you and I were meant to work together. But I can assure you that I would only accept the chairmanship for a period of one year, or a year and a half at the most, after which I will return it to you." He added that he recognized that what I was offering him was purely an honorary position and that was all he wanted; and he said that he wouldn't even preside at our annual meetings in Canada, because he did not intend to cross the Atlantic any more. All that he was looking for, he said, was an opportunity to retire honourably from the hustle and bustle of business, and devote himself to other interests which were close to his heart.

Harry Ferguson then got up, put his envelope on which he had noted our conditions in his pocket, shook hands with me, and said, "I am satisfied with this arrangement. We require no signatures. Your word and mine are all that is necessary. Your people and mine can now work out the details and it will be quite in order for you to send for your legal and other advisors who can meet with their opposite numbers over here."

It was on this informal note that we concluded what was often referred to by our competitors as the most important merger effected by the North American farm-implement industry since the House of Morgan was instrumental in bringing together five American implement companies and forming them into the International Harvester Company of Chicago in 1902.

By the time we had completed our discussions it was nearly six o'clock. Ferguson said good-bye somewhat unceremoniously to the president of his American company and to our comptroller, and then turning to me announced that dinner would be served at seven, and that there was just time for me to have a bath and dress.

I was amused to see his shocked expression when I suggested that dinner might be delayed by fifteen minutes so as to give me time to call Eric Phillips, the chairman of our executive committee in Toronto, to advise him of the completion of our arrangements, and to ask him to send over John S. D. Tory, our legal counsel, and any directors who wished to be present at the official signing.

Ferguson, a little flustered, said that he never changed his dining hour, but since this was a very exceptional circumstance he would go and discuss a slight postponement with Mrs. Ferguson.

I stayed behind to have a few words with our comptroller, and as I returned to the house, I met Ferguson on the terrace. "I am sorry," he said, "but we cannot change our usual dining hour. We will meet at seven as arranged."

By accomplishing a miracle, I succeeded in making my telephone call to Canada, having a bath which I had greatly looked forward to after my overnight trip from Canada, and with the assistance of my wife, getting into my dinner jacket in time to meet the Fergusons in their drawing room at five minutes to seven for a glass of sherry.

After all this, to Ferguson's discomfiture, no sooner had we settled down to enjoy the sherry than the butler came in and said that, owing to some mischance in the kitchen, dinner would be delayed three quarters of an hour!

My wife and I stayed with the Fergusons for a few days. We were soon on a first-name basis, and enjoying one another's company immensely. Friends were invited to meet us and I was always somewhat embarrassed by Ferguson's uninhibited praise of my ability and his frequently repeated assertion that under my leadership our enlarged company was destined to enjoy an unrivalled future. To my wife he kept repeating that his only regret was that our paths had not crossed much earlier in his life.

On August 5th, the president of our United States company, Herb Bloom, accompanied by two engineers, Elliott A. Adams and Arnold Pitt, whom I had sent for urgently, arrived in Coventry and Ferguson demonstrated his full line to us. None of us were impressed by his experimental large tractor, nor by his small mounted combine of which he had spoken with such enthusiasm. We greatly doubted whether either of them would make a substantial contribution to our future business, and later events proved that we were right.

In the course of our many conversations while I was staying with him at *Abbottswood*, Ferguson mentioned one morning, as we were walking through his grounds, that one of his problems had always been that some of his engineers were perpetually trying to modify details of his tractors and mounted implements. He felt there was a great danger that after he was no longer in a position to see that his system was not interfered with, his engineers or ours might embarrass me by recommending numerous detailed changes.

"It would be helpful," he said, "if I were given the right of refusal or acceptance of any modifications." This, he said, would greatly strengthen my hand as I could always refer to him any suggestions coming from his old engineering department. If he found that these were not constructive, he would dispose of the suggestion without involving me in the details.

This sounded eminently reasonable and I agreed to the inclusion of a clause to this effect in our agreement. Had I known him better I would not have done so. As events turned out, this was an error in judgement on my part which I lived to regret. Although I was not aware of it at the time, this was the second error I had made during our negotiations.

The first had been to give him the temporary title of chairman.

On August 7th, Eric Phillips, J. A. McDougald, M. Wallace McCutcheon, and our legal counsel, John Tory, all directors of the Company, arrived in England and were installed in the Welcombe Inn, close to Stratford-on-Avon.

The following day, Ferguson demonstrated once again all his implements and our directors were duly impressed. They were equally impressed by the eminently satisfactory deal which had been made with Ferguson. They had reason to be because, although Ferguson's business, as was the case with our own at the time, was going through a period of minor recession, we had made a purchase which was to lift our Company into the second position among all the world manufacturers of farm machinery.

We had acquired all the manufacturing rights and patents covering what was generally admitted to be the best engineered tractor and mounted equipment in the world at that time; a highly efficient distribution service in Britain and abroad; a predominant position in Britain, the Scandinavian countries, Australia, New Zealand, and many other countries throughout Europe, Asia, the Americas and Africa.

We had fallen heir to an excellent staff of designing engineers, both in England and in the United States; a well staffed manufacturing plant in Detroit; a number of excellent sales and administrative executives; a built-in demand for replacement parts for the vast numbers of Ferguson tractors and equipment which had been sold throughout the years; all this, including good will, for $16.3 million, which sum included properties conservatively valued at approximately $3½ million.

On our way to the demonstrations, Eric Phillips, John Tory

and I were travelling in Ferguson's car, when he referred to a slight disagreement which had arisen between himself and me on a matter of interpretation, involving approximately $1 million. I was not concerned over the matter because I was persuaded that Ferguson would not have insisted on his interpretation against my better judgement, and because he was too honourable a man to go back on the gentleman's agreement we had entered into.

Ferguson, however, always unpredictable, suddenly proposed that we should settle this difference of $1 million by the toss of a coin. I was just about to turn down this unorthodox procedure when Eric Phillips, who always enjoyed a gamble, agreed to it. This impulsive and quite unnecessary gesture might have proved expensive.

The motorcar was stopped on the country road along which we were travelling, a coin was flipped on a "heads or tails" basis, and Ferguson lost. To his credit, he accepted this loss of a million dollars without even turning a hair.

The story of this incident was played up by the local press and others and given an entirely wrong interpretation. In reality, Ferguson had not lost a million dollars because he would not have received it anyway. What really was at stake was the risk that our Company had unnecessarily taken of losing a million dollars by resorting to the flip of a coin to settle a matter which could have been settled to our satisfaction without any risk to ourselves.

The sales agreement was signed in Ferguson's home on August 12th, 1953 in the presence of those of our directors and senior officials who were in England at the time, legal representatives of both parties, Mrs. Ferguson, and my wife.

It was a pleasant ceremony during which we presented Ferguson with a handsome gold cigar case which my wife and I had purchased for him at Asprey's, and on which we had arranged to have inscribed an amusing phrase, composed by our talented legal advisor and director, John Tory, referring to the million dollar toss.

The honeymoon was to be of short duration.

The only troublesome question which now required to be dealt with was the sanction of the British authorities to the take-over of Harry Ferguson's important British interests by a Canadian company.

Fortunately, owing to my work in the Dollar-Sterling Trade Council, I was favourably known to most of the Ministers and senior officials of the British government, and to those of the Board of Trade, the Treasury Department, and the Bank of England, with all of whom I had worked very closely.

John Tory and I called on the Governor of the Bank of England, who agreed to what we were proposing to do, providing we could obtain the sanction of the Board of Trade.

Fortunately, the Rt. Hon. Peter Thornycroft,[1] who was President of the Board of Trade at that time, was a friend of mine. With his support and that of Sir John Henry Wood, previously Permanent Undersecretary of this Ministry, with whom I had made the arrangements to establish our manu-facturing plants both in Manchester and Kilmarnock, and with the agreement of the then incumbent of the post, Sir Frank Lee, John Tory and I received acceptance of our proposal by 5:00 p.m. on August 14th. Afterwards, we returned to Strat-ford-on-Avon, where we worked on a press release until 3:00 a.m.

On August 19th, John Tory and I held a press conference at the Savoy Hotel which was attended by a very large number of correspondents from British, American, and continental news-papers. The amalgamation between our two companies, as I described it to them, was given the widest possible coverage throughout the world, and judging by the number of cables and letters we received, it was favourably accepted by the public as a whole. The statement given out was approved of whole-heartedly by Harry Ferguson, who did not, however, wish to attend the conference.

Before leaving London, I went to call on some of our principal competitors to give them first-hand information about our take-over of the Ferguson interests.

The strongest competitor of the Ferguson tractor in Eng-land and in many Continental countries was the Ford Company of Dagenham, which was naturally included in my visiting list.

Sir Patrick Hennessy, the very able president of the British

[1] Now the Rt. Hon. Lord Thornycroft

Ford company and a great friend of the late Lord Beaverbrook, said to me when I had finished explaining our negotiations, "Well, Jimmy, I will give you three months before you have quarrelled with Harry Ferguson."

"You couldn't be more wrong," I said, laughing, "because Harry Ferguson and I get along splendidly. Furthermore I don't happen to be of a quarrelsome nature, so there is no reason to assume that our relations will not continue as pleasant as they are at present."

"My prediction still stands," said Patrick, as I was opening the door of his office. "I didn't mean that you will quarrel with Harry Ferguson within three months. What I meant was that he will quarrel with you. He has done so with all his associates, and you will find that you will be no exception." This was said on August 19th.

Unlikely as his prediction appeared at the time, his forecast proved, unfortunately, to be only too true—but his timing was wrong. It was only eleven days later that the first trouble with Ferguson arose.

Back in Toronto again, John Tory and I spent all weekend preparing our presentation to the board and a letter to all our shareholders, and on the following day the whole-hearted and unanimous approval was received from our board.

On August 26th, I flew back to England to meet all the senior members of the Ferguson staff and our own and to explain to them the procedures we proposed to follow in connection with the amalgamation.

On Ferguson's invitation, my wife and I and our two daughters, who had just returned from Spain, spent the weekend at *Abbottswood*.

The morning after our arrival, Ferguson suggested that we should get together to discuss a few matters in his library. I could see that he was very upset. Presently he said, "Jimmy, I have heard from some of my previous employees that you have called a board meeting of one of your local sales companies in London and I have not received an invitation to be present. How could such an oversight have taken place?"

I replied that it had not been an oversight, because, as chairman of the board of our Company, which as he and I agreed was purely an honorary position, the only meeting he would be expected to attend would be our annual meeting in Toronto.

To my surprise he said with much animation that he was the chairman of our board and, as the chairmanship in Britain was the senior executive position, he expected to be invited to and to attend every meeting of all our local companies throughout the world.

To begin with I didn't take him seriously. I recalled to him our conversation in the tea-house, his desire to retire from all active participation in business, his request that he be given some honorary position for a short transitory period, my suggestion that to meet these wishes he should take over the chairmanship for a period not exceeding five years, and my explanation that the chairmanship is purely an honorary position carrying with it no executive function. I mentioned his remark that he would not wish to hold the position for more than a year and a half, and that he didn't even intend to be present at our annual meeting during this period.

It was all of no avail. From then onwards, Harry Ferguson's attitude changed radically. He claimed that I had misinterpreted his wish to retire, and he proposed to function as head of our organization. Moreover, he said, he considered my position as president subservient to his.

I endeavoured to throw oil on the troubled waters, but he was adamant and showed a degree of irresponsibility in his statements that I attributed to an emotional strain due, perhaps, to the fatigue engendered by our recent negotiations. Believing that he was overwrought and that time would ultimately bring about a change in his attitude, I endeavoured to keep our relationship on as pleasant and friendly a basis as possible.

Our accountant had now had an opportunity to examine in greater detail the figures of the Ferguson organization. I was disappointed to find that their percentage of profit was even smaller than we had anticipated, and that they were paying the Standard Motorcar Company too high a price for the tractors they were purchasing from them.

It was urgent that this situation be remedied without delay. Accordingly, on August 31st, I called on Sir John Black, the president of the Standard Motorcar Company. Sir John, I found, was scarcely on speaking terms with Ferguson, and carried on all his negotiations with him through a third party. To my surprise, he had not even been informed of our negotiations and only learned that we had purchased the Ferguson company when he read the news in the morning paper two days earlier.

Sir John was greatly perturbed because the production of tractors meant a great deal to his company. As he knew we were manufacturers, and amply financed, he was concerned lest we would undertake the manufacture of the Ferguson tractors after the conclusion of his contract.

The occasion was propitious. I insisted that the price of our continued collaboration was that he should reduce his selling price to us by twenty pounds per tractor as of September 1st. This was a hard pill for him to swallow, but I was adamant and before leaving his office I obtained his written agreement to this effect. This was undoubtedly a very important concession on his part and one which he came to regret in subsequent years.

After spending a few days with the Ferguson organization in France, where I found a number of unsolved problems which required to be attended to, I returned to Canada. In November, I flew back once again to Europe where many pressing matters concerning the welding together of our two organizations were awaiting my arrival.

Once again, at Ferguson's invitation, I spent the weekend at his home. Although our relationship was friendly, the almost overwhelming cordiality of the early days was no longer present.

Ferguson's views on the farm-implement industry were based on his personal conviction that anything which did not conform to his pattern of mounted equipment, or to the design of his tractor, must be wrong.

On that Sunday morning, while walking through the grounds surrounding his home, I was astonished to hear him propose that we should give up "immediately" the manufacture of our self-propelled combines in which we were the world leader, to concentrate solely on the production of the small mounted combine fitted to his tractor. As events showed, his combine never proved successful, and its manufacture was discontinued.

On the following morning, while I was taking leave of him

in his beautifully panelled library, he almost bowled me over by suggesting that we should "immediately" cease the manufacturing of our Pony Tractor in France which, at that time, was sweeping the French market. A simple, inexpensive design, it took the place of a team of horses. It was immensely popular during the post-war years when tractor farming-mechanization in France was just beginning to come into its own. The Pony Tractor at that time was making a substantial contribution to the growing prosperity of our French organization.

I listened to these and other fantastic proposals he made to me about the manner in which we should be running our business, with equanimity, based on the knowledge that I did not propose to do anything about them.

The next month, at Ferguson's urgent request, I attended a demonstration of his experimental four-wheel-drive car, together with a small group of influential guests from London, including the Rt. Hon. Lord Bruce of Melbourne;[1] Sir George Bolton of the Bank of England; Sir Robert Sinclair,[2] Chairman of Imperial Tobacco; and Henry Tiarks, of Schroeder & Company, the private bankers.

I had an excellent opportunity of appreciating Ferguson's skill as a demonstrator of his product. Everything was arranged with the most meticulous care, and he treated me to a preview of what was going to take place on the following morning.

Slides were shown, during which Ferguson gave us a most dynamic and convincing sales talk. His car, he claimed, was a great leap forward in the automotive industry in which it was destined to play a leading role. Ford, General Motors, and Chrysler, according to him, were out-engineered and outdated. His was the car of the future. It was all very impressive.

We were then invited to a field in which Ferguson's Rolls Royce had been skillfully bogged down the night before. After his chauffeur had made valiant if fruitless efforts to extricate the Rolls, Ferguson, at the wheel of his four-wheel-drive car, appeared on the scene, hitched up to the bogged-down Rolls, and pulled it out of the mud with the greatest of ease.

After lunch, we were driven in the pouring rain to a steep, muddy, and slippery hill. Predictably, the Rolls got stuck again.

[1] Previously Prime Minister of Australia.
[2] Now the Rt. Hon. Lord Sinclair of Cleeve.

When its inability to negotiate the hill had been sufficiently well established, we were all invited to get into Ferguson's four-wheel-drive which climbed the hill with both ease and speed. This impressive demonstration was unfortunately somewhat marred by the fact that, having the top down for better visibility, we all got showered with mud and soaked by the rain! The chief victim was Lord Bruce, who got more than his share of the slush, and didn't like any part of it. In somewhat of a huff, as soon as we got back to the house, he called up his car and drove back to London, mud and all, while the rest of us gathered round the fire in Ferguson's house, with a liberal supply of Scotch and soda, while his butler removed as much mud as possible from our garments.

One of the problems I had to face in the early stages of our amalgamation was to retain the services and the loyalties of the many excellent members of the Ferguson organization. I was aided in doing so by the loyalty of our own Massey-Harris executives who, while naturally expecting that, since we had purchased the Ferguson organization, all the senior posts would go to them, willingly agreed with my decision that in many cases they should accept a secondary role. They were, no doubt, disappointed, but they knew that I considered it essential both from the point of view of retaining Ferguson know-how and ensuring the loyalty and co-operation of able executives, that the latter should feel they were being not only welcomed in our midst, but on occasion, appointed to positions senior to those they had held in the Ferguson organization.

During my early negotiations with Ferguson, he requested that two of his executives be appointed to our board. His candidates were E. W. Young, who in his time was sales director of Harry Ferguson Limited, and Hermann Klemm, director of engineering of the American company. Although I was greatly impressed with the ability, the forcefulness and the excellent technical background of Hermann Klemm, I suggested to Ferguson that he should consider appointing Albert Thornbrough to our board in his place. Ferguson brushed my proposal aside, saying that Klemm was the obvious choice, as he ranked him above any of the executives of his organization, either in

Britain or the United States. His wishes were therefore carried out.

After my return to Toronto, serious differences arose once again with Harry Ferguson, this time by correspondence. He vetoed, among other things, the modifications which all of us, including his own engineering department, felt were necessary to provide the original Ferguson tractor with facilities for row-crop cultivation essential in the North American market.

It was then that I realized the serious error I had made when I agreed to allocate to him veto powers over design changes in his tractors and equipment. His unreasonable attitude toward any changes, including those recommended by Hermann Klemm, his senior engineer, in whom he had previously expressed the most complete confidence, was threatening to interfere with the smooth running of our business.

During the months that followed, Ferguson bombarded me with letters, sometimes twenty pages in length, received as frequently as three times a week, embodying various suggestions for the conduct of our business, objecting to some of the moves we were making, and at times ending up his letters by saying that if we didn't adopt his suggestions, he would resign from the board and sell his stock.

In May, 1954, I went to see Ferguson at his home in Coventry in the vain hope that we could arrive at an agreement to work together more amicably in the future.

I was persuaded that a smooth working arrangement was essential to the success of our amalgamation. I had a personal interest in the matter, because Ferguson and I between us had virtually working control of the Company which, had our relations continued in the spirit which prevailed at the time of our purchase, would have sheltered me from some of the pressures to which I had been subjected over the past few years.

It was all in vain. I got nowhere at all, and upon my return to Toronto, the voluminous correspondence continued. Ferguson's harassment was proving disturbing at a time when our organization was devoting its energies to the difficult task of working out the broad lines of an amalgamation between two organizations, both of which were operating in nearly every country throughout the world.

On June 4th, 1954, I called a special meeting of the board.

On my recommendation, they came to the conclusion that Ferguson's irrational conduct was such that it left us no option but to accept both his resignation and his oft-repeated suggestion that we repurchase from him the shares he owned in our Company. The following resolution was passed unanimously.

Resolved

THAT THE BOARD OF DIRECTORS OF MASSEY-HARRIS-FERGUSON LIMITED

(1) Sincerely regrets the unfortunate differences which have arisen with Mr. Ferguson on questions relating to the general policy and administration of the affairs of the Company; but

(2) Having thoroughly considered the correspondence and the documents referred to by the President, together with his report on the matter, and having regard to the President's proper and customary function as the Chief Executive Officer of this Company and to generally accepted principles of organization and administration of public companies, *cannot consent to nor approve of any division or diminution of the President's exclusive responsibility for and control over the conduct and administration in all respects of the affairs of the Company*; and

(3) *Hereby expresses its confidence in and unqualified support of the President*; and

(4) Hereby authorizes the President in connection with the questions at issue to take all such action and do any and all such things as in his sole discretion may in the circumstances be necessary or desirable in the interests of the Company and the conduct of its affairs.

Armed with a certified copy of this Resolution I proceeded to London accompanied by John Tory, and there we met Eric Phillips and Bud McDougald, who had agreed to join me in Coventry to settle our differences with Ferguson.

The negotiations which took place were lengthy, arduous, and unpleasant.

On June 16th, 1954, all of us motored to Stowe-on-the-Wold where we met Harry Ferguson at his home.

After the necessary preliminaries, I presented him with the Resolution from our board, accepting his resignation, and informing him that we were prepared to buy back all his holdings.

It turned out to be an unpleasant interview. Harry Ferguson was very emotional and claimed that he had not intended to resign, and had merely written us that he would do so in order to bring pressure to bear on us. However, faced with our insistence on accepting the resignation he had offered us on so many previous occasions, he agreed that he would retire and sell his stock providing a fair price could be agreed upon.

There followed prolonged negotiations carried out with Ferguson through a third party by Bud McDougald and myself. Finally, on July 6th, after receiving the assent of the Governor of the Bank of England, Cameron Cobald, to the purchase of Ferguson's shares, McDougald and I proceeded to Coventry, where, after further discussions and another unpleasant scene with Ferguson, the necessary documents were drawn up whereby he agreed to resign from the Company and sell all his shares to us at a price which, although eminently satisfactory to our Company, was extremely disadvantageous to Ferguson himself.

The negotiations which had taken place in the presence of his legal advisor and ours were not concluded till about seven in the evening. As we had insisted that the documents should be signed that day it was agreed with Ferguson that we would drive to Leamington Spa for dinner while our lawyers were preparing the documents and that we would return at 10:30 to affix our signatures.

Bud McDougald, wise and experienced in these matters, and having serious doubts of Ferguson's rationality, decided that he would stay behind just in case Ferguson changed his mind during our absence.

It was well that he did so, because no sooner had the first course of our dinner been served than I was called to the phone and Bud informed me that Ferguson had indeed changed his mind, that he wanted to go to bed and had said that unless we got back to sign the documents immediately, he would no longer be available.

Bud and I had agreed that, come what may, the documents would be signed that evening so, leaving our dinners untouched, we drove back at once to *Abbottswood*. Here, after further lengthy discussions, Harry Ferguson finally signed the documents and retired to bed. McDougald and I, together with our lawyers and Ferguson's, returned to Leamington Spa, where we dined at 1:30 in the morning.

We were all feeling a little shopworn by that time, but

happy in the thought that our prolonged negotiations with Ferguson had been successfully concluded.

Patrick Hennessy's forecast had proven to be correct.

It was distressing to me that Ferguson, who had so many lovable and admirable qualities, was apparently unable to get along with any of his associates. This unfortunate proclivity broke up an association which, under normal circumstances, would have worked out greatly to the benefit of all concerned.

In prior discussions with our board I had expressed the desire that Ferguson's stock should be fairly widely distributed. (Wood, Gundy & Co. were particularly anxious to share.) But I was overruled in this and although I participated myself in the purchase of an important block of Ferguson stock, the bulk of it was taken over by the Argus Corporation, which gave that group unchallengeable control of the Company.

At a subsequent board meeting, the title of chairman, which I had gladly—if, as it turned out, erroneously—relinquished in favour of Harry Ferguson, was returned to me so that once again I became chairman and president of the Massey-Harris-Ferguson Company.

A few days after Harry Ferguson's resignation from our Company the *Daily Mail* carried the following news item:

> Harry Ferguson confirmed today his intention to enter the motor car industry on a world-wide scale in the near future. His new car will be revolutionary he declared. "I promise it will not be long until the farmers of the world have really low cost transportation for themselves and for their goods, over good roads, bad roads, and where there are no roads and over the plowed land."

These enthusiastic if somewhat visionary predictions did not materialize. The car never got beyond the experimental stage during his lifetime.

A few years later, when I was no longer connected with Massey-Ferguson, but was Chairman of Ontario Hydro, Harry Ferguson came to Jamaica on a winter holiday, and by a strange coincidence rented a house a stone's throw from my home at Round Hill in Montego Bay.

To my surprise, all the unpleasantness was forgotten. Harry used to come to my house every other day for afternoon tea. The day I left for Toronto, he came to see me with the surprising proposal that I should give up the Chairmanship of Ontario Hydro, take up residence in England and become his partner in the promotion of his four-wheel-drive car, which he felt was now at the point where he could go into production. According to his enthusiastic statements it would soon become the dominant element in the North American and European automotive industry.

I need hardly say, I turned down this proposal. One experience of being in business with Harry Ferguson was quite enough for me. But from then on, until his untimely death, he wrote me long and interesting letters, and with certain reservations on my part, we became good friends once again.

He carried his eccentricities with him, even on holidays.

The first time he came to call on us at our home at Round Hill, he told us that, much as he liked the hotel of which I was part owner, he considered the meal hours to be quite outlandish. "Imagine expecting me," he said, "to dine at eight-thirty or nine, and lunch between one-thirty and two-thirty, when at home I invariably lunch at one o'clock and dine at seven."

"I told them," he said, "that if they wanted me to stay, they had to serve our meals in the dining-room at one p.m., and seven p.m., and that I didn't propose to change my meal hours because I happened to be in the Caribbean."

I suggested that he would probably have a lot more fun if he conformed to the Jamaican habit of lunching and dining later rather than having all his meals alone in an empty dining-room, but he was adamant.

His idiosyncracies on this occasion might have cost him his life. It happened this way.

One evening around nine o'clock, a prowler, assuming that the Fergusons, like all the other hotel guests, were down at dinner, broke into their cottage and, holding a gun in his hand, made his way stealthily into Harry's bedroom with the intention of searching for valuables. To his surprise and horror, he found Harry in bed, and, just as he turned to rush out of the door, Harry, undaunted by the fact that the intruder was a big, athletic coloured man of over six foot two, (whereas he himself did not weigh more than 130 pounds) jumped out of bed intent on grappling with the intruder, who, in his agitation and eagerness to get away, accidentally fired off his gun. Wrenching himself loose, the thief jumped through the open ground-floor window.

Unfortunately the bullet ricocheted off a steel plate in the ceiling and wounded Harry in the foot.

Doctors were summoned. The wound, if painful, proved to be quite superficial. The six-foot intruder was never found, and Harry, on crutches and in a high dudgeon, left for home, reviling Round Hill, threatening suit for damages, and vowing that never again would he venture into the Caribbean.

My wife and I had left our home in Jamaica a week before these untoward events took place.

When the news of the assault came out in a Toronto paper, a friend who knew of our quarrel in Coventry exclaimed, "Gee, weren't you lucky to be back home when it happened. They might have thought it was you who tried to shoot him." My humorous friend didn't know that the volatile Harry and I were the best of friends once again. Besides, the only gun I ever fired in my life was an 18-pounder during World War I.

Although Harry's irascible and quarrelsome nature was immensely irritating at times, I never found it in my heart to dislike him.

He was the victim of his ever-changing moods and in many respects he was his own worst enemy. Even when he was at his most querulous and volcanic, I rather liked him, recognizing that he probably didn't mean half of the dreadful things he was saying; that basically he was kindly and generous. If quick to pick up a quarrel, he was also quick to make amends.

Regardless of his idiosyncracies, Harry Ferguson made an outstanding contribution to tractor design and manufacture, and his name will always find an honoured place in the annals of the farm-implement industry.

22

The Growing Pains of Expansion

OUR EXPANSION had been so rapid over the past fifteen years or so that our organization had been frequently called on to face up to many strenuous challenges. No year had been more absorbing, more arduous, or in some respects more rewarding than 1954.

The recession was still with us. Over the previous two and a half years, the farmers of North America, and in varying degrees those of many other countries throughout the world, had witnessed a gradual decline in the price of the things they had to sell, and frequently an increase in the price of those they required to purchase.

Weather conditions continued to be unusually unfavourable. Large agricultural areas in the United States suffered from drought, whereas in western Canada we were experiencing a disastrous year due to excessive and untimely rains, followed by rust, which substantially reduced the grain crop, and the farmers' incomes.

These factors cut deeply into farmers' purchasing power, and they seriously affected the earnings of the farm-implement industry. Those of Massey-Harris and Ferguson were no exception. Indeed, the drive to maintain our position in the highly competitive United States market was cutting deeply into our profit margin.

These were far from ideal conditions in which to deal with the world-wide problems of our amalgamation, and there were those who were disappointed when greater earnings did not immediately flow from the expansion of our operations.

The combining of our organizations was not made easier by the fact that we and other full-line companies were operating under a branch system throughout the world, whereas the Ferguson organization, being a relative newcomer, operated largely through distributors.

These, in the majority of cases, were well organized and highly successful operators and all of us were unanimous in our viewpoint that to withdraw too hurriedly the representation of the Ferguson line from many of its loyal and effective distributors would not only be running counter to my verbal undertaking with Harry Ferguson, but might well result in a very substantial reduction in the sale of Ferguson tractors and equipment, particularly in the initial years of the amalgamation.

On the other side of the picture, our Massey-Harris branches with their numerous small agencies were vociferously claiming the franchise for the Ferguson line. They were badly in need of a small Ferguson-type tractor. We had been endeavouring to design one for them over the past three years, but without too much success. The bald fact was that no one in the industry up to that time had been able to develop a small tractor which compared favourably with Ferguson's.

We found ourselves, therefore, before two claimants, the Ferguson distributors who wished to retain the exclusivity of the Ferguson line; and our world network of branches who were arguing that since we had purchased the Ferguson company they should be given the right to market the Ferguson tractors and equipment.

While common sense dictated that we should make a careful survey of the conditions in each of the countries concerned, an early determination of policy was being forced on us, particularly by the Ferguson distributors throughout the world, who were clamouring for a decision on the continuity of their franchise. Indeed, the Ferguson dealers in the United States had already met in conference to discuss bringing suit against our

Company for damages running into many millions of dollars should we decide to cancel their contracts.

To gain time and avoid hasty decisions, we announced, with the concurrence of our executive committee, that we were contemplating the marketing of two lines of tractors and equipment, one under the name of Massey-Harris, the other under the name of Ferguson.

This decision was approved at our annual meeting of February 19th, 1954.

In the meantime, our engineering department had been actively investigating the possibility of developing a satisfactory dual line with common basic features but differing in appearance through superficial design changes and colour. We built up a few samples bearing these dual characteristics, with a view to submitting them to a group of executives including some of our directors whom we called together at a conference at San Antonio, Texas, to determine the soundness of the course we proposed to follow.

The conference took place between the 6th and 12th of March, 1954. Our new models were demonstrated in operation, and discussions followed covering the whole range of problems inherent to the amalgamation of our companies, with special emphasis on the policy of establishing a dual line. At the conference we recognized that, if our policy were to be successful, it would be necessary to incorporate into the design of our two lines appreciable variations, but never to such an extent as to affect our ability to produce both with the same basic toolage and manufacturing equipment.

It was conceded that the dual-line policy would involve greater engineering expenditure, but if the results were to be as successful as a similar policy of the automotive industry had been, our reward in larger volume and profits would amply compensate us for this additional expenditure.

This procedure would have to be embarked on, on a gradual scale. It was pointed out at the San Antonio conference that should we adopt the dual-line policy, we would have to accept the handicap of too much similarity between the two lines during the initial years of production.

The consensus arrived at in San Antonio was overwhelmingly in favour of marketing the Company's products under Massey-Harris and Ferguson trade names. At the same time, the conference recognized that such a move could only be progressively undertaken, and that its application would be dependent on the various circumstances existing in each country, circumstances which we were frankly unable to assess until we had time to appraise the situation in each of the countries concerned.

In other words, we would leave the door open to apply the dual-line policy in certain countries and not to apply it in others.

In reaching out towards this solution which would harness the sales energy of both organizations, we were not showing any particular originality of thought. We were only considering the possibility of applying a pattern which had been successfully followed for many years by our chief competitor, the International Harvester Company, a policy which was being followed by General Motors, Ford, Chrysler and many other automotive companies. It had played a dominant role in the vast expansion and profitability of these organizations.

As far back as 1930, Alfred P. Sloane Jr., the eminent president of General Motors and one of the chief architects of the phenomenal growth of this organization, wrote in his annual report: "It is perfectly possible from the engineering and manufacturing standpoint to make two cars at no great difference in price and weight, but considerably different in appearance and to some extent in technical features, but both built with the same fundamental tools and equipment."

Whether it would have been possible or desirable to apply the dual-line policy in the course of time to any or to all countries is something we shall never know, because it was never tried out in its final form. Nor were we in a position to supply a suitably designed dual line of tractors and equipment at the time of my resignation in the spring of 1956.

My personal impression is that if, following the policy of all successful automotive firms and that of the International Harvester Company over a period of very many years subsequent to their amalgamation, we had adopted the dual-line policy, gradually increasing the distinctive features of each and capitalizing on the names of Massey-Harris and Ferguson, both regarded throughout the world as hallmarks of quality, our sales would today be considerably larger and more profitable than under the single-line policy which has been pursued.

With all these problems to solve, the repeated trips to Europe on organizational matters, the purchase of H. V. McKay Massey-Harris Company of Australia, which involved a six-weeks visit to that country, the numerous arrivals in Toronto of important Ferguson dealers from all over the world, each anxious to stake his claim for the continuance of his franchise, the vexatious difficulties with Harry Ferguson which culminated in the parting of the ways, and last but not least the problems inherent in a continuing recession in consumer demand, the year 1954 turned out to be one of the busiest and most challenging in my experience. Its burden, however, was easily and enthusiastically carried by management, knowing as we did that in the purchase of the Harry Ferguson Company we had set the stage for increasing the important role we were already playing in the world-wide activities of the farm-equipment business, and recognizing that the problems we were facing in 1954 were the growing pains of expansion.

The purchase of the McKay interests in Australia was both so difficult and yet so important to our Company that they are worthy of special mention here.

In the spring of 1954, Cecil McKay, the majority shareholder of the H. V. McKay Massey-Harris Pty. Ltd., flew over from Australia to see us. Our contract with his organization, which had been in force for twenty-four years, expired at the end of 1954. This could not have come at a more inopportune time.

Cecil McKay took the position that he would not renew our contract unless we cancelled the franchise of the Ferguson dealers and handed over the sale of the Ferguson line to his organization. This did not suit our purpose: we were not overly impressed with the quality of Cecil McKay's organization, while the Ferguson interests in Australia were in the hands of the most successful and best organized distributorship in Harry Ferguson's world-wide network.

I was convinced that if we acceded to McKay's demand, the

sales in Australia of the Ferguson line would be seriously affected. Our discussions in Toronto were abortive and McKay returned home.

Immediate action on our part was necessary, as our contract would expire within seven months. I decided, therefore, to proceed immediately to Australia to survey the situation, and, if my views were confirmed, to initiate negotiations to buy out the H. V. McKay interests.

I also arranged with the board before my departure that if my decision favoured the purchase of the McKay interests, my fellow director, J. A. McDougald, with whom I had so recently negotiated the purchase of the Harry Ferguson stock in England, and with whose ability as a negotiator I was greatly impressed, should fly out to Australia to assist in the negotiations.

McDougald was an able, if somewhat ruthless, negotiator, who had had a broad experience in the successful handling of financial situations, similar in many respects to those with which it was expected we would have to deal in Australia.

It is interesting to reflect that in April, 1930, one of my predecessors, Thomas Bradshaw, beset by the financial difficulties into which the great depression had plunged our Company, travelled to Australia to sell the assets of our Australian organization to our chief local competitor, the H. V. McKay Company. As a result, the H. V. McKay Massey-Harris Pty. Ltd. was formed, in which we were very minor shareholders.

Now, twenty-four years later, I was returning to Australia as head of one of the two largest implement companies in the world to reverse the operation and negotiate the purchase of the McKay interests, thus re-establishing Massey-Harris-Ferguson in a position of leadership in Australia.

A rapid tour of our sales outlets in Australia, both of Massey-Harris and Ferguson, confirmed the impression I had already formed in Canada that our best interests would be served by arranging to acquire all the family assets of the McKay group.

I cabled McDougald, as arranged, and he arrived in Melbourne on November 2nd, 1954.

The negotiations were difficult, the progress was slow, but the procedure was at times relieved by amusing situations over which Bud and I had many laughs in subsequent years. After weeks of long, drawn-out negotiations, agreement was reached in the middle of December.

The purchase was not a bargain as the purchase of the Ferguson interests had been, but we had acquired a valuable asset including a manufacturing plant as large as any we possessed in Canada or the United States; a sales organization comprising five branches; six hundred sales outlets; a staff of approximately 2,500; a leading position in this vigorously developing country; and a new dimension to our rapidly expanding world organization. It was not without satisfaction, therefore, that we undertook the return journey to Canada.

Before leaving Australia I had appointed three Canadians of proven experience and ability to positions of authority. With these exceptions, all the Australian staff were retained. By so doing, we gave them job assurance, preserved the Australian atmosphere of the organization, and retained the good will and experience of both executives and workers.

My action here was in accordance with my firm conviction that it is essential to retain as much experience as possible in an organization, and to ensure the loyalty and the whole-hearted co-operation of the workers. No doubt there were certain members of our Australian organization who didn't measure up in every way to our standards, but as I said to Tom Ritchie, our newly appointed general manager, no credit ever accrues to management by firing people.

On the contrary, an enlightened executive brings out the best in his fellow workers by raising the required standards of efficiency through personal example, dedication, fair play, hard work, and loyalty to his company, his fellow workers, and to the staff as a whole.

Nineteen fifty-four had been a year of solid achievement. The deepening of the recession and the costs incidental to the integration of the two organizations were, however, exacting a heavy toll from our margins of profit. This was particularly noticeable in Canada and the United States.

We were now suffering to a major degree, as were all our competitors, from the cyclical nature of the farm-implement industry, of which so much had been said and so little believed during the exceptionally prosperous years we had so recently experienced.

There was nothing in the situation, however, to cause anxiety. The recession had none of the earmarks of a full-fledged depression, and none of us believed it would be of long duration.

Our North American sales, including defence work, were down fifteen percent. On the other hand, our exports from North America showed a very substantial improvement.

Our total world sales, including defence work, which amounted to approximately $42 million, reached the figure of $349 million, which was a far cry from our $14 million turn-over in 1936, only eighteen years previously, (my first year in the active management of the Company).

We were justifiably proud that we had maintained our position as the second ranking company in the farm-implement business.

23

Choosing a Successor

THE PURCHASE of the Ferguson organization carried with it a problem of succession, which had not existed to the same degree before the amalgamation. The rapid strides the Massey-Harris organization had made over the years were unquestionably due to the quality, experience and ability of our senior executives. Among these were men who, in my estimation, would be fully capable, after a few more years' experience, of assuming the presidency of our organization as it then stood.

The purchase of the Ferguson organization changed the picture. I was most disappointed when, at the time of the amalgamation, Harry Ferguson stated categorically that none of his senior executives was qualified for top responsibility. But, meeting his executives, I had to disagree with his judgement, and I set out immediately to keep as many of his senior men as possible within the ranks of our Company.

During my preliminary negotiations with Ferguson, I met A. A. Thornbrough on two occasions, and was favourably impressed by him. His experience had been somewhat localized. He spoke no foreign language, his knowledge of sales and manufacturing was superficial, and he was unfamiliar with conditions outside the United States. On the other hand he was intelligent, had an excellent educational background, was ambitious, and had the great advantage of being young.

I decided to give him every opportunity to broaden his experience in the organization. I first transferred him to our American headquarters with the title of vice-president. Shortly afterwards, I moved him to our Canadian headquarters with a similar title. I sent him on important missions to Europe and elsewhere, travelled considerably with him, saw to it that he attended our engineering conferences, and followed the operations of our equipment in the field so that he would have the opportunity to familiarize himself gradually with the various aspects of our organization, and to become acquainted with our personnel.

Among the Massey-Harris executives who, given time and more experience, would, prior to the amalgamation, have been considered for promotion, was H. H. Bloom. He had been brought up in our organization, he had unequalled experience in the sales end of our United States and Canadian organizations; he was able, indefatigable, of sound judgement, and exceptional sales promotional ability. He was fiercely loyal to the organization, and although a hard driver, was popular with his staff.

Unfortunately, like Al Thornbrough, he spoke no foreign language and was unfamiliar with our export business, but what he didn't know about merchandizing our line in North America wasn't worth knowing.

My high opinion of Herb Bloom's ability and incisiveness was shared by the Canadian government and by our competitors. Early in 1942, I was approached by Donald Gordon, the eminent and successful chairman of the Wartime Prices and Trade Board, and by M. W. McCutcheon, his deputy, with the request that I should release Herb Bloom to become administrator of farm-equipment and construction machinery.

Although I knew we would miss him greatly, I agreed to his being transferred to the service of the government. He carried out his important administrative functions with aggressiveness, tact, and diplomacy and when he left government service to return to our Company in 1945, his contribution to the war effort was rewarded with an O.B.E. in the King's Honours List.

At the time of the amalgamation, Herb Bloom was, however, not in the running for a promotion. His health was giving him serious anxiety, and his doctors had strongly recommended that he decrease rather than increase his responsibilities.

John Beith was another man in whom I had great confidence, and whose qualifications undoubtedly fitted him for promotion. He was young and had a very broad experience in our export business. He was energetic, resourceful, and spoke French, German, and Spanish without a trace of accent. He was popular with the staff and his colleagues, and had given proof of his managerial abilities by successful handling of our branches in both the Argentine and France, and had spent a few years in an executive position in our offices in Toronto.

There were others in our American and European organization who would have qualified for senior responsibility.

Many executives labour under the delusion that a company's best interests are served by hiring expensive outsiders only to find after a year or so that they are still teaching them the business. Yet all the time there were excellent candidates within the organization who if promoted would have risen successfully to handle their enlarged responsibilities. Besides being inefficient, this policy of giving the top jobs to outsiders destroys the morale of the organization.

I had both Ferguson and Massey-Harris men to choose from. Following my constant policy of retaining within our organization the greatest amount of experience possible, I decided that this could be better accomplished by choosing a man with a Ferguson background for the top position. I was confident that our Massey-Harris executives, recognizing that it was essential to retain in our organization men who were well versed in the Ferguson line, would be willing to serve under a Ferguson-trained president.

I was much less confident, on the other hand, that the reverse would hold true if a Massey-Harris man was appointed to the top position. The Ferguson executives, being so recently absorbed into our organization, might quite understandably have felt a lesser loyalty towards it.

Thus my choice for the top position fell on Al Thornbrough. I felt assured that, with a few more years of collaboration, he would familiarize himself with the Massey-Harris line, the policies and philosophy of our organization, and would develop an apreciation of the sterling qualities of those senior executives who had contributed so greatly to the spectacular growth of our Company over the past twenty years.

I hoped that he would gradually sell himself to the organization, and develop a sense of loyalty to those who were engaged in it so that when, in the course of time, he was ready to occupy the senior position, the transition would be made without serious upset within the ranks of the organization.

I am certain that this would have worked out as I foresaw it had my plans not been upset in the following year.

After we had repurchased Harry Ferguson's shares, the board unanimously reappointed me chairman and president of the organization. I was convinced, however, that with the increased Phillips-Taylor financial control and my unwillingness to follow policies which I did not consider to be in the best interests of the Company, their assumption of the management function was only a matter of opportunity and timing. They had been for some time frustrated by the extreme loyalty of the senior Massey-Harris executives to the policies we were pursuing, and to myself personally.

I had provided an alternative in the promotion of Al Thornbrough, and I was therefore not surprised when it was suggested to me by Phillips, in early October of 1955, that Thornbrough should be immediately appointed executive vice-president.

Although I fully understood the motives behind Phillips' suggestion, I disapproved of it. I did not differ with the choice, which coincided with my own, but with the timing. Al Thornbrough was a relative newcomer to the organization. He was a Ferguson man, an American and still inexperienced in many aspects of our business. It was obvious to me that such an untimely appointment was bound to be unpopular and disruptive, and I felt strongly that it was unfair to him personally that he should be projected into a position of such authority until the way had been tactfully prepared for him.

Furthermore, from an organizational point of view, it made no sense at all that a man who was not a director of the Company and still inexperienced in merchandizing policies should be given authority over another, who was not only a director, but senior vice-president of the Company and had forgotten more about merchandizing than many of us ever knew.

I believed that with just a little patience and tactful handling under my guidance, within eighteen months or so, Al
Thornbrough could have been made a member of our board
and that his subsequent promotion to executive vice-president
would have been readily accepted by all concerned.

I pointed all this out to Phillips at the time, but we were
by now operating on different wave-lengths. However, as I felt
that the issue, although a very important one, did not warrant a
break at this particular time, I agreed under protest and with
much foreboding to make this appointment.

While these events were taking place I received a cable from
Vladimir Matskevich, the Soviet Minister of Agriculture, inviting us to spend two weeks in the U.S.S.R. as guests of his
government to familiarize ourselves with Soviet agriculture and
bring in our recommendations on the adaptability of the Ferguson tractor to Soviet requirements.

I will not deal here with this trip which was followed up
by a return visit to Coventry by the Minister of Tractor Production, because I described it subsequently in a booklet entitled
Russia's Bid for World Supremacy, which was given wide
circulation in Canada.

About this time my health, undermined, perhaps, by the
constant strain of heavy responsibilities and an inordinate
amount of travelling, began to give me concern. This was an
unusual experience for me, as I had always enjoyed wonderful
health, and my resistance to fatigue, constant travel, and long
hours of work had become almost legendary in our Company.
In 1953 I had developed an ulcer which bothered me throughout our long and strenuous negotiations with Harry Ferguson,
but due, perhaps, to a milk diet, but more likely to the rugged-
ness and longevity of my Scottish ancestors, I soon regained
my usual good health.

I fell ill, however, in the early fall of 1955, and was feeling
under the weather throughout a trip to the U.S.S.R., and subsequently to France and Spain. I therefore cancelled my air
passage from France, and returned to New York, on the S.S.

Liberty, hoping that the rest would be helpful. The sea trip, however, did not improve matters and I cabled my Toronto doctors to meet me at my home on my arrival in the late afternoon of November 30th, 1955.

Arrangements had been made for me to address a large gathering of our organization at a dinner on the evening of my arrival. It had always been my custom to address as many of our executives as possible on my return from distant trips so as to keep them in touch with the developments taking place, and to acquaint them with the policies we were pursuing. On this occasion, however, my doctors would not hear of it, and I was ordered to bed suffering from phlebitis. I remained there for over three weeks.

This was about the only time throughout my long career with the Company that my health had ever interfered with my work schedule or attendance at my office. Unfortunately, over the next seven months or so it was not going to be the last.

24

The Parting of the Ways

NINETEEN FIFTY-FIVE was to be the last full year during which I presided over the destinies of our Company.

When one considers that we were still being adversely affected, particularly in the United States, by the three-year-old recession, the results we obtained in 1955 were most gratifying.

Our world-wide sales had reached a record level of $367 million. Excluding our defence production, which was rapidly declining, our increase in sales over the preceding year was approximately 14.6%.

Our net earnings after taxes on a world-wide basis amounted to approximately $12.6 million which was approximately 41% higher than the comparable figure of 1954.

One is apt to forget how seriously the farmers of North America suffered during the recession. In 1955, the prices received by them for the sale of their produce dropped a further five percent after having fallen thirteen percent during the two previous years.

In Canada, there were signs of improvement, but the farmers had not yet recovered from the disasters of 1954 when unwieldy grain surpluses and excessive rain and rust cost them an estimated $400 million in revenue.

Conditions in the United States in 1955 were not conducive to increased volume of sales. The net realized farm income for 1955 declined approximately ten percent and yet our United States sales of regular goods showed an increase over the previous year of twelve percent. This spoke well for the wide acceptance of our product, and especially for the strength and aggressiveness of our sales and distributors organizations.

On the other hand, higher labour and material costs in the United States, together with stronger competition and the heavy expenses involved in our amalgamation, were continuing to take a heavy toll of our earning power. They would undoubtedly continue to do so until the recession had run its course.

On the other side of the Atlantic, conditions were generally favourable, especially in France where our sales exceeded those of the previous year by fifty percent. Meanwhile, throughout 1955, we continued to expand our manufacturing facilities to take care of the stepped-up demand forecast for 1956. Our French plant had been more than doubled since 1949 and further extensions were on the drawing boards. Our plant in Germany had been almost tripled in size, and those in the United Kingdom had been substantially increased, and now totalled approximately one million, three hundred thousand square feet. Since we had opened our second plant in Scotland, our volume there had multiplied approximately eight times.

In Britain, we secured approximately fifty percent of the total United Kingdom tractor business, both domestic and export, and our sales of combines, which at one time represented eighty percent of the total, continued to dominate the market by a large margin.

For a period of depression, then, we were giving a good account of ourselves. Our Company's performance was a clear demonstration of the wisdom of our policy of establishing manufacturing facilities in the United Kingdom, and enlarging and rehabilitating those in France and Germany.

Had we concentrated our industrial efforts in North America our Company, shorn of its traditional and lucrative exports to the sterling and other dollar-short areas, deprived of its opportunity of acquiring Harry Ferguson's business—as he would not have been interested in a company operating predominately in North America—and buffeted by three years of recession on this side of the Atlantic, would have been in deep trouble. Today, we would neither have been an international organization, nor to use the more modern terminology, a multinational one, but a relatively small organization operating largely on only one continent.

As is frequently the case in times of recession, we were carrying heavy inventories aggravated by our recent amalgamation, and energetic steps were being taken to reduce these. Beyond these measures, the size of our inventories was giving us no undue concern because the sovereign remedy to heavy inventories of manufactured goods and raw materials is increased sales, and by the end of 1955 our bankers, our competitors, and ourselves had all come to the conclusion that the tide was turning in our major markets. They and we believed that the recession had nearly spent itself and that we were on the threshold of a large pent-up demand for our equipment which would carry the Company forward to new heights of achievement, and go a long way towards solving our inventory problems in the process.

Furthermore, we had, over the years, been following the very conservative policy of setting to one side from our consolidated net earnings an inventory and contingency reserve, which in 1956 amounted to over twenty-four million dollars. On a large portion of this sum taxes on income had already been paid. Its purpose was to protect the Company against losses resulting from unusually heavy inventories, the closing of plants, or other unforeseen occurrences which are prone to take place in times of recession.

My health was continuing to deteriorate, and once again I was hospitalized. After I had recovered sufficiently my doctors recommended that I should go down to my home in Jamaica for a couple of weeks to recuperate in the warm sunshine of that pleasant island. This didn't work. I had another relapse on my arrival and as I was running a temperature of 104 degrees, Norman Appleton, the secretary of the Company, who was in contact with me over the phone, became alarmed and sent the Company's plane with Dr. Fletcher Sharp on board to bring me back to Toronto, where I was laid up until the end of March.

As the spring of 1956 approached, it became evident that

the industry's expectations of improved conditions in the early part of the year were going to be disappointed. In the United States the recession continued. Spring and summer demand for farm equipment dropped sharply, adding to our already heavy inventories.

This unexpected decrease in sales was largely due to uncertainties concerning produce prices, the government's farm program, and persistent drought in a number of important grain-growing areas. It was only in the fall of the year that the expected strong improvement became manifest, heralding a sustained demand which continued uninterrupted over the next ten years.

Meanwhile, our important British market was over-shadowed by restrictive legislative measures, poor growing conditions following an exceptionally hard winter, and labour difficulties affecting the production of Ferguson tractors. As a result, sales dropped twenty-four percent below those of the previous year, and inventories in the United Kingdom were unfavourably affected.

There were, however, encouraging signs. The upswing in farm-implement income throughout Canada was gathering strength from month to month. The unfavourable conditions prevailing in the United Kingdom were obviously seasonal. Sales and profits in France were spectacular, and isolated signs of improving conditions in the United States were showing up. All of this justified our opinion that we were witnessing the last phase of the three-and-a-half-year-old recession.

This view was shared by our bankers. George Moore, chairman of the First National City Bank, who was in close touch with the farm-implement industry of the United States was optimistic. I spent the morning with him in New York in early April, 1956, and, after reviewing our situation in detail, he and the vice-president of the Irving Trust agreed without hesitation to my request for a line of credit of $45 million for the following twelve-month period.

My only serious concern was whether I would regain my usual good health in time to bring the Company the kind of leadership required to take full advantage of the improving situation. Of my ultimate recovery I had no doubt. It was the timing that was giving me concern.

Unfortunately, in mid-April, I was hospitalized once again and underwent another operation which kept me away from business until May 14th.

Meanwhile, E. P. Taylor, somewhat unfamiliar with the actual operations of the farm-implement business, and growing panicky over the heavy inventories we were carrying, advanced the view that a massive price reduction was the only answer to a slow-moving inventory. I pointed out to him that in our case this would be applying the wrong remedy at the wrong time. Our inventory was heavy largely because agricultural conditions this spring had been more unfavourable than we had anticipated, and not because our product was less acceptable. Furthermore, we were preparing an exceptionally strong sales campaign to take advantage of the greatly improved conditions we expected would take place in the fall, and much of our heavy inventory would be lightened as a result.

The effect of price cutting in our industry is unfailingly nullified by competitive retaliation unless justified by outdated or defective equipment. With the exception of the odd line, this was not our case in 1956.

Although I was in close personal touch with our sales organization both in Canada and the United States, I did not wish to be arbitrary and I told Taylor that since he was worrying about it, I would convene a meeting of our senior sales executives in the United States and Canada to consider the situation once again, just as soon as I was able to leave the hospital.

This was duly arranged. At the conclusion of the conference, everyone, excepting Al Thornbrough, expressed the view that across-the-board price cuts would be exceedingly costly and damaging to our credit; nor would they produce the required results. In any event, it was agreed, price-cutting was not called for in view of the improved fall prospects.

I would have liked to carry our executive vice-president's approval but his experience in our business had not until very recently brought him into close contact with the sales activities of the Company. I felt that the unanimous view expressed by all our senior sales executives in North America, including those of Herb Bloom, our senior vice-president and director of the Company, should not be disregarded.

Further, I was under the impression that Thornbrough's

views were, in some measure at least, influenced by those of Taylor, or vice-versa, as I was given to understand that Taylor had held discussions with him on the matter when I was in hospital.

Following my usual custom, I discussed the conclusions of our meeting with Eric Phillips, who fully agreed with the majority decision. When I pointed out to him that this would probably involve a clash with Taylor, he answered that I need not worry about it as he was seeing him that afternoon, and would inform him that, as chairman of our executive committee, he approved of the decision taken.

Over the past decade I had found myself in frequent opposition to some of Phillips' and Taylor's objectives. These differences had, however, been largely confined to dividend policies, relationships with Argus, or the composition of our board. I could live with these issues; but when, during my absence in hospital, although I remained available for discussion over the phone, they began to interfere with the commercial policies of the Company, and to undermine my authority by discussing policy with members of my staff, I determined that we had come to the parting of the ways.

The issue of the across-the-board price reduction was the first in which an attempt had been made to interfere with the commercial policies of the business. I made up my mind that I would make no compromise on this issue. I had no valid choice in the matter. It was obvious that I could not effectively discharge my functions as chairman and president of the organization if my judgement and that of my experienced senior executives was to be seriously challenged, or if disaffection on the part of any of my executives was to be encouraged.

Until a few years before, I had always dealt with men who shared my values—men like Harry Gundy, John Tory, Gordon Leitch, Tommy Russell, and my own senior executives. Now I found myself faced with some whose values were no longer mine, and I was growing weary of the situation.

Much that was fanciful has been said and written about my departure from the Company in June, 1956. The facts, however, are simple.

The Taylor group had acquired financial control and felt, no doubt with some justification, that they were entitled to a more direct say in the management of the Company and its relations with Argus.

I, on the other hand, believed that my primary responsibility and loyalty must always be to the Company, to its thousands of small and medium shareholders, to its staff, and its traditions, and not simply to one large shareholding group.

The Taylor group wished to establish closer ties with Argus. I considered this to be disadvantageous to the Company.

They wanted more docile management, appointed by and fully responsible to themselves. I obviously did not fit into this picture.

The much discussed issues of price cutting, inventories, and organization were merely the excuse. Had it not been these issues, others would have been found to take their place.

There was no time for niceties. By the end of June it was becoming obvious that the recession was all but over and that we were on the threshold of a great demand for our product. The occasion of my ill health, which was temporary, and the low point of the recession were not to be by-passed by the Taylor-Phillips group. It is not easy to dislodge management when all is going well!

When Phillips came to see me on June 25, 1956, at my home where I was still laid up, I was neither surprised nor disconcerted when he informed me that, owing to my ill health, he and his colleagues had reluctantly come to the conclusion that it would be unfair to me and, if my health did not improve, unfair to the Company were I to continue to assume the heavy responsibilities of the chairmanship and presidency of the Company.

Owing to my unchallenged authority within the Company, my intimate knowledge of every phase of business throughout the world, and the extraordinary loyalty which I enjoyed from the executives and personnel of the organization, he believed an incoming president would never be able to develop into a top independent operator if I remained in the organization.

He had, therefore, decided, with the concurrence of his colleagues, to take on the chairmanship himself, "with the greatest possible reluctance, but strictly for one year only."

They knew me well enough, he said, to realize I would never be happy in the position of a chairman without responsibility, and he added, "Our group is absolutely opposed to the principle of the chairman being the senior executive officer of the Company. Under these circumstances, we felt that you would not wish to remain on the board." His assumption was quite correct.

Things had worked out as I expected they would. Six weeks prior to this interview, I had set forth the only conditions under which I was prepared to remain as chairman, president, and senior executive officer of the Company. One of these was that there should be no further interference with the commercial policies of the Company after these had been agreed upon by the chairman of the executive committee and myself.

I outlined the conditions under which I was prepared to resign, without resorting to a proxy fight which I was loath to contemplate because it would be injurious to the Company and incompatible with the state of my health at the time.

As the financial settlement worked out between us was adequate, I immediately tendered my resignation.

It is an amusing footnote to this conversation that Eric readily overcame his "absolute opposition to the principle of the chairman being the senior executive officer of the Company," by assuming this dual responsibility less than a week after my conversation with him, and continuing in this position until his premature death several years subsequently.

At this stage I was much more interested in the effect of my resignation on the immediate future of the Company and its personnel than in the manner in which it affected me. I strongly urged Eric Phillips to make as few changes as possible during the early months of the take-over. To this he agreed whole-heartedly, but did quite the contrary.

Whereas I was entirely confident that under my continuing leadership the effects of the recession could be readily overcome, and that by the fall of 1956 we would resume our rapid growth and expanding profitability, I was seriously concerned about what might take place if the organization became greatly disturbed.

I enquired of Eric what steps he proposed to take to appoint a president. In his opinion, there was no one in the Company at the present time capable of assuming the presidency, and his group had arrived at the conclusion that they should hire an American whom they had already interviewed, and who was occupying a top position in the motor-car industry. "We feel," he went on, "that we should finalize our arrangements with him and make him president right away. He proposes to bring with him twenty members of his staff."

I told him that I disagreed fundamentally with this concept, and that I could not conceive of a plan better calculated to wreck the Company than to bring in an inexperienced president, unfamiliar with the farm-machinery business, together with a staff of inexperienced assistants. I don't know whether my protest was effective or not, but two days afterwards Eric came back to tell me that he had given up the idea and that no appointment for the presidency would be made for the time being.

This episode was an example of the conflict which seems to occur more frequently these days between the company executive conversant with the business, dedicated to the organization which he has helped to create and has been serving over the years, to all its shareholders, and to its staff who have co-operated in building it up, and, on the other hand, a financial group owning a controlling interest in the Company.

Following our meeting of June 25th, the question of how my departure from the Company was to be presented to the public and to our own organization arose. I would have preferred to make a statement to the press that I was severing my connection with the Company owing to a disagreement on policy, but it was felt that it would be more readily accepted by the public and the organization if I related my departure to the state of my health. I recognized the validity of this point of view, especially insofar as our staff was concerned, and I prepared a release to the press which was accepted by all concerned. Although it was understood by all of us that my statement was a half-truth, it was agreed that we would all stand by it in the future, and that no other explanation relating to my departure from the Company would be given out either privately or publicly.

In due course, my press release[1] was carried in the majority of the dailies and weeklies throughout Canada. It was also given

[1] Appendix

wide coverage in the United States and the United Kingdom, and sent to all our senior executives.

On the morning of July 6th, 1956, although I was still running a temperature, I went down to my office to address all our vice-presidents and senior members of the staff, to inform them of my resignation, and the official reasons for it before this became public knowledge. At the end of my address to them, I made a statement which was uppermost in my mind, and which ran as follows:

Perhaps my deepest regret is that I am leaving you all. It has been a wonderfully successful association, based on hard work, mutual appreciation, respect and good fellowship.

We have worked together as a team striving successfully towards a common objective. We have been proud of what we have achieved, and we have had a lot to be proud about.

You have always been splendidly loyal to me, and I have tried to reciprocate.

From tomorrow onwards the Company will operate under new management. Col. Phillips will become chairman of the board, and chief executive officer.

I know you all well enough to realize that the news of my resignation will be a disappointment to you, but I would like to say in closing that although I am no longer connected with the Company I will continue to have its best interests before me, and if each one of you could find it in your hearts to continue on as you are doing and give the new management the same support which you have always so generously given to me, it would make me very happy indeed.

At 10:00 a.m. on the same day I took the chair at our board meeting where the documents in connection with my resignation were duly ratified. This was the last episode in my career with the Company which had started almost half a century before.

I left with regret but without bitterness. For forty-six years I had served the Company with unquestioning devotion, and I was at ease in my own mind. Others might have done better, but at least I had always done my best. I felt, in leaving my office for the last time, that the Company presidents who preceded me would not have been dissatisfied with what had been accomplished.

Arthur Meighen, probably the greatest intellect and certainly the finest exponent of the English language ever to occupy the prime ministership of Canada, said in his farewell speech in 1927, when he withdrew from public life, "Now that I stand apart after nearly two decades of heavy responsibility, there is a conviction within me which means a great deal. I can look in the face of all the world who care to listen, and say that there was no falsity or faltering. There is no matter over which I want to make petition. The book can be closed, and I am content."

I knew Meighen well and admired him greatly. The thoughts running through my mind, as I left the Company, were the same as his, but he expressed them with greater eloquence than I could have aspired to.

After saying good-bye to my secretaries and wishing them well I got into my car and was driven to my home on Highland Avenue, where my wife was waiting for me on the doorstep. My doctors were also there; they ordered me to bed, where I stayed until my temperature returned to normal ten days or so later.

My wife, who had been worrying considerably over my health, was relieved that the burden of responsibility which I had been carrying for so many years was lifted from my shoulders. We both turned with zest and enthusiasm to the plans we had formulated for the future and which we had never had the leisure to carry out.

25

The Aftermath

I WAS REASONABLY AT EASE about the future of the Company
because I had confidence in Eric Phillips' undoubted ability and
the undertaking he had given me that he would make no important changes in the personnel of the organization, during
the early stages of his management.

Within a few days of his take-over, however, a ruthless
purge of senior Massey-Harris executives took place. H. H.
Bloom was first to go. His departure was followed by the resignation or dismissal of a large group of executives including Ed
Burgess, the dynamic vice-president in charge of manufacturing; Norman Appleton, the experienced, able, and loyal secretary of the parent company; the comptroller; the sales manager
of our Canadian operations; the executive vice-president of our
North American company; his manufacturing manager; his
general sales manager; and many others too numerous to mention. Most of them were members of the managerial team, men
of proven ability and experience.

It is always difficult to understand other people's motiva-
tions; I have always assumed that much of what took place was
the result of the undue haste and lack of preparation for the
take-over.

The new management had had little opportunity to appreciate the value of the men who had served our Company so long and so well; they, on their part, perhaps showed resentment at the action which had been taken.

All this could have been avoided had Phillips listened to the advice I gave him at the time of the appointment of Al Thornbrough to the position of executive vice-president in October of 1955.

I was saddened that so many of my old colleagues were no longer with the Company, but nearly all were snapped up by our competitors. I was grateful to note that some were appointed to positions senior to those they had held with us. I rejoiced in the knowledge of their success in other fields of endeavour, where their abilities and experience, and their prestige as members of the successful Massey-Harris executive team were recognized and rewarded.

To cite one example, Cecil Milne, who had successfully assumed senior responsibility for our important defence work in the United States, and subsequently became the executive vice-president of our American organization was appointed to the highly responsible position of Assistant Under-Secretary of the Navy (Procurement) under the Eisenhower government.

Reorganization, in my opinion, should always be approached with patience and discernment. The new pattern may look splendid on a chart but, if too hastily or ruthlessly undertaken, it may well affect the spirit and morale of an organization, and create confusion and disorder.

No company can overnight divest itself of a large group of able and experienced executives without serious repercussions. Our North American companies were no exception to this rule.

Fortunately, the eastern hemisphere group, operating out of London, required people with specialized knowledge of languages, habits, and customs of the foreign countries in which they were operating. This was uncertain ground for the new management, inexperienced as they were in European affairs. Consequently, the purge which had decimated the North American operations did not take place to the same extent in Europe; the operation of this very important division was less affected and the careful balance of experienced Massey-Harris and Ferguson men which I considered to be so essential was largely preserved.

I will refrain from comment on other events that took place after my departure. Many things were done which I would have done differently but my advice was not sought and my responsibility was not involved.

As had been foreseen, the fall of 1956 heralded a period of unparalleled prosperity for both the farmer and the industry. Over the next ten years or so, sales volumes and profits reached unprecedented heights. This was the golden era in North America and in many other parts of the world for both the farmer and the implement industry.

Our chief competitor, for instance—Deere & Co., from whom we had wrested the second ranking world position a couple of years before, and who had regained it—saw their sales soar from $313 million in 1956 to $1,062,000,000 in 1966, and their net profits rise during the same period from $20 million to $78.7 million.

As was bound to happen, the new management came under considerable pressure, from within the organization and from without, to explain more fully the reasons for my departure and that of so many of my executives. People simply did not understand why an organization which had been so conspicuously successful over the past twenty-odd years should suddenly have allegedly gone into reverse, nor why so many of our outstanding executives, well known in manufacturing, sales, engineering, and labour relations, had suddenly been caused to leave the Company.

I was far from being unknown throughout Canada. I was a director of many of the largest Canadian enterprises. My government and public service had kept me in the public eye. Only a month before my resignation, I was chosen by the National Sales Executive Club of the U.S.A. as Canada's Businessman of the Year.

It was no doubt all very disconcerting and embarrassing to my successors. People began to wonder and to question whether my much publicized release to the press told the full story. The press besieged me with questions about my resignation. I refused to discuss the matter and simply referred them to the press release which I had made on the day of my resignation.

If the Company had followed the same policy—as they had agreed to do—the whole thing would have no doubt blown over, but harassed by awkward questions, they made statements designed to leave the impression that they had been reluctantly obliged to step into the picture in order to save this great Canadian company from bankruptcy.

No one who was informed took this seriously, least of all myself. I was content to rest on the Company's record and my own.

Massey-Harris has always been a part of my life and is still. I have watched its progress over the years with interest, and generally with approval.

Its strength continues to lie in its world-wide export business which has always been its greatest asset, and was my greatest concern. Its weakness is in its relatively small share of the great American market just as it was in my time, but progress until the recent recession is being made in both fields.

As a strong believer in a tight and uncomplicated form of organization, I am opposed to extravagance and I have reservations concerning a multiplicity of functions and of titles. They cost money and, when in times of recession they require to be dismantled, the process is both painful to management and disheartening to the staff. Having led the Company through three depressions, I have always been opposed to making optimistic statements concerning the future, and particularly to forecasting earnings.

Management consultants notwithstanding, I am not a believer in the excessive use of charts. They look well on paper, but if too frequently used, tend to demoralize those on the lowest levels, or those who don't, in the eyes of management, rate high enough to be on the charts at all.

Over the past twelve or thirteen years, noteworthy progress has been made both in North America and abroad. The Company has kept pace with the great developments which have taken place in the economies of most of the countries throughout the world.

Decisions have been taken which were sound, imaginative,

and courageous, and they have brought the Company strength and vitality.

As I write these words, the Company is suffering from one of these recurring periods of recession which have always bedevilled the farm equipment industry. Sales are hard to come by, and increased competition is cutting into profit margins. Inventories and receivables are high, both in the Company's hands and in those of their distributors. Strikes are taking their heavy toll, factories are operating well below capacity, and earnings are being drastically affected.

As they say in French, "Plus ça change, plus c'est la même chose," but I am confident, as I was in 1955 and 1956, that these difficulties, although much more distressing, will be overcome and that, when the recession is over, Massey-Ferguson, chastened and strengthened by its management's first experience of a serious recession, will continue to grow and to maintain its proud record as a great Canadian institution.

26

New Horizons

IN JULY OF 1956, for the first time in my life, I found myself, at the age of sixty-three, with leisure and the chance to make my own plans for the future. I rather enjoyed it. My wife and I spent many agreeable hours arranging the priorities of the things which we wished to do. The first among these was to take the children to Europe for two months' vacation.

Our plans did not work out; Dr. Farquharson would not hear of it. Under no circumstances, he said, should I travel abroad until I had fully recovered. Instead, he proposed that I should go to my fishing camp in Quebec for a short holiday.

Ten days in the woods, far removed from all the trappings of civilization, with no human beings within miles other than my own family and the French-Canadian guide, did wonders for my health and spirits.

Our log cabin was rough but comfortable in a primitive sort of way. My guide had supervised its construction and the trees of the forest had supplied the raw materials. It possessed no bathroom, no gas or electricity, and best of all, no telephone.

We bathed in the soft brown waters of Lake McCracken; I shaved on the shore in the early morning sun with the aid of a small mirror nailed to an overhanging silver birch. We caught a lot of speckled trout. I shot the odd partridge. My son Jimmie went bear hunting and my wife, who is clever at many things, prepared the most delectable meals on a primitive wood-fired stove. She adored doing this.

Even in August the nights were cool, and of an evening we would gather around the great stone fireplace, watching the huge logs burning brightly in the hearth, while our guide, an accomplished woodsman, sang *habitant* songs, accompanying himself on a guitar, which he handled with dexterity.

Back in Toronto again I sat in at several conferences with a number of my friends who were active in the organization of a large gathering to be held at St. Andrew's-by-the-Sea, to consider the important subject of engineering and technical education. I was being urged to take on the chairmanship, and finally agreed to do so.

It involved a lot of work, the reading of numerous papers and reports on a subject with which I was not too familiar. In the early part of September I left for the Algonquin Hotel at St. Andrew's-by-the-Sea, where a very large group of educationalists, engineers, technicians, and university leaders had assembled.

The conference was not only well attended, but highly successful, and out of it grew the Exploratory Committee for the Advancement of Education of which I was later prevailed upon to accept the chairmanship.

To recuperate from these activities, my doctors suggested that I should return to Boisclair, since my short stay there had been so beneficial. Accordingly, in the third week of September, my wife and I, accompanied by our family, left once more for our fishing lodge.

The weather was beautiful, although occasional snow flurries in the evenings would remind us that the winter in this north country was not far away.

The days, however, were delightfully warm and we swam and fished in Lake McCracken to our heart's content. In the early mornings, before the sun had warmed the air, and in the chill of the evenings, a mist would rise from the warm waters of the lake, and the bay which surrounded our fishing lodge would be shrouded in an eerie haze from which only the upper branches of the forest trees would emerge.

It was time to return to Toronto. We left reluctantly. The Indian summer was at its best and the trees, clothed in their autumn foliage, and shining in the morning sun, were unbelievably beautiful.

We crossed the river in a large, red-painted wooden barge. As we drew up to the shore on the Ontario side, Valois, the owner of the Valois Lodge, came down to meet us, excitedly calling out to me, as I was stepping ashore, that Premier Leslie Frost had been trying to get me on the phone for two days and had left messages asking me to call him without delay. A plane, he went on, was standing by to fly me to Toronto.

As we were unloading our luggage, I reminded Valois that I had no phone at my fishing lodge and asked why he had not sent out a runner to advise me of Premier Frost's request. "I did," he replied, "but a mother bear with her two cubs was on the trail, and wouldn't allow the boy to get by. He made several attempts," Valois said, "but the bear became so menacing that he took fright and ran half way back to the river."

I called up Mr. Frost as soon as I reached the Valois Lodge. He asked me to fly to Queen's Park without delay as he wished to see me on an important matter. I explained that I had all my family with me, and preferred to drive to Toronto, but added that if he didn't object to my going to his office in my fishing outfit, I could be with him by 1:30 in the afternoon. He grumbled a little at this, having a luncheon engagement, but he agreed to cancel it and wait for me in his office.

When I got there, the Premier told me that Richard Hearn, the distinguished Chairman of Ontario Hydro, had resigned, that the position was in many respects second only to his in importance in Ontario, and that, from a political point of view, it was most desirable that it be filled as quickly as possible and by an executive of broad administrative experience whose appointment would be well received by the people of Ontario. Dick Hearn and those of his Cabinet colleagues whom he had consulted, he went on to say, were unanimous in their views that I was the man for the job. He asked me to accept the chairmanship, adding that he hoped he would be in a position to make the announcement in the House in the following week.

I should have felt flattered, but I didn't. I told the Premier that my health was still giving me some concern, that I had always been an independent operator, and shrank from a civil service appointment, however exalted it might be, and that I did not wish to get tied down to any full-time responsibility as I had other plans in mind.

I turned down the Premier's proposal for these reasons. He does not accept defeat easily however and I finally agreed to withhold my decision until I had discussed the matter with the outgoing Chairman.

I had no intention of changing my mind, but a number of influential Canadians—no doubt emissaries of the Premier—called at my home during the weekend. All urged me to take on the chairmanship as a matter of public service.

Dick Hearn described in considerable detail the wide-ranging activities of the organization. Ontario Hydro was big business indeed. It ranked with the leading electrical utilities of the world as well as being the largest in Canada, and was only exceeded by one in the United States. He enlarged on the financial and other problems which the organization was facing over the next few years, and assured me that if I would take on the job I would receive the full support of the organization and the government.

I have always thrived on problems, and the more Dick Hearn told me of the difficulties attendant on the vast expansion Ontario Hydro was facing over the next few years, the more interested I became. I decided that same evening, therefore, with the whole-hearted approval of my wife, that I would accept the Premier's offer of the chairmanship for a limited period.

No financial consideration influenced my decision. Although the salary attached to the chairmanship at that time was the highest paid for any governmental post in Ontario, it bore no relationship to salaries earned in industry. This aspect of the job was unimportant.

I called on Premier Frost and accepted the chairmanship for a maximum period of two years on the understanding that, although responsible to him personally, I would be in sole charge of the administration of the Commission, that no government pressure would be brought to bear on me about the appointment of personnel, or any other matter dealing with the administration of the Commission, by any members of the government.

Premier Frost accepted these conditions. Throughout my four-and-a-half-year term of office, no attempt was ever made either by himself, or any other member of the government, to interfere with any of my prerogatives.

I found myself, however, faced with a difficulty I had not foreseen. Premier Frost pointed out that unless I resigned from all my directorships to avoid "conflict of interest," I would lay myself open to constant criticism from members of the legislature and others, which would no doubt be painful to me and might reflect adversely on Ontario Hydro and his government.

I had accepted the position as a public service and because I had become interested in the challenge. I felt, therefore, that I would have to go all the way. With great reluctance I resigned from all the boards which could in any way conflict with the interests of Ontario Hydro.

It was agreed that I would be appointed officially on November 1st. This gave me a little over three weeks to wind up some of the interests I had taken on, resign from the various boards, squeeze in an interesting visit to Montreal and Quebec City, and address gatherings in Montreal, Winnipeg, and Toronto, whose invitations I had previously accepted.

I also put in a good deal of time answering the very large number of letters of regret I had received on the announcement of my resignation from Massey-Harris-Ferguson. They came from all parts of the world, from employees, from agents, from Ministers of the Crown, from British leaders and from competitors. All expressed the bewilderment and the deep regret of the writers.

On November 1st, 1956, I attended a meeting in the Lieutenant-Governor's suite at Queen's Park, where, in the presence of the Hon. Louis O. Breithaupt, Premier Frost, and several members of his Cabinet, I was officially sworn in.

The appointment was well received by the press throughout Canada.

On the day I was sworn in, the ambassador for the U.S.S.R., Aroutounian, who was making his first official visit to Toronto, joined a few of our friends at a dinner I gave for him at our home. He was a Georgian and very helpful to me when, a few years later, I made an extended tour throughout the Southern Republics of the U.S.S.R.

After dinner, he brought up the subject of his reception at City Hall by Mayor Phillips, the "mayor of all the people." His pride had been hurt. It happened this way.

As he was signing the guest book, the mayor asked him to pronounce his name. The ambassador pronounced it—A-rou-tu-nian. Mayor Phillips, in his jocular way, replied, "Well we can't pronounce that. We'll just have to call you Rootin Toot-in," and laughed vigorously at his own joke.

The Ambassador was not amused. The great Soviet Union had been slighted. I told him—in vain— that this was only intended as a joke, and that our mayor's sense of humour was at times somewhat unorthodox. I agreed that his joke wasn't all that funny, but added that the mayor had not intended to be disrespectful. Aroutounian was not fully appeased. His diplomatic feathers had been ruffled.

The dinner party had a sequel.

The first caller at my new office on the 15th floor of the Hydro building, the next morning, was a member of the Royal Canadian Mounted Police. His visit was merely a formality, he said, but he knew that the Russian ambassador had dined with me on the previous evening, and wondered if there was any special significance to be attached to the matter. I was impressed by this efficiency, but explained that I had been received warmly during a trip to Russia, and that I was merely repaying the hospitality that had been so generously offered to me in the ambassador's own country, and that his dining with me had no political significance.

My first impressions of Ontario Hydro were excellent. I liked what I saw and I knew from the very beginning that I was going to get along well with the executives and the other members of the staff to whom I had been introduced. They seemed to me to be an absolutely first-class group of men, and throughout the four-and-a-half years I spent with Hydro I never found reason to change my mind. I sensed immediately that an atmosphere of good will, loyalty, and of common endeavours permeated the whole organization just as it had in

Massey-Harris until a short time before. It made me feel very much at home. Executives and staff gave me a heart-warming welcome.

Most of the previous chairmen had been leading engineers steeped in the skills of design, construction, and distribution. Some had left their mark on the history of Ontario, of Canada, and indeed of many countries where hydro-electric power was produced and distributed.

I sensed, however, that those senior executives with whom I came in contact were looking forward to working under the leadership of one whose experience was in an entirely different field, and whose contribution would be that of an executive who had spent his life building up an organization on a world-wide scale. They felt, I believe, that I would bring with me to Ontario Hydro the fresh approach of an outsider.

At all events, no group of men was ever more loyal or more co-operative to a leader than they proved to be, and it is perhaps for this reason, more than any other, that I remained with Hydro much longer than I had agreed to do, and that the four-and-a-half-years I spent with it were among the happiest in my business career.

I was embarrassed when, shortly after assuming the chairmanship, I had a recurrence of my previous trouble and was taken to hospital where I underwent a third operation.

Two weeks afterwards my doctors allowed me to get up to attend a dinner given by my friend H. M. Turner, in honour of the outgoing and incoming chairmen of Ontario Hydro. I would indeed have felt badly if I had not been present to pay tribute to Dick Hearn, my predecessor, who throughout the years had made a valuable contribution to Ontario Hydro and to many other public utilities both in Canada and abroad.

Together with Dr. Otto Holden, a man of great ability and charm, and one who was internationally known as a leading hydro-electric engineer, I travelled to Cornwall to visit the site and the preliminary construction of the St. Lawrence Power Project and its ancillary structures which, in partnership with the United States, we were building on the St. Lawrence River.

Ontario Hydro was responsible for the Canadian half of this spectacular engineering project, while the Americans under

the leadership of Robert Moses, the distinguished and controversial New York Parks Commissioner—to mention but one of
his numerous responsibilities—were in charge of the American
half.

Those late December days during which we visited the St.
Lawrence project were intensely cold. Snow was falling, glacial
winds were blowing, and the temperature had dropped to below zero. The flowing waters of the St. Lawrence, with ice
gathering along the shore and around the concrete structures,
seemed to make the cold feel colder still.

But these untoward weather conditions could not dull the
enthusiasm I felt for this great project, nor my satisfaction in
the thought that I was to become associated with it.

It was on this note that 1956 drew to a close. It had been an
interesting year crowded with dramatic events, during which I
had been under the weather, had severed my connection with
the organization with which I had spent most of my life, and
finished up as Chairman of Ontario Hydro, fascinated by the
unfolding opportunities which lay before me, and looking forward to my new career with enthusiasm and satisfaction.

My term of office with the Commission, always referred to
as Ontario Hydro, coincided with several of the most eventful
periods of the long and colourful history of this great organization. I was not responsible for them. They merely came to fruition or were embarked upon during my chairmanship.

When I joined the organization, it was deeply involved in
converting a major part of the entire system from twenty-five
to sixty-cycle frequency. This operation, which took ten years
to complete, was the largest of its kind ever undertaken in the
world.

It involved the transformation of our own equipment, and
of millions of items in use in homes and factories as well. It was
a triumph of organization and planning. A maximum of 3,600
men and 1,300 vehicles were engaged in the task, and on the
average over the entire ten-year period, six appliances were converted every minute of the regular working day. The cost was
over $352 million.

When I first became associated with Ontario Hydro, by far the largest amount of the power generated came from the falling waters captured from the numerous fast-flowing rivers of southern Ontario. Niagara Falls was the most outstanding among these.

The St. Lawrence Power Development, however, tapped the last major source of cheap hydraulic power in southern Ontario, and our engineers turned their eyes towards the undeveloped potential of our rivers in the wilderness of the far north, the James Bay area.

The problem was how to carry this potential power from these remote northern rivers to the densely populated areas of southern Ontario at a lesser cost than power produced by coal-fired plants. The solution was to be found in the complicated process of transmitting a larger flow of power over higher voltage lines. High priority was therefore given to the complex experimental work involved, and finally the feasibility of this project was satisfactorily established.

In the course of time, the first extra-high voltage towers which were to carry this yet untapped power to southern Ontario were erected, four to a mile, on the frozen muskeg of northern Ontario, by crews clad in special Arctic clothing. In the vanguard, an army of slashers cut a right of way approximately 220 feet wide through dense areas of spruce, jack-pine, poplars, and birch.

The first hundred miles of this right of way was covered almost entirely with muskeg, as deep as thirteen feet, and impassable excepting in winter when, with up to fifty degrees of frost, the ground was frozen solid. In some sections, eighty feet of piling had to be driven in to secure a firm footing for the tower foundations.

It was a titanic task. Temporary roads had to be built, bridges constructed across swamps, boggy areas, and small streams. Sixty-five tons of fabricated material had to be handled for every mile of line. The construction force was housed in temporary Arctic buildings all along the right of way.

Supplying the construction force posed a staggering problem. Trucks, aircraft, helicopters, and specially designed wide-track muskeg vehicles were pressed into service.

As I write, this mammoth project has been completed. Toronto is linked to the James Bay area, a distance of 440 miles, by an extra-high voltage, 500-kilovolt transmission line, the performance of which is living up to our earlier expectation.

The cost of the entire project was approximately $200 million. It is only the forerunner of further developments along similar lines.

Another event of great and lasting importance was the construction of Canada's first nuclear power plant on the shores of the Ottawa River. This was carried out in co-operation with Canadian General Electric and Atomic Energy of Canada Ltd., whose scientific and research departments had for many years grappled with the problems of designing an effective natural uranium-fueled heavy-water-moderated power reactor. It was only a small unit, generating 20,000 kilowatts of electricity, but it was the important forerunner, the prototype of the vast expansion in nuclear-powered plants which was to take place in Ontario.

Probably the most colourful event that marked my tenure of office was the building at Cornwall, in conjunction with the power authority of the State of New York, of one of the then largest power plants in the world, which stretched all the way across the St. Lawrence River and drew power from the International Rapids section of the St. Lawrence. The cost of this undertaking was in the neighbourhood of $600 million and its total capacity exceeded 1,800,000 kilowatts.

The construction of the St. Lawrence power plant, with its attendant upstream structures, proved to be one of the great engineering and social undertakings of our time. It involved the flooding of approximately 38,000 acres of which 20,000 were on the Canadian side of the river, and the creation of a body of water subsequently named Lake St. Lawrence, which covered an area of approximately 100 square miles.

This resulted in the submergence of seven-and-a-half villages, some of them quite important, and 225 farms. In turn, it involved the relocation and rebuilding of these villages, and of nine schools, fourteen churches, four shopping centers, ninety-six multiple-dwelling units, five municipal and public buildings, the construction of 349 homes and the moving of 525 others, which were picked up by special lift trucks built for this purpose, and deposited on foundations prepared for them in the new villages.

Dykes, waterworks, sewage treatment plants, roads, highways, double-track railways, had to be built, and all the services for the new communities from telephones to paved streets and sidewalks had also to be assured.

It was a mammoth task, larger than anything of its kind ever undertaken in Canada. It called for a great expenditure of money. More important still, it required the exercise of a high degree of diplomacy and co-operation with the inhabitants of the flooded areas, the majority of whom did not relish the thought of losing their homes, their farms, their schools, and their churches, notwithstanding that Ontario Hydro strove to rebuild these, retaining where desired the original design, and assured these citizens that no financial loss would be suffered by anyone.

One of the most baffling, controversial, and time-consuming problems was the relocation of cemeteries, of which there were eighteen of different denominations in the area.

On the American side, the problem was, fortunately, much less staggering because their 18,000 acres of flooded land was sparsely populated and included no villages.

This vast engineering and rehabilitation program stirred the imagination and awoke the interest not only of the peoples of the United States and Canada, but of those living in distant countries. Hundreds of thousands of visitors (1,800,000 during 1958 and '59 alone) were conducted to the points of interest by thoroughly trained Ontario Hydro guides attached to our information services set up in Cornwall for this purpose.

Special tours were organized at Ontario Hydro's expense to enable political, financial, and industrial leaders from the U.S.A. and Canada to see for themselves the magnitude of the operations involved. The manner in which these throngs of visitors to the St. Lawrence valley were taken care of was a triumph of organization.

As the project advanced towards completion, I was beset by the problem of receiving numerous important delegations from the United States and from abroad, and of outstanding individual visitors such as former Presidents Hoover and Truman, His Royal Highness Prince Bernhard of the Netherlands, Governor Harriman and Governor Rockefeller of New York, prime ministers and premiers from various countries including our own, members of the Senate and House of Representatives from the United States, and from our own Senate and House of Commons. It was all very interesting, but great inroads were made upon my time.

By far the most colourful event was the visit by Her Majesty Queen Elizabeth II, and His Royal Highness Prince Philip on June 27th, 1959.

Accompanied by George Hees, federal Minister of Transport, Her Majesty Queen Elizabeth, and Prince Philip sailed up the St. Lawrence Seaway on the Royal Yacht *Britannia*, and were received officially at the Eisenhower Lock by Vice-President Richard M. Nixon and Mrs. Nixon, Governor Nelson Rockefeller, and Premier Leslie M. Frost and Mrs. Frost.

After a brief reception on the American side, the party proceeded to the center of the powerhouse structure for the unveiling ceremony. At this point, I presented to the Queen, Prince Philip and Mr. and Mrs. Nixon a number of our senior Hydro officials. After the usual round of speeches, I called on Her Majesty to unveil a great block of black granite placed on the headworks of the power dam, at the dividing line between our two countries. On the smooth surface of the block, the following words were carved:

> This stone bears witness to the common purpose of two nations, whose frontiers are the frontiers of friendship, whose ways are the ways of freedom, and whose works are the works of peace.

It was our hope that those who read these simple words in the years and the generations to come would be conscious of the co-operation, understanding and good-will between the two nations which had presided over the building of the St. Lawrence Power Project.

Contrary to what I had expected, the chairmanship involved a considerable amount of travelling in connection with inspection trips to our various power plants throughout Ontario, and to annual meetings and other important gatherings of the municipalities, our valued partners in the development of Ontario Hydro. I was also called on to make frequent trips abroad, in connection with atomic energy developments, or to meet our opposite numbers in the United States, England or France.

Although my recuperative powers have always been excellent, and I was persuaded that the ill health from which I had suffered during my last seven months with Massey-Harris-Ferguson was a thing of the past, I probably overdid it, and on my return from a very strenuous trip to England I was taken from the airport to the hospital with a blood clot in one of my lungs, and remained there for a period of three weeks. Dr. Pugsley, who was looking after me, recommended that I should curtail my activities and lead a quieter life, but I was never very good at accepting this kind of advice, and after five days' rest in Bermuda, I resumed my usual activities.

It was during this short visit to Bermuda, where my wife and I had never been before, that at her suggestion we decided to purchase a home on this charming island. Before we returned to Toronto we bought *Somerset House*, built in 1740 and beautifully located on high ground overlooking Hamilton Harbour and the surrounding bays and islands.

Our intention then was to use the house for short vacations in the spring or fall of the year. It never entered our thoughts at the time that this lovely old home would become our permanent residence.

One of the factors which gave me the most satisfaction while I was in office was the contribution our organization was making towards holding in check the upward spiral of inflation. In 1957 and again in 1958 and '59, I was able to point out in our annual reports that while the price of most articles of consumption, of labour, and of raw materials was rising on every side, electrical energy alone was delivered to the homes of the Province of Ontario at a lower average unit cost than that prevailing in 1940.

This unequalled performance was due to many causes. Important among these was that Ontario Hydro was a thoroughly well organized, efficient and hard-hitting organization which, while keeping salaries and wages at a high level, tolerated no extravagances in its set-up, and through its effective and im-

aginative research department kept its equipment in the forefront of every cost-reducing development. As was the case in
Massey-Harris in my time, Ontario Hydro never suffered from
the obsession for charts and complicated organizational patterns
so characteristic of organizations with rapid personnel turnover.

Our staff was composed of some 16,000 men and women,
and all knew where they stood and to whom they were responsible.

When I took over the reins of office, I was careful to avoid
any violent changes. I set out to strengthen the authority of
those in charge of their various departments, to avoid as much
as possible time-consuming conferences, and to insist on well
prepared and short board meetings where discussions were always confined to the problem at hand, and where the questions
being brought before the board were clearly and concisely set
forth, and were dealt with quickly and effectively.

The senior officials of a number of organizations producing
and distributing electricity in the United States, our opposite
numbers, had made two extensive and rewarding visits to the
U.S.S.R. It became apparent that it was both desirable and
timely that a delegation composed of senior executives of our
Canadian public utilities should be given an opportunity to see
something of the very remarkable progress the U.S.S.R. was
making in our field. I took the matter up with the Minister of
Power in the U.S.S.R. and after protracted negotiations it was
arranged that I should bring over a Canadian delegation, and
that in turn we would welcome a number of U.S.S.R. delegates
to make a tour of our power plants in Canada.

The trip turned out to be a most valuable experience. During
a stay of almost three weeks we covered some eight thousand
miles, travelling as far as Irkutsk in Siberia, and visiting such
important centers as Bratsk, Sverdlovsk, Beloyarsk, Kubyshev,
Stalingrad, Stalino, Lugansk, Kharkov, Voronesh, Leningrad,
and Moscow.

We were afforded every opportunity of examining in considerable detail a number of thermal and hydro-electric plants,
and saw something of two nuclear electric stations. We were

particularly interested in their extra-high voltage transmission grids which brought power from Siberia to the more densely populated areas of European Russia.

In the transmission of large blocks of power over long distances, the U.S.S.R. was considerably more advanced than either Canada or the United States.

We were received everywhere with the greatest hospitality. Our group was surprised at the accurate and detailed knowledge the Soviet engineers had of our Canadian hydro and thermal power plants, obtained, of course, through the literature so freely published in Canada on the subject.

The Intourist representative who was looking after our party advised us that our program had been slightly modified to enable us to visit the special exhibition that had been hastily set up at the Gorki Park in Moscow to house the remains of the American U-2 spy plane brought down a few days before our arrival.

Huge crowds of people had queued up to await their turn to enter the buildings, but, as is customary in the U.S.S.R., we, being foreigners, were allowed to enter first.

The exhibition was well arranged and included an important part of the plane itself which had been surprisingly little damaged. A large number of instruments were displayed on counters. There were the personal belongings of the pilot, including American and Russian currency, his gold ring and watch, and the needle which, it was claimed, was to have been used for suicidal purposes in case of an emergency.

A group of interpreters was placed around the room at strategic points to supply the visitors with all the required details.

It was interesting to observe that whereas the papers were carrying violent anti-American articles every day, and the propaganda services were working overtime, the people with whom we came into contact during our trip reflected no hostility towards us. Even those with whom we spoke in the exhibition hall itself could not have been more friendly.

Of all the hydro-electric stations visited, the one which retained our attention most was in the process of construction at Bratsk on the Angara River which flows out of Lake Baikal and is situated approximately 290 miles downstream from

Irkutsk. Irkutsk was famous in Tsarist history as the Siberian town to which thousands of political enemies of the regime were exiled.

The power plant at Bratsk on the Angara River is in an area which, a few years ago, was covered with primeval forest. In some respects it reminded me of the wilderness of Newfoundland and Labrador, or of the far north of Canada.

Construction on this plant started in 1955. It was planned to produce five million kilowatts of power and when completed it would be the largest plant in the world, its output being two and a half times greater than the St. Lawrence Power Plant.

According to their advance planning, the Bratsk unit was to be one of a cascade of five plants on the Angara River, with an ultimate total capacity of 17 million kilowatts.

Keeping pace with the construction of the power plant, the town of Bratsk was already well advanced and boasted of a population of 60,000. Its buildings, situated on either side of very wide concrete boulevards, were of logs cut from the primeval forest which surrounded the town. They were most attractive and solidly built.

The local mayor, an energetic looking young man, wagered that if I returned to Bratsk in four years' time, the population of the city would then be a minimum of 250,000.

In our capitalistic countries, we bring the power sometimes long distances to our great manufacturing centers. The U.S.S.R. reverses the process. They bring the manufacturing plants to the source of power. Accordingly, major industries were under construction in the Bratsk area at the time of our visit. Some were to produce aluminium, others chemicals, machine tools, or paper.

In the modern hotel where we spent the night, we were guests of the mayor. On the morning of our departure at 6:30, he entertained us at a most lavish breakfast accompanied by numerous speeches, and many toasts drunk in vodka. Hardly my idea of an early morning breakfast!

As we were leaving, the mayor asked me to sign the visitors' book, and I was interested to note that both Chairman Khrushchev and Averell Harriman had been guests there just a few weeks prior to our arrival.

Although the U.S.S.R. has made noteworthy progress in the development of electrical power, her output at the time scarcely exceeded one-third of that of the U.S.A. Just as the U.S.S.R. believes in guns rather than butter, their electrical production is predominantly directed towards their larger industries; very little effort is made to bring the benefits and comforts of electrical living to the homes of the people.

While I was still active in the Massey-Harris Company, my wife and I had planned that upon my retirement I would devote several years to intensive travelling in Red China, the U.S.S.R. and those countries which were dominated or influenced by communism, and, through my writings and speeches, endeavour to alert the people of Canada to a situation and a danger with which they were all too unfamiliar.

After retiring from Massey-Harris it had been my intention to put these plans into force but at Premier Frost's urging I had postponed my plans. But I had never given them up, and as the years rolled by and I was approaching my sixty-eighth year, my wife and I realized that since travel in many of the countries concerned was very strenuous, I could not postpone my plans much longer if I were to carry them out at all.

Accordingly, in the fall of 1959, while returning with Premier Frost from the opening of our Silver Falls plant, I brought up the question of my retirement. He was reluctant to discuss it, and asked me to carry on for one or two more years. I agreed to stay on until the spring of 1961. He was, I believe, influenced by the fact that he also was giving thought to his retirement in 1961 or early '62. He agreed, therefore, that I should sever my connection with Ontario Hydro in May of 1961, and he accepted my strong recommendation that Ross Strike should be appointed in my place.

It was not without the sincerest regret that I had come to this decision. My period of office with Ontario Hydro had been a most exhilarating experience and I had enjoyed it all immensely, notwithstanding the fact that I had, from time to time, come in for my fair share of criticism from the legislative opposition who were looking, no doubt, for an opportunity to embarrass the government. The opposition had a lot to say concerning a trip I made to mainland China and about a luncheon

I attended in New York for Nikita Khrushchev. When a picture
appeared in the paper showing me shaking hands with the Chairman of the Council of Ministers of the U.S.S.R., a howl of
disapproval was to be heard from the opposition benches. The
Premier had apparently appointed a communist to the chairmanship of Ontario Hydro!

Neither the Premier nor I took this type of criticism to heart.
He recognized, as I did, that everyone in public life must accept
unfair criticism of this type. If a public servant allows it to
upset him, he shouldn't be in public life at all.

In May, 1961, the time came for me to leave Ontario
Hydro. I was buoyed up by the thought that I was leaving it in
good hands, and at a time when it was operating smoothly and
efficiently. I had every confidence in the leaders of the organization. They were men of proven ability. They all got along
splendidly together, no jockeying for position, no disloyalty
to the Commission or to their fellow workers. Ross Strike who
was to be my successor was highly regarded and I knew that
under his guidance the managerial team would continue to work
happily together and to perform effectively.

Our 16,000 employees were taking our rapidly increasing
activities in their stride. Our revenues, at $229 million, had
reached an all-time high; our recent $100 million debentures
issue had been readily taken up, thereby attesting to the high
credit standing of the organization which, as a whole, was enjoying the unprecedented good will of the people of Ontario. The
problems of the future, and there were plenty of them, were
the problems of growth and expansion, and the ever greater and
insatiable demand for more electric power.

Had I been ten years younger I would have undoubtedly
retained my position. The exhilaration of leading an organization set on a course of doubling its already mammoth activities
every ten years or so would have proven irresistible.

But it was not to be. The retirement age in Ontario Hydro
was sixty-five, and I had already reached sixty-eight. I have
never belonged to those who wish to hang onto their jobs regardless of advancing years.

After attending a number of dinners given to my wife and
myself by the government and by the senior members of On-

tario Hydro, and by the leaders among our partners in the municipalities, my resignation became effective on May 31st, 1961.

Leslie Frost had been right that day in 1956 when, offering me the chairmanship of Ontario Hydro, he said that the years I was about to spend with the Commission would be among the most challenging and fulfilling of my long career in business. I didn't believe this at the time, but I found it to be true. I will always be grateful that I accepted his offer.

27

After Hydro

PERHAPS THE MOST IMPORTANT and certainly the most time-consuming of my extra-curricular activities was the organization of the Dollar-Sterling Trade Board of which I assumed the chairmanship from 1949 to 1961. It came about this way.

In the pre-1914 days, Great Britain had on balance a greater net foreign investment than all other powers put together. This, combined with her willingness and ability to accept goods freely from any source, made the multilateral trading pattern automatic and self-correcting.

At the end of the first world conflict, Great Britain's position had been so adversely affected by the cost and sacrifices of the war that her trading pattern was seriously upset. Throughout the inter-war period, the Anglo-American group of trading nations endeavoured to maintain relative freedom in exchange rates, in conversion of currencies, and in trade and capital movements, and continued to fight what at times appeared to be a losing battle against the forces which were restricting the flow of international trade.

Had the world been granted a long period of peace during which the normal processes of recovery might have made themselves felt, the situation might conceivably have righted itself.

Unfortunately this was not to be; the Second World War went far towards destroying the whole mutilateral trade pattern. Britain's share of the cost of the two wars was nearly $4,000 per capita. Canada's was less than $2,000, and that of the United States, $2,860. Only defeated Germany suffered a loss comparable to that of Britain.

The United Kingdom had survived World War I still the largest creditor nation in the world. By the end of World War II, she was, and still is, a net debtor.

These untoward happenings seriously affected Canada's trading position. Since the days of Confederation, Britain had been Canada's largest overseas customer, but now she found herself unable to purchase the goods she required from Canada, because she had not dollars to enable her to pay for them.

The loss of income of her foreign investments throughout the world, plus the decline in her income from services abroad, could no longer offset the difference between her imports from Canada and her exports to Canada.

Thinking people both in the United Kingdom and Canada realized that if England was to continue to build up her export trade, which is the life-blood of her economy, and if Canada was to continue to find in Britain her greatest market for her agricultural products, something had to be done about it.

I was aware that a group of public-spirited citizens in Britain had, with the strong support of the British government, set up an organization called the Dollar Exports Council, which was manned by some of the most powerful and distinguished men in Britain. I knew they felt very strongly that they were handicapped in stimulating their exports to Canada because no corresponding body had been set up in our country.

The situation was a serious one for Canada, whose grain exports to this important market were seriously affected. C. D. Howe spoke to me of this troublesome situation on many occasions, and every time I went to England, members of the Dollar Exports Council were in touch with me in the hope that I might interest myself in their problem. While sympathetic, I consistently avoided the issue, believing that, in view of my many responsibilities, there were others in Canada who could better afford to devote their energies to this problem.

In 1948, Sir Graham Cunningham, the first Chairman of the Dollar Exports Council, came to Canada to see me with the definite request that I should set up a Canadian organization. I turned down the request and introduced Sir Graham to several influential Canadians in the hope that one of them would take on the job. Sir Graham failed to secure the services of anyone who, in his judgement, fulfilled the requirements, and he returned home empty-handed.

A few months later, while I was attending a sales conference in Edmonton, I received a telephone call from Sir Stafford Cripps, then Chancellor of the Exchequer, who was in Washington. He asked me as a favour to meet him the next day in New York at the home of Gardner Cowles, the well-known publisher of two important daily papers, and of several magazines. He went on to say that he was leaving for Britain on the night flight and wished to discuss a matter of importance with me.

I agreed, flew to New York, and after lunch at the Cowles home, the Chancellor outlined at some length the difficulties Britain was experiencing in connection with her exports. He then expressed the hope, in terms I found difficult to resist, that I should organize and take on the chairmanship of what became subsequently known as the Dollar-Sterling Trade Board, without which, he felt, the efforts of the Dollar Exports Council would be abortive.

In view of his insistence, and of the difficulties I knew Britain was experiencing, I agreed to set up such an organization providing the Canadian government favoured my doing so.

I discussed the situation in Ottawa on the following morning with the Prime Minister, the Rt. Hon. C. D. Howe, and the Rt. Hon. James Gardner. All three felt it was definitely in the interests of Canada that such a body should be set up. They strongly urged me to take on the task.

I agreed, therefore, with the proviso that the government would suppply me with a senior civil servant who would be seconded to the new organization to act as general secretary. With the blessing of L. B. Pearson, A. G. S. Griffin was appointed to this post. The government could not have made a more felicitous choice.

As the formation of the Dollar-Sterling Trade Board was deemed to be a matter of considerable urgency, I proceeded immediately with its organization, and selected fourteen potential directors, located in various parts of Canada, all the way from the eastern provinces to Vancouver, men of stature who would give prestige and weight to the organization. I had no time to call on them, so I spoke to each over the telephone, explaining our objectives, which, in the simplest terms, were to reduce our massive imports from the United States and endeavour to switch a portion of these to the United Kingdom, thereby enabling her to earn more dollars with which she could increase her imports from us.

It was for me a source of great satisfaction and a tribute to the patriotism and generosity of such men as H. R. MacMillan of Vancouver; N. R. Crump, President of the C.P.R. in Montreal; John David Eaton, of the T. Eaton Company; Donald Gordon, President of the C.N.R., to mention only a few, that without a single exception, they all agreed to serve on the board, knowing that it involved a certain amount of personal work and responsibility. By the following morning the Dollar-Sterling Trade Board was set up.

We were in business. A press release was made in time to catch the evening papers.

Offices had been placed at our disposal in Ottawa; Tony Griffin and his staff had taken over. An imposing flare of governmental publicity gave us a good start.

Our Board operated in several different ways. Canadian imports from all sources, for instance, were thoroughly analyzed to determine which items imported from dollar areas could be transferred to the sterling area. Where it appeared that a commodity was transferable, and met Canadian requirements in price, quality, and service, we brought heavy pressure to bear on Canadian purchasers to obtain these from the sterling area.

Information and guidance were supplied to British exporters on such important factors as acceptable advertising, marketing procedures, packaging, styling, pricing, and distribution. We assisted Canadian importers in procuring supplies from the sterling area. These were not always readily available, and we brought pressure to bear on the United Kingdom suppliers to expedite deliveries.

We engaged in publicity and educational work to inform the Canadian public of the nature and the urgency of the Dollar-Sterling Trade problem. Speeches were made, articles published, press conferences were held, and nationwide radio talks were given.

Our efforts were crowned with success. In the first quarter of 1950 I was able to report that the British exports had forged ahead and that in March for the first time in recent history we actually had an unfavourable balance of visible trade with the United Kingdom. They sold us more than we sold them.

We hastened to point out that this was not a recurring phenomenon, but it was significant of the energy which had been placed behind the British export drive, of which the sale of automobiles was an excellent example.

I retained the Chairmanship of the Dollar-Sterling Trade Board until I retired from business in 1961 and took up my official residence in Bermuda.

I believe that it is generally acknowledged by both Britain and Canada that a great deal had been accomplished towards the stimulation of our trade relationships, and in developing a better understanding and closer commercial relationship between our two countries.

For me, it had been a challenging experience. I spent more of my evenings and weekends in its service, put in more hard work, wrote more articles, and made more speeches, than I had ever been called upon to do for any other extra-curricular activity. It was strenuous but I enjoyed it all. I was greatly privileged to be working throughout the years of my tenure of office with a splendid group of patriotic and dedicated men on both sides of the Atlantic. With many of them, I continue to enjoy a rewarding friendship.

When I retired from Hydro I was sixty-eight. I believed I had fully regained by usual good health, but Trini persuaded me, without too much difficulty, that before undertaking the strenuous travelling we had planned we should go to Europe for a few weeks' holiday.

My decision to do this was influenced by a telephone call from Vincent Massey urging us to join three other couples in chartering a yacht for a three weeks' cruise in the southern Aegean.

Accordingly, the day after the last official dinner marking my retirement from Ontario Hydro, we left for New York, where we were to embark for Europe. In New York we caught a slight glimpse of the life of the international jet-set.

The S.S. *Bremen* was sailing at midnight, and my friend, George Moore, then President of the First National City Bank, arranged with Aristotle Onassis to include us in a small dinner he was giving for the Moores on his yacht *Christina*, which was anchored in the port of New York. We were a small party: Maria Callas who acted as hostess, Prince and Princess Rainier of Monaco, the Moores, and the Wristons. Wriston is now President of the First National City Bank, succeeding George Moore.

Ari Onassis is an excellent host, friendly, and forthcoming. He met us at the top of the gangway, as the motorboat which he had sent to pick us up came alongside. After cocktails and introductions to Maria Callas and the Rainiers, who were already on board, Onassis took us on a tour of his fabulous yacht. As Onassis showed us through the spacious reception rooms, the dining-room which could comfortably seat thirty people, the wide and magnificent staircase covered with heavy white carpeting leading to the staterooms, we lost all sense of being on a ship and felt as if we were in a luxurious and well appointed home.

Onassis took special pride in showing us the large stateroom, the dressing room with the sunken inlaid mosaic bath and solid gold fixtures, which Churchill always used during his many cruises on the *Christina*.

What impressed me most, as Onassis took us over his yacht, was not so much the luxury of it all, but the equipment on the top deck, which included a four- and a two-engine aircraft, a helicopter, a four-wheel-drive truck, two Cadillacs, two jeeps, a large and a small motor cruiser, and two sailing boats.

Another remarkable feature was the large swimming pool adjoining the reception room and bar, with mosaic inlay floors and walls. At the flick of a switch the water was drained out, and the bottom of the pool rose to the level of the deck and became a spacious dance floor.

After an excellent and amusing dinner, accompanied by a connoisseur's choice of wines, Onassis saw us off in a launch which took us to the S. S. *Bremen* where we arrived shortly before sailing time.

Before travelling to Greece, we spent two weeks at Claridge's in London. My daughter, Maruja, who was studying at the Sorbonne, flew over from Paris to spend a few days with us, and later accompanied us to Rome.

Having now retired from active concerns, I gathered together for lunch at Claridge's some of the men who had been helpful to me over the years, both when I was Chairman of Massey-Harris and later of Ontario Hydro, many of whom had become valued friends.

Among the guests was Ted Heath,[1] whom I had seen something of while he was Minister for the Common Market. I had greatly admired the dexterity with which he handled his difficult task.

Later at a Bilderberg meeting I had the great satisfaction of watching him in action at close quarters. De Gaulle had sent one of his senior officials to the meeting to defend his veto against Britain's entry to the Common Market. Ted Heath answered him in one of the most brilliant speeches ever made within the very select confines of the Bilderberg meetings.

He spoke for half an hour without a note of any kind. Like all my fellow members I was immensely impressed by the lucidity with which he marshalled his facts, and the fluency of his delivery.

Ever after that memorable occasion I was of the belief that Ted Heath was headed for the leadership of the Conservative Party. I greatly rejoiced when, notwithstanding the criticism levelled against him by members of his party, he led the Conservatives to victory in 1970.

Selwyn Lloyd,[2] who also has had a remarkable political

[1] Rt. Hon. Edward Heath, now Prime Minister.
[2] Now speaker of the House of Commons.

career, and whom I saw frequently when he was Anthony Eden's Minister of State for Foreign Affairs, was also among my guests, as was Oliver Chandos,[1] who made such an outstanding contribution to his country in the Churchill War Cabinet.

I have a great admiration and friendship for Chandos. I know of no other man who has made as great a success of everything to which he has turned his hand. His war record was splendid, his business career both notable and extremely successful. He was chosen by Churchill to serve in his Cabinet as Minister of Supply, President of the Board of Trade, member of the War Cabinet as Minister of State in Cairo, and in many other ministerial posts until the end of hostilities. In each of these he served with distinction.

He is erudite, friendly, witty, and has another qualification which always rates high in my esteem: he is a connoisseur of the fine wines of France, and his choice of a menu speaks of his good taste and broad experience.

In recognition of his outstanding administrative ability, he has been called on, since the war, to take over the Chairmanship of the National Theatre Board, of the English Opera group, the Institute of Directors and many other artistic and charitable bodies too numerous to mention.

In addition to all this, he has found time to write two excellent books, one of which was his autobiography, and both of which bear the hallmark of classical training, wit, and the fascinating experiences of a long and interesting life.

It was with joy—shared by many of his friends—that we had read in 1954 that Oliver Chandos had been made a Knight of the Garter, the greatest honour Her Gracious Majesty can bestow on one of her subjects.

There were many other guests, too numerous to mention, all of whom were making a useful contribution in finance, industry, and public life.

Our cruise on the *Daphne*, a 130-foot yacht, with a crew of ten including the captain, was a great success. We visited a

[1]Viscount Chandos, K.G., D.S.O., M.C.

number of Aegean Islands and sailed through the Corinth Canal to the Islands of the Ionian Sea, up the coast of Yugoslavia with its fjords of surpassing beauty and its medieval towns and villages. We finished our trip tied up to a mooring at the mouth of the Grand Canal in Venice, almost in front of the Doge's Palace.

After spending a few days in Venice, we flew back to Toronto. This was the first long holiday I had ever taken away from the cares and responsibilities of office, and we both enjoyed it thoroughly.

Our house at 49 Highland Avenue had been sold to John Craig Eaton, and while Trini, with her usual efficiency, attended to the despatch of our belongings to Bermuda, I spent most of my time in Ottawa putting the finishing touches on preparations for our forthcoming trip which was to take us to Turkey, Iran, the republics of the southern U.S.S.R., Afghanistan, Pakistan, India, and back to Iran to make a six weeks' survey of the country.

I knew from experience that if one is to make a useful study of a foreign country it is essential that one should go there under suitable auspices and armed with official introductions. Iran presented no problem in this respect, because following a meeting with the Vice-Premier at the home of John Bassett in Toronto, and an introduction to the Shah-en-Shah which Prince Bernhard had given me, I received an official invitation to spend six weeks in that country.

Ambassador Aroutounian had been most helpful in arranging my visit to the southern republics of the U.S.S.R., and between the Canadian External Affairs Department, the British Foreign Office in London, and Paul Hoffman of Marshall Aid fame, I was well equipped for my visit to Turkey, Afghanistan, Pakistan and India.

Our arrival in Istanbul, on the first leg of our four months' tour, coincided with the barbaric hanging of both the ex-prime minister, Menderez, and his finance minister. The city was in a turmoil.

I had met both of these men, who had attended the opening meeting of the Bilderberg group in Turkey a few years before. Menderez at that time was the uncontested ruler of Turkey and headed the largest political party.

On our arrival in Tehran we were met by Dr. Ali Majd, secretary to the Prime Minister, who was to look after us during our preliminary and subsequent visit to Iran, and who arranged an interview for me with His Highness the Shah-en-Shah at the summer palace.

By way of introduction, Canadian Ambassador Somers gave a dinner for us, which included members of the diplomatic corps, the ambassador to the United States and the United Kingdom, and two ex-premiers. Ex-premiers are fairly numerous in Iran.

I was greatly impressed by the Shah. His knowledge of every aspect of the political and economic life of Iran was quite remarkable.

The security service surrounding him is extremely rigorous. Entry to the grounds of the summer palace and progress through them is made tiresome by repeated scrutiny of the visitor's papers, a procedure which is continued and intensified within the palace itself. But when finally one is ushered into the Shah's presence, all formalities cease.

He received me with the utmost simplicity and cordiality, and was interested in the objectives of my visit. He told me that all arrangements would be made on my return so that I could obtain the clearest picture of the economic and political life of the country, its relationship with the U.S.S.R., its land reform which was in its infancy, and its point of view about its principal source of revenue, oil resources.

The Shah promised that on my return to Iran, a few weeks after, I should immediately call on the prime minister, who was arranging for me a tour of the country, which would take me all the way from the Caspian Sea to Abadan.

All arrangements having been made, we left the following day by train for the U.S.S.R.

To arrive in that country on a direct flight from London, or Stockholm, or Paris, as a guest of the government, or as leader of a Canadian power delegation, as was my lot on other occasions, is one thing. To arrive there over a remote frontier in northern Iran, and do so without any official status, is quite another.

I was accompanied by my wife and eldest daughter. We

were to cross the border at Julfa, a little town between Iran and the Soviet Socialistic Republic of Armenia.

A police van took us to a small guard-house on the Iranian side of the bridge dividing the two countries, and we were told to wait there. On the other side, a red-painted barrier surmounted by the outsized red star of communism marked the Soviet border.

Our luggage was carried across the bridge by two Iranian guards and deposited in front of the red barrier. Meanwhile we were kept in the evil-smelling guardhouse until a Soviet jeep drew up behind the iron barrier. From the jeep an officer descended, accompanied by two soldiers armed with machine-guns held at the ready.

This was evidently our cue. The Iranian officers, leading the way, marched us across the bridge while two Iranian soldiers, also armed with machine-guns held at the ready, fell in twenty paces behind us. Feeling somewhat self-conscious at this display of melodramatics, we crossed the bridge and handed our passports to the Russian officer through a slit in the red barrier. These were examined, found in order, the gates were swung open, and we were admitted behind the iron barrier, if not the iron curtain.

We were driven to the station in a Soviet jeep indistinguishable from its American prototype. After prolonged border formalities, we boarded a local train to Tiblisi in Georgia, our first port of call.

Throughout the first part of our journey to Yerevan, the capital of Armenia, the railway wound its way along the banks of the Aras River which separates Turkey from the U.S.S.R. Heavy barbed wire and high watch-towers, closely spaced troops on the tracks, and at all the stations, armed guards walking in pairs up and down the corridors of the train in which we were travelling, provided an atmosphere of tension and of military preparedness which served as a reminder of the sad state in which this troubled world finds itself today, even in these remote and impoverished areas.

A little later in the afternoon, Mount Ararat came into view. It was on this peak, rising 17,000 feet like a great pyramid, that, so the Bible tells us, Noah's Ark came to rest when the great floods covered the earth.

From Tiblisi in Armenia we followed the itinerary I had arranged with Aroutounian before leaving Canada. We covered a lot of ground, spending some time in the fabulous Caucasus, where 72 different languages are reportedly spoken; but most of it in the ancient world of central Asia, vast, remote, arid, dusty, but flowering like a tropical garden when water is brought to the parched land.

We visited Ashkhabad, the capital of the Republic of Turkmen, the scene of the deepest penetration of Czarist troops in central Asia which started in 1864 and led to the present Russian position on the frontiers of Afghanistan and Iran by 1896.

We visited Samarkand, the rallying point of the caravans which travelled on the silk route from China to Persia. This ancient city was destroyed by Alexander the Great 300 years before Christ, overrun by Ghengis Khan, and finally captured by Czarist Russia in 1868 after the defeat of its ruler, the Emir of Bukara.

We visited the fascinating town of Bukara and then proceeded to Tashkent, the thriving capital of Uzbek, and the largest industrial, scientific, and cultural center of central Asia. Tashkent was occupied and sacked by Ghengis Khan in his western march from Outer Mongolia.

We were accompanied on our trip by a most efficient interpreter who had been sent specially from Moscow to meet us at Tiblisi. She stayed with us until we finally left Tashkent for Kabul in Afghanistan at the end of our visit to the U.S.S.R.

In each one of these republics, arrangements had been made for me to meet the chairman of the council of ministers and cabinet members. These invariably gave me generously of their time, answering all my questions, including the indiscreet ones. I was impressed by the calibre of these members of the various governments visited. They were young, able, dynamic, well informed, and on the average as well dressed as their opposite numbers in North America.

I met no Russians among them. All were from their native republics.

It would be redundant for me to deal with the southern republics of the U.S.S.R. at length, or our fascinating visit to Afghanistan, one of the very backward countries in the world today, or Pakistan where British influence was still strong, or my six weeks' trip through fascinating Iran, after having visited India, because all this is covered in a small book I published, entitled *In the Shadow of the Red Star*, which describes the conditions under which people were living in the various countries concerned, the relationship of some of these to the U.S.S.R., the progress being made, and the political implications involved.

From Iran, after spending ten days in Switzerland with our children over the Christmas holidays, we travelled to London, where I reported to the Foreign Office. After an excellent trip across the Atlantic on the *Caronia*, we arrived in Bermuda and drove to *Somerset House*, which was to become our permanent home. The trip had taken us just over five months.

Many of my friends, knowing of the active life I had always led, predicted that, after the first few weeks of leisure, retirement would become a burden to me. I never shared their anxiety. Retirement to me merely meant a change of pace and of location, and an opportunity I was looking forward to, of doing many of the things an active business career had prevented me from enjoying in the past.

As I write, it is approximately ten years since I retired from Ontario Hydro. These last ten years have been as interesting and as rewarding as any like period in my life.

My time has been fully occupied by such activities as the completion and publication of *In the Shadow of the Red Star*, trips to Amsterdam to attend meetings of the Steering Committee of the Bilderberg group at the Soestdijk Palace, the residence of Prince Bernhard and Queen Wilhemina of the Netherlands, the attendance at the Bilderberg meetings in Cannes in 1963, and Williamsburg in 1964.

Another time-consuming task has been the chairmanship of the Round Hill hotel in Jamaica, the reorganization of which took over one-third of my time for a period of nearly three years, and necessitated numerous visits to Jamaica.

On the lighter side, some of our more enjoyable experiences were the yearly visits of Vincent Massey and many of our old and valued friends from England, Canada, and the United States.

We made a trip to Spain and Ireland followed by a second

unforgettable cruise on the *Daphne* which I chartered for a two-week trip through the historic islands of the southern Aegean.

My activities were interrupted briefly in 1962 when I had a heart attack in Venice. This resulted in my being hospitalized in Italy and London for over five weeks.

In the summer of 1964, following an invitation from the People's Republic of China, Trini and I left for that country, travelling via Honolulu and Japan.

Following my usual practice, I spent several days in Japan gathering as much official information as possible about China. In this I was greatly assisted by Richard Bower, the Canadian ambassador, and by Edwin O. Reischauer, the United States ambassador to Japan, who, having been born in that country, and having travelled widely throughout Asia, was particularly knowledgeable about Red China.

I carried letters of introduction from the State Department to the American Consul General in Hong Kong, Edward Rice, who arranged for me to obtain such information as I required from his staff of senior executives. Our Canadian officials in Hong Kong were equally well informed and helpful.

I had made arrangements with a professional English photographer, Allan Cash, to accompany my wife and me to mainland China to make a visual record of our trip.

Our party left Hong Kong on the morning of August 31st, 1964, and crossed the border at Shum-shun, a frontier station dividing China from the new territories of Hong Kong. The station had been rebuilt since our last visit. It was enlarged, modernized, adorned with clusters of red flags surmounted by a great red star, and enlivened with the usual propaganda posters, depicting happy industrial workers, and smiling peasants, bronzed, healthy-looking, and obviously loving their work, and stern-faced military-looking young men and women, ready to defend their country, rifle in hand, against all intruders. Most prominent of all were the inevitable pictures of Lenin and Chairman Mao Tse-tung.

"We welcome you as a friend from Canada," said the official who had travelled from Canton to meet us in Shum-shun. "You are to be our honoured guests, and everything you wish to see will be shown to you. When you return to Canton, we hope that you will give us the benefit of your observations, because we are a very backward people, and we want to profit from your experience." After this gracious and modest speech, which I was to hear *ad nauseum* throughout our visit to China, and which caused me at times to doubt the sincerity of our hosts, we were served the ever-present pots of steaming tea which my wife and I had grown to like during our previous visit, while we were awaiting the departure of the train for Canton.

We spent six weeks in China as honoured guests of the government. We travelled widely throughout the land, frequently in areas closed to the mill-run of tourists. We visited schools, universities, factories, communes, hospitals, recreation centers, communal homes, creches for children, and homes for the aged and the infirm.

We were received everywhere with kindness and hospitality. Delegations of senior officials met us everywhere, entertained us lavishly, and, after we had completed our visit in their town, saw us off as we departed by train or by air.

Interviews were arranged for me in Peking with senior officials of all the government departments in which I was interested and I spent considerable time visiting embassies and ministries in Peking including those of the U.S.S.R., the U.K., Pakistan, Sweden, and the Netherlands.

A full account of this fascinating and informative visit, and of the two weeks spent subsequently in the dynamic and progressive island of Taiwan, has been related in my book, *A Businessman Looks at Red China*, the first edition of which came out in 1965, and the second in 1966. I will not therefore burden the reader with a further recounting of our experiences.

Both Trini and I are fond of sea travel. After spending a week in Hong Kong, during which I reported my observations on China and Taiwan to those who had been so helpful to me on the outward journey, we returned to San Francisco on the S.S. *Oronsay* with stop-overs in Japan and Honolulu. We reached home in November of 1964.

My return from Red China coincided with a salutary quickening of interest in both the U.S.A. and Canada about conditions behind the Bamboo Curtain, and as my visit had been fairly widely reported on in the press, I found myself involved in numerous requests to address or take part in university-sponsored conferences, symposiums, and discussion groups. All of these were most interesting, but they involved a lot of travelling and proved to be time consuming. I was also the recipient of invitations to address gatherings and conventions, and accepted some, among which were the National Association of Manufacturers in New York, and a convention of the Society of American Newspaper Editors which was held in Montreal.

I appeared before a meeting of the Foreign Relations Committee of the Senate at the request of Senators Fulbright and Hickenlooper, and in 1966 was invited to address the Foreign Relations Committee of the House of Representatives.

I spoke before clubs in Washington, Ottawa, Montreal, Detroit, and Toronto, and at the request of the State Department in Washington and External Affairs in Ottawa, I appeared before a group of their Asiatic specialists.

While this was going on I accepted an invitation from the government of Israel to spend two or three weeks in their country, and we worked out a program which included travel to the most interesting areas of that country, and an opportunity to discuss the economy and the political orientation of Israel with the Cabinet ministers concerned, and with senior civil servants.

I had agreed to write a few articles on this subject. Accordingly, in mid-summer Trini and I sailed for Genoa on the *Michelangelo* on the first lap of our trip to Beirut, Jordan, and Israel, after having spent some time in Italy, Spain and London.

This visit to Israel, coming as it would have shortly before the Seven Day War, should have proved most interesting, and I feel the poorer for not having been able to undertake it.

Unfortunately I could not go. Instead, I spent the next two and a half months in hospitals in London and Chelmsford, and underwent two serious operations, at the hands of Britain's most famous arterial surgeon, Peter Martin.

Although I rapidly regained my usual good health, my doctors felt that I should only visit countries where first-class hospitals were readily available, and this limited, for the time being at least, the journeys I had planned to make to Southeast Asia and to some of the newly emerging republics of Africa. This was disappointing but it is an ill wind which blows nobody any good, and this contretemps gave me the opportunity of settling down to the writing of this present journal out of the memories of a long, happy and varied life.

Now, however, my wife and I are resuming our program of travelling to distant lands and, in 1971, we are undertaking an extended visit to the South Sea Islands, Australia, Indonesia, Malaysia, Singapore, Thailand, Hong Kong, Taiwan and Japan and, if it can be arranged, a return visit to mainland China.

28

The Harvest of the Years

TRINI AND I, much as we enjoyed living in Canada, where we have many valued friends, have never regretted our decision to set up our retirement residence in Bermuda. This island has much to commend it. Its climate is varied, but, for those who live here, its very changeability is among its most attractive features. We both enjoy its sunshine, fresh air, and sea breezes.

Bermuda is a beautiful island. It is clean and orderly, and its people enjoy a remarkably high standard of living. Poverty as it exists in so many of the Caribbean islands, in Africa, India, or in many countries in Europe is unknown here.

The coloured people are dignified, friendly, well educated, and likeable. Many among them have risen to positions of eminence in the professions, in public life, and in business. The colony is not entirely free of agitators and racists who love to dwell on the injustices of bygone days, but their extravagant gyrations and unreasonableness only serve to bring into relief the basic harmony and mutual respect which exists between both races.

In a world in travail, Bermuda is a good place in which to live.

We enjoy our gracious home, that has a charm only age

can impart; but what we enjoy most in Bermuda are the friends we have made here, among old Bermudian families, many of whom have played an honoured role in the development of this colony, and among peoples of many countries who, like ourselves, came to visit the Island and stayed to make it their home.

We seem never to have an idle moment. This is the secret of happiness for those who have retired. Trini is always happy and busy with her manifold household duties, her flower garden, the slat house where she is skilful in growing orchids, her children and grandchildren and the entertainment of our many friends from Bermuda and abroad.

My time is largely spent at my desk. At the request of the Governor-General, I have served as chairman of a commission which studied the problems of devaluation of the Bermudian currency. On another occasion I chaired a committee dealing with the problems of education. Both of these activities gave me great pleasure and an opportunity to become acquainted with facets of the financial and educational life of this Island which otherwise would have escaped me.

The harvest which I have reaped during fifty-odd years of business life has brought with it satisfactions far beyond material rewards. Of course, I have enjoyed making money, and I enjoy the independence which money brings as much as the other fellow. But I have never had much time for those whose approach to business is tough and ruthless, and whose interests are centered in financial gain.

The other day my son, on leave from his University, asked me to outline for him my basic philosophy concerning human relationships in big business. A good question, and one that any businessman should be willing to answer out of his own experience.

There is, to my mind, no element in business more essential than loyalty. Loyalty—to the organization, to its management and to other workers—is the cement which binds an organization together. It is necessary to the success of any undertaking. Once established, loyalty remains remarkably constant.

Loyalty cannot be bought with high salaries and bonuses alone. A delicate plant which must be carefully nurtured, it grows gradually in an atmosphere of participation, of belonging, of fair dealing and of job security. Unfettered opportunities, promotions made strictly on merit, appreciation shown for a job well done are all necessary elements in the cultivation of loyalty.

Loyalty is not a one-way street. No organization is loyal to a leader unless he, in turn, is loyal to those who are working for him. The example must always come from the top. No leader should ever ask his staff to do more than he is prepared to do himself. Come in late and leave early and you cannot expect your staff to keep to strict office hours.

In times of stress and difficulty, which most businesses experience, a loyal staff will be willing to work longer hours and accept less pay if they know that the leader is imposing similar sacrifices upon himself.

Unfairness and harsh treatment will weaken loyalty, but the most destructive thing that management can do to any organization is to make a practice of bringing in people from outside to fill the top positions.

When a manager complains of lack of able people around him, it is a sure sign of lack of leadership. In any large organization there are always men capable of greater things than they perform; all that is required is the opportunity to measure up to broader responsibilities.

Arbitrary decisions should be avoided by management. If a difficult decision must be made, the executives concerned should be called together and given an opportunity to express their views. When the decision is made, the reasons for it must be explained to them. You will find that even if some of your executives do not agree they will carry out a decision loyally because they have been given an opportunity of expressing their point of view.

However large the organization, the senior executives must always be ready to go out on the firing line. It means a lot of travelling, a lot of hard work, a lot of sacrifice, but it pays rich dividends and binds the organization together. The "ivory tower" executive who deals with other peoples' opinions and reports, and does not go out to see for himself, is to be avoided.

Discipline is necessary. No big business can be well run, and no staff can work happily, unless both fairness and discipline prevail, but I believe most profoundly in the human approach and in understanding the problems and aspirations of one's subordinates. At the same time, the senior executive is wise to avoid familiarity with his staff, not because he believes that he is superior to those who are working for him, but because special relationships make impartiality more difficult.

I have always felt strongly that the head of a large organization must, at all times, be prepared to play his part in major community, provincial or national activities; to give leadership in fund-raising campaigns for good causes; to serve on the board of hospitals and institutions of learning; and to be prepared to take a stand and express an opinion on matters of public interest.

These things are not only an obligation on the part of the leader, but they are good business for the company. A sense of humanity improves the company's public image, both within the organization and without.

I am a strong believer in keeping an organization simple, and avoiding a multiplicity of functions. Experience should never be sacrificed to "advanced management techniques" so dear to the heart of the academic theorist.

The number of committee meetings should be reduced to a minimum, and a limit to those attending them should be rigorously applied. These time-consuming committee meetings frequently result in no recommendations or in the tabling of a recommendation that could have been arrived at by experienced management without a committee at all.

Business consultants should be brought in with caution. There are occasions when they can fulfill a useful purpose, such as advising on an activity or a method new to the organization. But they are costly, encroach upon the time of senior executives and tend to upset and demoralize the staff. The business consultant is usually the refuge of inexperienced management. Put a man in charge of a business which he does not understand, and his first step is to hire a business consultant. Someone has said that a management consultant is a person who knows less about the business than you do yourself, but who is prepared to advise you how to run it for a fee you can ill afford.

I have never believed in Conglomerates. I distrust the ability of an executive, however able he may be, to be a successful leader of a multiplicity of businesses quite unrelated to one other.

The pattern of business is never static, nor should it be. The organization which was suitable in 1951, is outdated by 1971, just as the present pattern will no longer be relevant twenty years hence. The approach to the human element in business will, however, remain basically the same.

Such are some of the lessons I have learned and want to pass on to young men like my inquiring son.

Life has been very kind to me. I have enjoyed it all immensely, and I am enjoying it today as much as I have at any time. I have never shared the views of those who feel that as the years roll by the zest for life becomes dulled and diminished. On the contrary, I have always felt that though the pattern of living changes as one grows older, the capacity for savouring it is just as great.

Today I find myself in the happy position of looking back with pleasure on the past, of thoroughly enjoying the present, and of looking forward to the future with lively interest and **anticipation.**

Statement to the Press, July 6th, 1956

THE IMPLEMENT INDUSTRY, following the historical pattern, is going through a period of recession. I do not believe that it will be of long duration; in fact, conditions in Canada are already showing signs of improvement and farm income in the United States is rising slightly. It is my firm conviction that the Company will emerge from these difficulties strengthened and in an enhanced competitive position.

To guide the Company successfully, however, through the next few strenuous years is going to require leadership, energy and driving force of the highest order.

As is well known, I have been under medical care for some months, and while well on my way to complete recovery, my medical advisers have recommended that, after more than 46 years of strenuous work in the Company, I would be well advised to take things a little easier. I have, however, expressed to our Board of Directors my confidence in my health and ability to lead the Company successfully through these difficult times, but after considering these factors of health, it has been agreed that to do so might prove to be both unfair to me and, in the event of my health not standing up to the strain, injurious to the Company.

I have never been a half-measure man, and under the circumstances, I have decided with great regret that the proper course is for me to retire completely, and my resignation as Chairman and President, and Director of the Company and its subsidiaries throughout the world will, therefore, become effective immediately.

Needless to say I have informed our Directors that I will always be available for advice or counsel, should they wish to call upon me for this purpose.